Johann Joseph Ignaz von Döllinger

Fables Respecting the Popes of the Middle Ages

Johann Joseph Ignaz von Döllinger

Fables Respecting the Popes of the Middle Ages

ISBN/EAN: 9783743309852

Manufactured in Europe, USA, Canada, Australia, Japa

Cover: Foto ©ninafisch / pixelio.de

Manufactured and distributed by brebook publishing software (www.brebook.com)

Johann Joseph Ignaz von Döllinger

Fables Respecting the Popes of the Middle Ages

INTRODUCTION.

Dr. von Döllinger's *Fables about the Popes in the Middle Ages*[1] was published more than ten years ago; the fruit, as the author says, of preparatory studies upon a larger work, the general History of the Papacy. The growing importance of all subjects bearing upon the development of the papal system, and the high reputation of Dr. Döllinger as a theologian and as the leader of the so-called Old Catholic party in Germany, led to its translation last year in England by Mr. Alfred Plummer, a Fellow and Tutor of Trinity College, Oxford, and a pupil and personal friend of the author. In the present edition that translation is retained, here and there, revised from a comparison with the original. Mr. Plummer added the Appendices B to F, and also wrote a long and interesting Introduction to the English edition, giving a general review of the main topics of the work. This

---

[1] Die Papst-Fabeln des Mittelalters. Ein Beitrag zur Kirchengeschichte von Joh. Jos. Ign. v. Döllinger. Zweite unveränderte Auflage. München, 1863. Literarisch-artistische Anstalt der J. G Cotta' schen Buchhandlung.

has been left out, in part to make room for another valuable essay of Dr. Döllinger. We are, however, indebted to Mr. Plummer's Introduction for many facts about Dr. Döllinger's life and writings. The paragraphs in brackets are by the English translator, excepting those signed with the initials of the American editor.

The essay of Dr. Döllinger, translated for this American edition, is on *The Prophetic Spirit and the Prophecies of the Christian Era*.[1] It was published last year in the new series of von Raumer's *Historisches Taschenbuch*. It is an attractive subject, treated with great learning and ability; and not the less interesting because of its silent bearing upon the questions and complications of the hour, especially the relation of the Italian Papacy to European Christendom. For now, as well as throughout mediæval times, it may be said, in a broad general view, that Latins and Germans, Guelph and Ghibelline, Ultramontanes and Cismontanes, the South and the North, the Papacy and the Empire, are arrayed against each other, and that the destiny of Continental Europe hangs, as it has for fifteen hundred

---

[1] Der Weissagungsglaube und das Prophetenthum in der christlichen Zeit: In the *Historisches Taschenbuch*, begründet von Friedrich von Raumer, herausg. von W. H. Riehl. Fünfte Folga. Erster Jahrgang. Leipzig: F. A. Brockhaus, 1871.

years, upon the results of this conflict. Besides this, however, the topic itself, as here treated, is one of profound interest in its psychological, as well as in its historical and religious connections. Such a historic review shows that man must look before as well as after; he must remember the past and also strive to anticipate the future,—especially in the great joints and crises of events. Belief in Providence, as well as faith in Scripture, prompts men of deep thought and feeling to ascend some mount of vision, whence they may perchance descry the shadows of coming events. Nowhere has this profound theme been treated in so full and compressed a manner as in Dr. Döllinger's admirable summary.

All of the dissertations of the present volume are important to a correct understanding of mediæval times, and, indirectly, to a just appreciation of those mediæval tendencies and institutions which still survive, and instinctively contend against reformation and progress. They are likewise valuable as indicating the process through which their distinguished author has passed in coming to his present position. History rather than dogma has brought him to oppose the decrees of the Vatican Council. He has examined and sifted the records, and found that the very tradition of the Church disproves the present pretentions of the Papacy. In his eloquent inaugural address last year, as Rector of the University of Munich, he declared that the Ultramontanists, unsuccessful in their warfare against science, are now striving to falsify history. In a recent lecture he is reputed to have said, that "the Papacy is based upon an audacious falsification of history. A forgery in its very outset, it has, during the long years of its existence, had a pernicious influence upon Church and State alike." The historic records must be altered, if the Papacy is to be upheld. And this is one reason why Roman Catholics all over the world are now contending for the ecclesiastical control of popular education. They want their own text-books in history as well as their own catechisms.

Dr. John Joseph Ignatius von Döllinger celebrated his seventy-third birth day on the 28th of February last; the celebration was in the Museum Hall of Munich, in connection with the fifth lecture of his recent course on the Reunion of Christendom. He was born at Würzburg in 1799, ordained as priest in 1822, and in 1826 he became professor of theology in the new University of Munich. The same year he published his earliest work, *The Doctrine of the Eucharist in the first three Centuries*. The first two volumes of his *Church History* came out from 1833 to

1835; from 1836 to 1843, he published a *Compendium of the History of the Church to the Reformation*. The English translation of his *Church History* is "an unskilful combination of these two." In 1838 he brought out a work on *Mohammed's Religion, its Development and Influence*. Between 1848 and 1851 appeared his three volumes on *The Reformation, its Internal Development and Effects within the Sphere of the Lutheran Confession* (Ratisbon); he had previously written, as far back as 1828, a *History of the Reformation*, which formed the third volume of Hortig's *Ecclesiastical History*. All of these works show great research, and ever-increasing largeness of view. He confessed to Mr. Plummer that his *History of the Reformation* was "a one-sided book written with the definite object of disproving the theory that the German reformers revived pure Apostolic Christianity in the presbytery." The whole of the third bulky volume is in fact devoted to an examination and refutation of the doctrine of justification by faith alone.

In the University he meanwhile read lectures on the Philosophy of Religion, Canon Law, Symbolism, Patristics, and for a time on Dogmatic Theology. He also published several occasional pieces:—*The Religion of Shakespeare; The Introduction of Christianity among the Germans; A Commentary on Dante's Para-*

disc, accompanied with the designs of Cornelius; *Mixed Marriages* (1838); *The English Tractarians; John Huss; The Albigenses; The Duty and Law of the Church toward those who die in other Communions* (on the occasion of the death of the Queen Dowager of Bavaria, 1842); *Error, Doubt and Truth*, 1845, being an address to the students of the University; a speech on *The Freedom of the Church*, 1849, before the Catholic Union of Germany; *Martin Luther, a Sketch*, 1852. He superintended an edition of his colleague Möhler's minor writings. For several years he was the editor of the *Historisch-politische Blätter* (for which however he did not write much), an able periodical devoted to the interests of the Catholic reactionary party in Southern Germany.

Dr. Döllinger has also taken a prominent part in the political movements of his times. He represented the University in the Bavarian Chamber from 1845 to 1847; several of his speeches have been published.[1] In 1847 he was deprived of his professorship, and consequently of his seat in the Chamber, where the ministers who had been raised to power by Lola Montez dreaded his eloquence and character. Having

---

[1] Drei Reden, gehalten auf dem bayerischen Landtage, 1846. 1. Die Kirchlichen Anträge des Reichsrathes. 2. Die Protestantischen Beschwerden. 3. Die Judenfrage.

been elected a deputy to the National Parliament in 1848, he spoke and wrote with great effect in favor of religious liberty; and the definition of the relation between Church and State, which was passed at Francfort, and afterwards nominally adopted both at Vienna and Berlin, is said to have been his work.[1] In 1849 he was restored to his professorship and also to his seat in the Chamber, which last he resigned two years later, to devote himself entirely to his literary labors.

He took part in the controversy excited by the discovery of the *Philosophumena*, 1851 (at first ascribed to Origen, but probably the work of Hippolytus) by the publication in 1853 of his *Hippolytus and Callistus; or, the Roman Church in the first half of the Third Century*, reviewing the writings of Bunsen, Baur, Wordsworth and Gieseler, and showing himself their equal in learning and skill and power of historic combination. His *Paganism and Judaism*, translated into English by the Rev. N. Darnell under the title of *The Gentile and the Jew*, is a very learned and able introduction to the general history of the Christian Church. In 1860 appeared *The First Age of Christianity and the Church*, translated by Rev. H. N. Oxenham; and the next year *The Church and the*

---

[1] Mr. Plummer's Introduction, pp. xi., xii.

Churches, translated by Mr. W. B. Maccabe—which more than any of his previous volumes made his name familiar in England and this country. His inaugural address, 1867, when first chosen Rector of the University, was on *The Universities as they Were and Are;* it was published in an enlarged form (p. 58). It gives an excellent account of the rise, growth and present state of the university system in Europe ; though it hardly does full justice to the provisions for higher education in Great Britain and this country.

His recent course is well known. The letters on *Rome and the Council,* by Janus, were doubtless inspired by him, though said to be written by Professor Huber ; the famous letters of Quirinus, chiefly from Rome, are of a kindred character. Döllinger's *Declarations* about the decree of Infallibility, his reply to the sentence of excommunication by the Archbishop of Munich, his speech at the Old Catholic Congress in Munich, his Inaugural Address when recently called for the second time to be Rector of the University, his recent lectures at Munich on the Reunion of Christendom, especially the one on Luther, and that on the past attempts to frame schemes for uniting the Roman Catholic and the Protestant Churches—these publications have followed in rapid succession, and their fame has gone abroad into all lands. They would be well worth gathering into another volume. He is said, by Mr. Plummer, to intend continuing his treatise on *Prophecies*, etc., by an essay on "Dante as a Prophet," in both senses of the word, i. e., as a great and inspired teacher, and as a seer, or foreteller of future events; aspects of the great mediæval poet which have hitherto been comparatively lost sight of. He is also engaged on a work treating of the "Constitution and Internal Government of the Church."

Many of the Old Catholics are hardly satisfied with Dr. Döllinger's present position, thinking it to be indefinite and untenable. But, in all great changes, untenable positions must be taken up for a time; some persons, some Churches, may remain in them for a long time; a vital and growing movement will soon pass beyond them. And we ought rather to rejoice that "the Nestor of the German Catholic theology" (as the able Canonist von Schulte, of Prague, calls Dr. Döllinger) has advanced so far, than blame him for not yet being a thorough Protestant. In his successive recent publications his tone is becoming firmer and clearer. In his last course of lectures he speaks of Luther as he has never done before: "The mind and heart of the Germans were in Luther's hands as the lyre in the hands of the musician. Did he not give to his nation more than any other man in Christian times ever gave to a nation,—language, books for all, the Bible, church hymns?..... Others were stammering, he spoke; he alone it is who has impressed the ineffaceable stamp of his genius, not only upon the German language, but also upon the German mind. And even those Germans who detest him from the depths of their souls as the mighty heretic and seducer of the nation, are forced to speak in his words and think with his thoughts." In his fifth lecture he discourses about the Papacy thus: "The opinion [that the Pope is Antichrist] has not been formed without the guilt of Rome. When the popes again and again encouraged religious wars, when they recommended and demanded the bloody extirpation of all who believed otherwise than themselves, when even in the seventeenth century men were executed at Rome itself on account of their Protestantism—the people could hardly fail to believe that the Papacy must be the Woman, of whom John says that she was drunken with the blood of saints, and the Man of Sin, of whom Paul prophesied as coming with lying wonders, and exalting himself above all that is called God, in that he as God sitteth in the temple of God, showing himself that he is God." (2 Thess: ii., 3, 4.) He may not adopt this "popular" view, but he thinks it natural enough.

INTRODUCTION.

Dr. Döllinger bides his time. He moves cautiously yet firmly. And who can tell what a few months may bring forth? It may be that in Southern Germany, a National German Catholic Church will yet be found necessary by the government, to prevent the newly shaped Vatican decree of Infallibility from overriding the old and ever-reserved rights and relative independence of the nations. For that decree claims for the Papacy, not only omniscience in all that man can know about faith and morals, but also the right to make its decisions directly binding on every Roman Catholic conscience, without appeal, and against any and every other earthly power.

In a recent conversation with an American citizen of high standing, Dr. Döllinger is reported to have said to him: "Do you in the United States comprehend what that doctrine (Papal Infallibility) involves? It imposes upon those who accept it the solemn obligation to violate civil law, to set themselves up in opposition to the ordinances of your Government, whenever the Pope shall pronounce his infallible judgment against any one of those ordinances upon moral or religious grounds. In a word, it is the assumption of power on the part of the Pope to proclaim a higher law, which, according to the dogma, his children must obey, though such obedience involves treason to the State, and the overthrow of your Government."

Sooner than many people suspect, we may begin to feel the effects of this new dogma in a new policy on the part of Roman Catholics. This must be so if the Decree is faithfully applied. Revision of many of our laws as to education, ecclesiastical property, and the amenability of the priesthood to civil tribunals, may soon be demanded. This portends serious disturbances in our political and religious life. We may soon have to face the question, whether the canon law or the civil law is to be the law of the land.—H. B. S.

AUTHOR'S PREFACE.

THE present publication is the fruit of a course of reading and study which I undertook with a view to a more considerable work, intended to embrace the history of the Papacy. It seemed to me, however, that the results of my researches, which are here given to the public, formed to some extent as a connected whole, because all these fables and inventions —however different may have been the occasions which gave them birth, and however intentional or unintentional may have been their production—have, nevertheless, had at times a marked influence on the whole aspect of the Middle Ages, on the history and poetry of the time, on its theology, and its jurisprudence. For this reason I may, perhaps, venture to hope that not only theologians and ecclesiastical historians, but lovers and students of mediæval history and mediæval literature in general, will find this book not altogether devoid of interest.

J. v. DÖLLINGER.

MUNICH, May 24th, 1863.

TABLE OF CONTENTS.

PART I.

MEDIÆVAL FABLES ABOUT THE POPES.

                                                                        PAGE.
1. POPE JOAN.

Not yet sufficiently proved to **be a myth**.................... 4
Not an inexplicable riddle.. 6
Eight explanations stated... 7
All eight assume that the story **is older than the 13th**
  century... 9
The Papess not mentioned by Marianus Scotus...................... 10
             nor by Sigebert of Gemblours...... 11
             nor by Otto of Freysingen.......... 12
Stephen de Bourbon the first chronicler who mentions
  her.. 14
Martinus Polonus **the chief** means of spreading the story.. 16
Even in his case **the story is an** interpolation............. 18
Various ways of **interpolating**................................ 20
In "Anastasius" also **the story is a later addition**........ 24
Reasons **for inserting the Papess between Leo IV. and**
  Benedict III... 25
Writers who **copy** Martinus Polonus........................... 28
Writers of the **14th** century who mention **her**............. 29
The Dominicans and Minorites spread the story.................. 32
Used as an argument at the council of Constance................ 34
The Dominicans might easily have exposed the story............. 36
Not known to the Greeks till 1450-1500......................... 38
Aventin and Onufrio Panvinio the first to deny it.......... 40

ANALYSIS OF THE STORY

Discrepancies about the name of the Papess..................... 40
             the date of her Pontificate......... 41
             her previous abode................. 42
             the mode of the catastrophe....... 43
Boccacio's version probably the popular one.................... 44

Origin of the Story.

Four elements of production.—1. A statue 47
                2. An inscription 49
                3. A seat of unusual shape 53
                4. A custom 58

Examples of similar Stories.

The two wives of the Count of Gleichen 59
The Püstrich at Sondershausen 61
Archbishop Hatto and the mice 62
Figure on the Riesenthor of Vienna Cathedral 64
The origin of the house of Colonna 65

Abode of the Papess.

Why represented as coming from England 66
                     Mayence 67
                     Athens 72

II. POPE CYRIACUS,

This fiction had a definite object 75
Visions of the nun Elizabeth of Schönau 75
St. Ursula and her maidens 76
Abdication of Cyriacus 77
Martinus Polonus the chief means of spreading the story.. 77
The story brought to bear on the abdication of Cœlestine V. 79

III. MARCELLINUS.

The story of his abdication very ancient 81
The whole story a tissue of absurdities 83
Its object, to prove that popes are above all tribunals 84
Probable date of its fabrication 85
Use made of it by Nicolas I., Gerson, and Gerbert 87

IV. CONSTANTINE AND SYLVESTER.

Multitude of writers who mention the baptism of Constantine by Sylvester at Rome 88
The true account seemed incredible in the Middle Ages ... 88
The story certainly originated in Rome 91
Probable date of its fabrication 92
Not generally accepted at first 93
Influence of the *Liber Pontificalis* 95
Attempt of Ekkehard to reconcile the two accounts 96
Theory of Bonizo of Sutri 97

Italian chroniclers who follow him.................... 99
The story appealed to by Hadrian I., Nicolas I., and Leo
  IX.. 99
Johannes Malalas the first Greek who accepts it.......... 100
The true account seemed incredible to the Greeks also.... 100
Æneas Sylvius and Nicolas of Cusa knew the truth....... 102
The truth spreads slowly............................... 102
Its final triumph due to French theologians............. 103
The story a favourite subject for poems................. 103

V. THE DONATION OF CONSTANTINE.

Account of the Donation in the *Liber Pontificalis* sus-
  picious... 104
Evidence of Hadrian I............................... 105
No traces of the Donation till about 750............... 105
Theory that it was a Greek fabrication disproved by the
  language of the document........................... 107
The Greek text an evident translation 110
Why the Greeks so readily believed in the Donation..... 113
Accepted in the West even before known to the Greeks... 114
The work of a Roman ecclesiastic...................... 115
Probable date of the forgery........................... 116
Roman horror of the Lombards......................... 116
Not ungrounded....................................... 118
Scheme of Gregory II. to make Rome independent....... 120
The Donation gave an historic basis to this scheme...... 121
Not fabricated by the pseudo-Isidore................... 122
Contents of the document.............................. 123
The momentous ninth clause........................... 125
Change of "or" into "and"............................ 126
The senate, patriciate, and consulate in the 8th century... 127
Papal officials an imitation of imperial officials........... 127
Stated object of the Donation......................... 131
Certainly known in Rome before 850.................... 132
Æneas of Paris treats it as authentic................... 133
Hincmar and Ado are more reserved.................... 133
Leo IX. shows full belief in it......................... 134
Remarkable silence of Gregory VII..................... 134
Urban II. claims Corsica on the strength of it........... 135
Hadrian IV. gives Ireland to Henry II. on the strength
  of it... 136
Neapolitan clergy fabricate a Donation................. 139
The Donation disputed in Rome when found inconvenient
          by monks.................................. 140
          by followers of Arnold of Brescia.. 141
But, though disputed, still largely used................ 143

Claims of the popes to the imperial insignia and homage.. 145
Dissatisfaction in Germany at such claims................ 147
Historians, more cautious than the clergy, limit without
    denying the Donation................................ 148
From the 12th to 14th century its authority increases..... 151
Innocent IV.'s statement of papal supremacy............. 153
Lawyers allowed the Donation only the right of pre-
    scription.. 156
Uncertainty as to its extent.............................. 158
Extension given to it by German law-books.............. 164
Two opposite views respecting it :—
    1. That it and similar endowments were admirable..... 166
    2. That the wealth of the Church was a source of infinite
        evil... 168
Hence the story of the angel's lament.................... 171
Mediæval sects adopted the second view................. 173
The fiction exposed by Æneas Sylvius.................... 177
Also by Bishop Pecock, Cardinal Cusa, and Lorenzo Valla
    its last defenders................................... 178

VI. LIBERIUS AND FELIX.

The true account...................................... 183
Felix an antipope...................................... 183
Liberius an apostate................................... 185
He is fairly called heretical............................ 186
He re-establishes his orthodoxy........................ 189
Felix more culpable, and without excuse............... 190
The fable.. 191
Object of it to whitewash the party of Felix........... 192
Not older than the 6th century........................ 192
Version of the *Liber Pontificalis* and of the *Acts of Felix*.. 193
Version of the *Acts of Eusebius*........................ 196
Name of Felix inserted into martyrologies, calendars, &c.. 197
He is confounded with the African martyr Felix......... 199
The fable originated in the *Liber Pontificalis*........... 202
Difficulties when the truth became known in the 16th
    century.. 205
A forged inscription................................... 206
Paoli's monstrous hypothesis........................... 207
The fable finally abandoned............................ 209

VII. ANASTASIUS II.

Anastasius II... 210
Dante selects him as an instance of an heretical pope..... 210
Was he a heretic ?..................................... 212
Dante's error the common belief of the time.............. 216
This erroneous belief created mainly by Gratian.......... 219

VIII. THE CASE OF HONORIUS.

Opposite fate of Honorius and Anastasius................ 223
Monothelitism an attempted compromise between monophysitism and orthodoxy............................. 223
Honorius confessedly a monothelite.................... 228
Anathematized by the VIth general council............. 229
For actual heresy, not for mere negligence............. 230
The papal legates vote for the anathema............... 233
Pope Agatho's vain attempt to avert the anathema....... 234
Leo II. confirms the anathema........................ 235
The *Liber Diurnus* requires every pope to confirm the anathema... 236
Marked silence of the *Liber Pontificalis*............... 237
The anathema treated in the East as a matter of course... 240
Hincmar of Rheims assents to it....................... 240
Silence of the *Liber Pontificalis* followed by historians... 241
The anathema on a pope is thus forgotten.............. 241
Leo IX. shows utter ignorance of it................... 243
A Greek first reminds the West of the fact............. 246
Torquemada sacrifices the council to save Honorius..... 247
The question not seriously debated till the 16th century.. 248

Various Hypotheses.

1. That the *Acts of the Council* have been interpolated.... 248
2. That they are really the Acts of another synod........ 249
3. That the letters of Honorius are forgeries............. 249
4. That Honorius was condemned for negligence only.... 250
5. That the letters of Sergius are forgeries.............. 253
6. That the letters of Leo II. are also forgeries.......... 254
7. That Honorius was condemned by the Greeks only.... 254
8. That Honorius wrote, not as pope, but as a private teacher.. 255

The Monothelitism of Honorius would never have been questioned, had he not been pope....................... 256

IX. POPE GREGORY II. AND THE EMPEROR LEO III.

Gregory II. represented as heading a revolt against Leo III.. 257
Martinus Polonus once more the propagator of error..... 257
Theophanes the source of the statement............... 258
Gregory headed no revolt, but helped to quash one..... 260
View of Gregorovius inconsistent with facts and itself.... 262
Difficult position of Gregory II....................... 264

X. SYLVESTER II.

Gradual defamation of his memory...... 267
1. That he was too fond of profane arts and sciences...... 267
2. That his election at Ravenna was due to sinister arts.. 268
3. That he was addicted to magic and black art.......... 268
4. That he sold himself to the devil.................... 269
The fable of Roman origin............................ 270
Its object.. 270
The Dominicans spread the fable...................... 272
The truth recognised in the 14th century............. 272

PART II.

THE PROPHETIC SPIRIT AND THE PROPHECIES OF THE CHRISTIAN ERA.

I. INTRODUCTION.

Contrast between the prophetic spirit in Heathendom and in Christendom................................... 273
Four orders of prophecies............................ 274
Ecclesiastical prophecies............................ 275
Three-fold origin of predictions..................... 275
Spontaneous prophecies............................... 276
Predictions with a purpose........................... 277
Dynastic prophecies.................................. 278
Predicted succession of the popes.................... 281
The predictions of Joachim........................... 282
The predictions of Malachias......................... 283
Hess' prophecy of the Reformation.................... 284
Cazotte and Beauregard............................... 284

II. PROPHECIES OF THE EARLIER TIMES; ANTICHRIST; THE END OF THE WORLD.

The Sibylline books.................................. 286
End of the Roman Empire.............................. 287
The Antichrist....................................... 288
The literature about the Antichrist.................. 290

III. NATIONAL PROPHECIES.

From a sense of national guilt.............................. 293
Among subjugated nations.................................. 294
Merlin and his prophecies.................................. 295
The ancient Britons, Cymri................................. 295
Merlin in Southern Europe.................................. 296
Galfried's History of the Britons........................... 297
The German Dragon and the Red Dragon................ 299
King Arthur... 300
Merlin's influence on the Welsh............................ 301
The Irish predictions....................................... 302
The Scotch predictions..................................... 303
The Portuguese predictions................................. 304
Sebastian and the Sebastianists............................ 305
The prophecies of Vieira................................... 306
Byzantine prophecies....................................... 308
Constantinople.. 311
George of Trapezium....................................... 312

IV. THE PROPHECY ABOUT ROME.

"The Eternal City".. 314
Rome and the end of the world............................ 316
Prediction of St. Benedict.................................. 317
Richard Rolle de Hampole.................................. 318
Charles V... 319
Bishop Berthold's Prophecy................................. 319
Bartholomeo Brandano and Clement VII.................. 320
The Church to be saved by fleeing from Rome........... 323

V. THE CHARACTERISTICS OF THE PROPHETS.

No special sanctity required............................... 324
A double consciousness.................................... 325
Thomas Aquinas on the Prophets.......................... 325
False prophecy of Peter Damiani........................... 327
False prophecy of St. Bernard.............................. 328
False prophecy of Vincents Ferrer......................... 329
Prophecy of Catharine of Siena............................ 330
St. Brigitta nearer right.................................... 331
Two currents of prophecy.................................. 331
Savonarola an unwilling prophet........................... 332
Campanella, his prophecies and persecutions............ 333
Dionysius Ryckel "the ecstatic teacher".................. 335
Nicolas of Cusa... 335
Robert of Usez.. 337
Holzhauser's visions.. 337

VI. THE COSMOPOLITICAL PROPHECIES.

Four periods of the same	339
From the ninth to the eleventh century	340
The Holy Roman Empire	340
Revelations of Methodius	341
The Abbot Adso on the last conflict	342
The Mongol Irruption	344
Gog and Magog	344
Brandt's edition of Methodius	346
The prophetess Hildegarde	348
Guelphs and Ghibellines in Italy	351
Separation of Empire and Papacy	353
Predicted destiny of the empire	354
Jordan of Osnabrück	355
The Belgian chronicler, Dynter	357
Roger Bacon	359
Influence of Astrology	359
The Flagellants, in 1260	360
The Papa Angelico in Bacon	361
The Emperor Frederick II	362
The Catharists	363
Dolcino in Italy; and the war he occasioned	364

VII. THE JOACHIMITES.

Joachim's prophetic gifts	364
His great repute and sanctity	366
Prophecies under his name	369
The unfulfilled prophecies	369
Salimbene's position	370
John of Parma and Bonaventura	373
General view of Joachim's system	374
The three great periods	374
The last period	376
The Empire misunderstood by the Guelphs	378
Difference between the true and false Joachim	379
French and not Italians first attack Joachim	380
William of St. Amour	380
Gherardino's Eternal Gospel	382
His "Introductorius" condemned	383
Exact dates given up	384
Seven periods	384
D'Olive on the Apocalypse	385
Ubertino's work (in note)	385
Antichrist to be on the papal chair	386
Boniface VIII. "the new Lucifer"	386
Summary about the "Spirituals"	388

TABLE OF CONTENTS.

The prophecy of Cyril from Constantinople 389
Arnold of Villanova..................................... 390
Prophecies about the religious Orders................... 391

VIII. THE PROPHETIC SPIRIT FROM THE FOURTEENTH CENTURY TO THE BEGINNING OF THE REFORMATION.

The Silver Tables of Cyril.............................. 393
Cola di Rienzo.. 393
The "Papa Angelicus".................................... 394
Petrarch's Sonnet on Rome............................... 395
Jean de la Rochetaillarde............................... 396
Catharine of Siena and Brigitta......................... 398
Rome canonizes these prophets........................... 399
Brigitta's Prediction applied to Pius IX................ 400
The Black Death... 401
The Crusades and Palestine.............................. 402
The Angelic Pope again.................................. 403
The fate of the Monk Theodore........................... 404
Savonarola as "Papa Angelicus".......................... 405
The "Papa Angelicus" quadrupled......................... 406
Joachimites and Anti-Joachimites........................ 407
Henry of Langenstein.................................... 407
The Predictions of Telesphorus.......................... 409
He revives the prediction about Frederick III........... 410
But applies it to the French King....................... 410
Gamaleon's counter German prophecy...................... 411
Theological refutation of Telesphorus by Henry of Langenstein... 412
Warning more general as the Reformation drew near....... 413
Bishop Grosseteste of Lincoln........................... 414
Macchiavelli and Pico of Mirandula...................... 414
The prophecies of Savonarola............................ 415
His sagacity like that of Cicero and Du Vair............ 416
His political prophecies true and religious false....... 417
German popular prophecies............................... 419
John Lichtenberger and the prophecies ascribed to him... 419
Aytinger and Grünpeckh.................................. 420
John Hagen's warnings................................... 421
Henry of Largenstein.................................... 422
German prophecies of a German pope...................... 423
Bishop Berthold's "Burden of the Church"................ 424
The Swiss poet Gengenbach on the Emperor Maximilian..... 425
Close of the fifteenth century.......................... 425

APPENDICES.

A. The Papess in the Tegernsee MS.................... 427
B. Further particulars about Pope Joan................ 430
C. Illustration of the growth of Myths................ 438
D. Pope Hadrian's Letter to Henry of England......... 444
E. Ex Cathedrâ Definitions........................... 447
F. Defenders of Honorius, etc........................ 456
G. The Prophecies of Malachias...................... 462

PART I.

MEDIÆVAL FABLES ABOUT THE POPES.

I. POPE JOAN.

THE subject of Pope Joan has not yet lost the interest which belongs to it as a fact in the province of historical criticism. The literature respecting her reaches down to the very latest times. As recently as 1843 and 1845 two works on this question appeared from the pens of two Dutch scholars; the one by Professor Kist,[1] to prove the existence of Pope Joan, the other, a very voluminous one, by Professor Wensing, of Warmond, to disprove Kist's position. In Italy Bianchi-Giovini wrote a book on the subject in the same year, 1845, without being aware of the works of the two Dutch writers. In Germany no one—at any rate of those who know anything of

---

1 [*A Woman in the Chair of S. Peter.* Another edition of this has lately appeared; Gütersloh, 1866. Professor Kist thinks that Pope Joan was possibly the widow of Leo IV.]

[Kist's Essay was first published in the *Nederlandsch Archief voor Kerkelijke Geschiedenis*, iii, 27. See Gieseler's *Church History*, New York edition, vol. ii, pp. 30-1,—a long note, summing up all the data in the case. H. B. S.]

history—will easily be induced to entertain a serious belief in the existence of the female pope. To do so, one must do violence to every principle of historical criticism. But with the banishment of the subject to the realm of fable all has not yet been completely accomplished. The riddle—how this strange myth originated—remains still to be solved.

Nothing but the insufficiency and ill-success of all previous attempts at an explanation can account for it that a man like Luden, in his *History of the German People*,[1] does all he can to make the reality of the well-known myth at any rate probable. "It is in-"conceivable," says he, "how it could ever enter into "any man's head to invent such a foolish, insane "falsehood. He must either have invented his lie "out of sheer wantonness in order to scoff at the "papacy, or he must have intended to gain some "other object by means of it. But of all the dozens "of writers who mention Pope Joan and her mishap, "there is not a single one who can be called an "enemy of the papacy. They are clergy, monks, "guileless people, who notice this phenomenon in the "same dry way in which they mention other things, "that seem to them to be strange, wonderful, "laudable, abominable, or in any way worth men-

---

[1] *Geschichte des deutschen Volkes*, vi., 513-517.

" tioning." "And it cannot be imagined," says Luden further on, "what object could seem to any one to be attainable by means of such a falsehood. Moreover, it is inconceivable how people in general could have believed in the story, and that without the slightest doubt, for nearly 500 years from the eleventh century onwards, if it had not been true."

It is here to be noted that Luden make the myth of Pope Joan a matter of general belief from the *eleventh* century onwards. It would be very much nearer the truth to say that it did not find general belief till the middle of the *fourteenth* century. The author, however, of the article on Pope Joan in the *Nouvelle Biographie Générale*, published at Paris by Dr. Höfer, as lately as 1858, goes much further.[1] "This belief prevailed in the christian world from the *ninth* century to the Renaissance." And to crown it all, Hase thinks it, at any rate, credible that the Church, not content with creating facts, annihilated them, also, whenever the knowledge of them seemed critical for the already tottering papacy.[2] According to Hase and Kist, then, we must state the matter thus: that soon after the year 855 an edict issued from Rome to this effect: " Let no one presume to say a word about the fact of " a female pope," for at that time Rome did not feel

[1] Vol. xxvi., p. 569. [2] *Kirchengeschichte*, 7. Aufl. s. 213.

her position to be as yet very secure. About the middle of the thirteenth century, however, a counter order issued from the same place: "Henceforth it "is lawful to discuss history; we now consider our "position safe, and can venture to let the narrative "appear in historical works."

The judgment of Kurtz is, at any rate, more sober and free from prejudice.[1] "The evidence before us," he says, "forbids us to assign to the myth any histo-"rical value whatever. We must, however, (quite "apart from the falsification of the acts, which, in "some cases, is manifest, in others is a matter of "suspicion,) characterize the myth as a riddle, which "criticism has as yet not solved, and *probably never* "*will.*"

That the riddle has not yet been solved, that all attempts at explanation which have been made up to the present time, must be held to have miscarried, is true enough; that a solution which may satisfy the historian is, nevertheless, possible, it will be the object of the following pages to show.

Let us first glance for a moment at the explanations which have been set forth up to this time. Baronius considers the myth to be a satire on John

---

[1] *Handbuch der Kirchengeschichte*, 1856, ii. Band, 1. Abtheilung s. 225.

VIII., "ob nimiam ejus animi facilitatem et mollitudinem," qualities which he exhibited more especially in the affair of Photius. Others, Aventine to begin with, and after him Heumann and Schröckh, prefer to reckon the supposed satire as one on the period of female rule in Rome, the reign of Theodora and Marozia under certain popes, some of whom were called John; in which case, however, it would have to be transferred from the middle of the ninth century to the tenth. The opinion published by the Jesuit Secchi in Rome, that it is a calumny originating with the Greeks, namely with Photius, is eqally inadmissible. The first Greek who mentions the circumstance is the monk Barlaam in the fourteenth century. Pagi's assertion also, which Eckhart supports, that the myth was an invention of the Waldenses, is pure imagination. The myth evidently originated in Rome itself, and the first to give it circulation were not the Waldenses, but their most deadly enemies—the Dominicans and Minorites.

Leo Allatius thought that a false prophetess called Thiota, in the ninth century, gave occasion to this myth. The explanation invented by Leibnitz[1] is also a forced attempt to meet the exigencies of the case.

---

[1] *Flores sparsi in Tumulum Papissæ*, ap. Scheid, Biblioth. His. Goetting., p. 367.

There might very well, he thinks, have been a foreign *bishop* (pontifex *i. e.* episcopus), really a woman in disguise, who gave birth to a child during a procession at Rome, and thus gave occasion to the story.

Blasco and Henke supposed that the myth about the female pope was a satirical allegory on the origin and circulation of the false decretals of Isidore. This interpretation, however, is entirely at variance with the genius of that century, an age in which men had no sense for satirical allegories; and then too it refutes itself, for the story of Pope Joan originated at a time when no one doubted the genuineness of the false decretals of Isidore. Nevertheless, Gfrörer has lately taken up this idea, and worked it out in a still more artificial manner.[1] "The whole force of the fable," he says, "resides in these two points, that the "woman was a native of Mayence, and that she came "from Greece (Athens), and ascended the papal-chair. "In the first particular I recognise a condemnation "directed against the canons of the pseudo-Isidore, in "the second an allegorical censure of the alliance "which Leo IV. wished to make with the Byzan- "tines. . . It is said that in the later days of Leo IV. "the papal power in Mayence and Greece was abused, "or to make use of a metaphor, of which the Italians

---

[1] *Kirchengeschichte,* III., iii., 978.

"are very fond in such cases, was at that time "*prostituted.*" Side by side with this explanation, which can scarcely fail to provoke a smile from any one who is acquainted with the Middle Ages, stands the extraordinary circumstance, that there is no authority whatever for this intention of Leo IV. to compromise himself more than was right with the Byzantines. It is purely an hypothesis of Gfrörer's. But the myth about Pope Joan, as thus interpreted, is in turn made to do further service as a proof of the correctness of this hypothesis, as well as for his assumption that the false decretals originated in Mayence.

In short, all the attempts at explanation, which have hitherto been made, split on this rock—that the myth had its origin in a much later age; when the remembrance of the events and circumstances of the ninth and tenth centuries had long ago faded away, or at most existed only in the case of individual scholars, and, therefore, could not form material for the construction of a myth. That is to say, I believe, that I can without difficulty produce convincing evidence, that the myth about the female-pope, though it may possibly have had somewhat earlier circulation in the mouth of the people, was not definitively put into writing before the middle of the thirteenth century. This evidence could not have been given with anything like certainty before the present time. For it is only during the last forty[1] years that all the stores of mediæval manuscripts in the whole of Europe have been hunted through with a care such as was never known before. Every library corner has been searched, and an astounding quantity of historical documents, hitherto unknown (what a mass of new material exists in the Pertz collection alone, for instance!), has been brought to light. Nevertheless, not a single notice of the myth about Pope Joan has been discovered, which is earlier than the close, or, at the very most, the middle of the thirteenth century. We can now say quite positively, that in the collected literature, whether western or Byzantine, of the four centuries between 850 and 1250, there is not the faintest reference to the circumstance of a female pope.

For a long time it was supposed that the myth, though certainly not to be found in any author of the ninth or tenth century, appeared as already in existence in the eleventh and twelfth centuries. Marianus Scotus[2] is said to have been the first to mention the

---

[1] [This was written in 1863.]

[2] [Born, probably in Ireland, about 1028; died at Mayence, 1086, not to be confounded with Marianus, the Franciscan, a Florentine writer of the fifteenth century. In 1056 Marianus Scotus entered the

female pope, and he certainly does mention her in the text as given by Pistorius. Now, however, that the text in the great Pertz collection has been edited by Waitz[1] according to the most ancient manuscripts, the fact has come to light, that Marianus knew nothing whatever of Pope Joan. In his case, as in the case of so many other authors, the short mention of the female pope has been interpolated at a later period. In the chronicle of Sigebert of Gemblours, and the supplements of the monks of Orcamp (*Auctarium Ursicampinum*), the notice of the papess is wanting in all original manuscripts. She was first inserted by the first editor in the year 1513.[2] Kurtz

abbey of S. Martin at Cologne; in 1059 he moved to the abbey of Fulda, and thence in 1069 to Mayence. He passed for the most learned man of his age, being a mathematician and theologian as well as historian. His *Chronicon Universale* is based on Cassiodorus, augmented from Eusebius and Bede, and the chronicles of Hildesheim and Würzburg, and extends down to the year 1083; published at Basle by Hérold, 1559.]

[1] *Monumenta German. Hist.* viii., 550. [v. 551. vi. 340, 470.]

[2] "In nullo quem noverimus Sigeberti codice occurrit locus "famosus de Johanna papissa, quem hoc loco editio princeps ex- "hibet," says the latest editor, Bethmann, ap. Pertz, viii., 340. Compare the remark, p. 470, where Bethmann says decisively, "nemo "igitur restat (as interpolater of the passage) nisi primus editor, "sive is Antonius Rufus fuerit, sive Henricus Stephanus." It is a mistake when Kurtz elsewhere (p. 228) says with regard to Sigebert and Marianus: "The oldest editors would scarcely have added the "passages in question out of their own heads; and therefore it is "probable that the passages were purposely omitted in the codices

has lately appealed again to the supposed evidence of Otto of Freysingen.¹ In the list of the popes, continued down to the year 1513, which is printed with his historical work,² Pope John VII. (in the year 705) is marked as a woman, without one single word of explanation. And in the edition of the *Pantheon*, as given by Pistorius, we find in the list of the popes these words, "the Papess Johanna is not reckoned."

Meanwhile a close investigation of the oldest and best manuscripts of Gottfried's *Pantheon* and of Otto's chronicle have brought it to light, that originally neither the word "fœmina" was placed in Otto's chronicle against the name of John VII., nor the gloss "Johanna Papissa non numeratur" in the *Pantheon*

"which they had before them." There are no signs whatever of anything being intentionally omitted or effaced; in many of the manuscripts, on the other hand, there are many signs of subsequent insertions and additions in the margin. [Sigebert was born about 1030, and died 1112. His chronicle extends from 381, where Eusebius ended, to 1112.]

1 *Kirchengeschichte*, ii., 226

2 [Otto, Bishop of Freysingen, went with his brother, Conrad III., on his crusade to the Holy Land, resuming his diocese on his return. He died in September 1158, having held the see twenty years. His chronicle in seven books extends down to 1146. The first four books are a mere compilation from Orosius, Eusebius, Isidore, Bede, &c.; the last three are of great value. He also wrote two books *De Gestis Friderici I. Ænobarbi*, which come down to the year 1157.]

between Leo IV. and Benedict III.; both of which insertions are given in the printed editions.¹

In the chronicle of Otto the addition to the name of John VII. is manifestly the work of a later copyist or reader, who inserted the word quite at random, because he was bound to have a female John somewhere among the popes. The fact that this John comes as early as the year 705 was the less likely to puzzle him, because the list of popes in this chronicle does not give the dates.²

The first who really took up the myth is the author of a chronicle, to which Stephen de Bourbon appeals without giving any more exact quota-

---

1 [That confusion prevailed in some of the lists of the popes precisely at this point is shown by an annalist, who apparently wrote in Halberstadt 854: "Benedictus papa, ut quidam volunt, "hoc anno factus est, et post hunc Paulus (!), post eum Stephanus "per annos quatuor sedisse inveniuntur."—Baxmann, *Politik der Päpste*, i., p. 361, note.]

2 In the good original manuscripts of the *Pantheon* in the royal library at Munich the addition about Pope Joan is wanting. These are:—Cod. Lat. 43 (from Hartmann Schedel's collection) f. 118, b. Cod. Windberg. 37, or Cod. Lat. 22,237, f. 168 b. Similarly in the oldest manuscripts of the chronicle of Otto in the Munich library the addition to the name of John VII. does not appear. These are Cod. Weihensteph. 61, or Lat. 21,561, which is of about the same date. Cod. Frising. 177, or Lat. 6,517. Cod. Scheftlarn. Lat. 17,1-4, in which the list of popes comes to an end with Hadrian IV., and therefore is also of the same date.

tion.¹ That is to say, Stephen, a French Dominican, born towards the close of the twelfth century, died in the year 1261, in his work on the Seven Gifts of the Holy Spirit,² which was written just about the middle of the thirteenth century, makes the first mention of Pope Joan, whom he asserts he has discovered in a chronicle. Now seeing that he refers with exactness to all the sources from which he has gathered together the collection of passages which contribute to his

1 [He merely says] "dicitur in chronicis." He means no more than *one* chronicle; Chronica is constantly used in the plural as a title. Otherwise Stephen would naturally have added "variis" or "pluribus."

2 It has never been printed. The whole, or portions of it, exist in the French libraries, one portion of it in the Munich library. Echard was the first to cite it at great length in his work, *Sancti Thomæ Summa Suo Auctori Vindicata*, Paris, 1708; and again in the *Scriptores Ordinis Prædicatorum*, pt. i.

[The passage from Stephen de Bourbon as cited by Gieseler (ii. 31) from Quetif and Echard, Scriptores Ordinis Pradicatorum, i. 367, reads: Accidit autem, mirabilis audacia, imo insana, circa ann. Dom MC. [CM?] ut dicitur in chronicis. Quaedam mulier literata, et in arte nondi (notandi?) edocta, adsunto virili habitu, et virum sefingens, venit Romam, et tam industria, quam literatura accepta, facta est notarius curiae, post diabolo procurante cardinalis, postea Papa. Haec impraegnata cum ascenderet peperit. Quod cum novisset Romana justitia, ligatis pedibus ejus ad pedes equi distracta est extra urbem, et ad dimidiam leucam a populo lapidata, et ubi fuit mortua, ibi fuit sepulta, et super lapidem super ea positum scriptus est versiculus: "Parce pater patrum papissae edere partum." The same story appears in an enlarged form in Martini Poloni († 1278), Chron., and here the passage is perhaps genuine, although it is also wanting in several MSS.   H. B. S.]

practical homiletic object, we can, at least with great probability, show from what chronicle he has obtained this mention of Pope Joan. Among chroniclers he names Eusebius, Jerome, Bede, Odo, Hugo of St. Victor, the "Roman Cardinal," and John de Mailly, a Dominican. We may set aside all but the two last· The "Roman Cardinal" (or Cardinal Romanus (?)—there were several of this name, but none of them wrote a chronicle) is probably none other than the author of the *Historia Miscella*, or continuation of Eutropius, whom the Dominican, Tolomeo of Lucca, also quotes later on among his authorities as Paulus Diaconus Cardinalis ;[1] but he cannot be distinguished with certainty. It remains then that the lost, or as yet undiscovered, chronicle of the Dominican Jean de Mailly,[2] who, moreover, must have been a contemporary of Stephen, is the only source to which the latter can have been indebted for his account of Pope Joan. And Jean de Mailly, we may be tolerably certain, got it from popular report.

We can, therefore, consider it as established—that not until the year 1240 or 1250, was the myth about the woman-pope put into writing and transferred to works of history. Several decades more passed,

---

[1] Cf. Quetif et Echard *Scriptores Ordinis Prædicatorum*, i.. **544**.
[2] On him see the *Histoire littéraire de la France*, **xviii., 532.**

however, before it came actually into circulation and became really wide-spread. The chronicle of Jean de Mailly seems to have remained in obscurity, for no one, with the exception of his brother Dominican, Stephen, notices it; and even Stephen's large work—great as was its value, especially to preachers, on account of the quantity of examples which it contained, was not possessed by very many, as is proved by the scarcity of existing manuscripts of it. The *Speculum Morale*, which bears the name of Vincent of Beauvais, was the chief cause of this. For this work appropriated most of the examples and instances given by Stephen, but was superior to Stephen's books both in convenience of arrangement and fulness of matter, and eclipsed it so completely, that the narrative about Pope Joan, in the form in which it appears in Stephen's work, is to be found nowhere else.

The chronicle of Martinus Polonus has been the principal means of giving circulation to the myth. This book, which gives a synchronistic history of the popes and emperors in the form of a dry, mechanical, and utterly uncritical collection of biographical notes, exercised a most extraordinary influence on the chroniclers and historians from the beginning of the fourteenth century onwards, especially on their ways of thinking in the latter part of the Middle Ages.

Wattenbach's[1] statement, that Martinus Polonus became almost the exclusive historical instructor of the catholic world, is not an exaggeration. Of no other historical book is there such an inexhaustible number of manuscripts in existence as of this. All volumes of the *Archiv für deutsche Geschichtskunde* show this. And indeed the book was held in estimation in almost all countries alike, was translated into all languages, was continued over and over again, and still more frequently copied by later chroniclers. That the effect of such a book, utterly unhistorical and stuffed with fables, was to the last degree mischievous, so that (as Wattenbach says) the careful, thorough, and critical investigation of the history of the early Middle Ages, prosecuted with so much zeal during the twelfth century, was completely choked, or nearly so, by Martin's chronicle, cannot be denied.

The position of the author could not fail to win for his history of the popes an amount of authority such as no other similar writing obtained. Troppau was his birth-place, the Dominican order his profession. He was for a long time the chaplain and penitentiary of the popes; as such lived naturally at the papal court, followed, everywhere, the Curia, which was

---

[1] *Deutschlands Geschichtsquellen*, s. 426.

then constantly on the move, and died [A.D. 1278] as archbishop designate of Gnesen. His book, therefore, was considered to a certain extent to be the official history of the popes, issuing from the Curia itself. And hence people accepted the history of Pope Joan also, which they found in Martinus Polonus, all the more readily and unsuspectingly. The form in which he gives the myth became the prevailing one ; and most authors have contented themselves with copying the passage from his chronicle word for word. Nevertheless, Martin himself, as can be proved, knew nothing about Pope Joan, or, at any rate, said nothing about her. Not until several years after his death did attempts begin to be made to insert the myth into his book. It is no doubt correct that Martin himself prepared a second and later edition of his work, which reaches down to Nicolas III., 1277, while the first edition only goes down to Clement IV. (died 1268). But the second is exactly like the first in arrangement. Each pope, and each emperor on the opposite page, had as many lines assigned to him as he reigned years, and each page contained fifty lines, that is, embraced half a century. Hence, in the copies which kept to the original arrangement of the author, additions or insertions could only be made in those places where the account of a pope or emperor did not fill all the lines assigned to him, owing to the short period of his reign. But the insertion of a pope had been rendered impossible by Martin himself and all the copyists who kept to the plan of the book, by means of the detailed chronology, according to which every line had a date, and in the case of each pope and emperor the length of his reign was exactly stated. But for this same reason Pope Joan also, if she had originally had a place in his book, could not have been *effaced*, nor have been omitted from the copies which held fast to the arrangement of the original.

Pope Joan then does not occur in the eldest manuscripts of Martinus. She is wanting especially in those which have kept to the exact chronological method of the author. Nor is the opinion tenable, that Martinus brought her into the latest edition of his book prepared by himself. That theory is contradicted by manuscripts, which come down to the time of Nicolas III., and, nevertheless, contain no trace of Pope Joan. Echard[1] has already noticed several such manuscripts. The exquisite Aldersbach[2] manuscript, now in the Royal Library at

---

[1] On this point see Quetif et Echard. *Scriptores Ordinis Prædicatorum*, 1. 367; and Lequien *Oriens Chr.* iii., 385.

[2] Aldersp. 161, fol. Pergam.

Munich, gives the same evidence. There are, however, manuscripts in which her history is written in the margin at the bottom of the sheet, or as a gloss at the side.[1] It was thence gradually, and one may add very violently, thrust in the text. This was done in various ways: either Benedict III., the successor of Leo, was struck out, and Pope Joan put in his place, as is the case in a Hamburg[2] codex reaching down to the year 1302. Or she is placed, usually by some later hand, without any date being given, as an addition or mere legend in the vacant space left after Leo IV. Or, lastly—merely in order to gain the necessary two years and a half for her reign—the whole chronological reckoning of the author is thrown into confusion; either by assigning an earlier date than is correct to several of Leo's predecessors, and that as far back as the year 800; or by giving to individual popes fewer years than belong to them. This eagerness to interpolate the female pope in the book at all hazards—so to speak,—without shrinking from the most arbitrary alterations in the chronology in order to attain this object, is certainly somewhat astonishing. Just the very circumstance which above

1 In the *Archiv für altere deutsche Geschichtskunde* quotations from several of these are given, e. g. vii., 657.

2 Archiv vi., 230.

all others conferred on Martin's book a certain amount of value, viz. the painstaking and continuous chronological reckoning line by line, has been sacrificed in several manuscripts,[1] merely in order to make the insertion of Pope Joan possible; or else only one year has been placed against the name of each pope, either in the margin or in the text, in order to conceal the disagreement between the insertion of Pope Joan and the chronological plan of the author.

It was in the period between 1278 and 1312 that the interpolation took place; for Tolomeo of Lucca, who completed his historical work in the year 1312, remarks[2] that all the authorities which he had read placed Benedict III. next after Leo IV.; Martinus Polonus was the only one who put Johannes Anglicus in between. By this means two facts are established; first, the industrious collector Tolomeo knew of no writing in which a mention of Pope Joan was to be found, except the chronicle of Martinus; secondly, the copy of Martinus with which he was acquainted was one which had her *already* inserted, and that in the *text*. Had the account of her merely been written

---

[1] "Nulla chronologia, sed adest fabula," says Echard of several manuscripts of **Martinus** which he had seen, p. 369.

[2] *Hist. Eccles.*, 16, 8.

alongside in the margin, this would undoubtedly have aroused Tolomeo's suspicions, and he would have noticed the fact in his own work.

Another main vehicle for circulating the myth about the papess was the chronicle *Flores Temporum*, which exists in numerous manuscripts under the names of Martinus Minorita, Herrmannus Januensis, and Herrmannus Gigas. It was printed by Eccard, and, in another form, by Meuschen; and after that of Martinus Polonus, was the most widely circulated of all the later chronicles. Unlike Martinus Polonus, however, it appears to have come into general use only in Germany. It reaches down to 1290, and is in the main not much more than a compilation from the chronicle of Martinus Polonus, as the author himself states. According to the conjecture of Eccard and others, Martinus Minorita is the original author,[1] and Herrmannus Januensis or Gigas the continuer[2] of the chronicle down to the year 1349. Pertz,[3] on the other hand, is of opinion that what is printed under the name of Martinus Minorita is only a poor extract from the work of Herrmannus Gigas, who brought his chronicle down to the year 1290, and died in 1336.

1 *Archiv der Gesellschaft für deutsche Geschichtskunde*, viii., 835.
2 Archiv i., 402 ff.
3 Achiv vii., 115.

The relation between the Minorite Martin and the Wilhelmite Herrmann of Genoa appears meanwhile to be this:—that the latter has copied the Minorite, with [1] many omissions and additions, but without mentioning him. Martin the Penitentiary—that is Martinus Polonus—is given as the main authority. It was **from him, then,** beyond all doubt, that the story about Pope Joan passed (embellished with additions) into chronicles of considerably later date; for manuscripts in which it is wanting have not come within my knowledge.

The story of Pope Joan has also been inserted in the so-called Anastasius [2] (the most ancient collection known of biographies of the popes), and in precisely the same form as that in which it exists in Martinus Polonus. The literal wording of the text does not allow the possibility that the story really formed any

---

[1] Bruns, in Gabler's *Journal für theolog. Lit.* 1811, **vol.** vi., p. 88, **etc.** Bruns had a manuscript before him in Helmstadt, which was marked as a work of Herrmannus Minorita. But at the end of the **document** the author **was** correctly styled Herrmannus Ordinis S. **Wilhelmi.**

[2] [Anastasius, the Librarian of the Vatican, took part in A.D. 869 **in** the eighth General Council at Constantinople, where his learning and knowledge of Latin and **Greek** were of great service to the **papal** legates. His celebrated *Liber Pontificalis* is a compilation of lives of the popes from S. Peter down to Nicolas I., first printed at **Mayence in 1602. Only the lives of** some of the popes of his **own times can be** regarded as his own composition.]

part of the original text. The interpolation must have been made with the most foolish wantonness, or just as has been done in the Heidelberg manuscripts, by striking out Benedict III., and then inserting Joan in his place. In other copies she has been added by a later hand in the margin, at the side, or quite at the bottom of the page.

The most natural supposition, and the one which Gabler[1] also follows, seems then to be, that the papess passed from Martinus Polonus into the few, and very much later, manuscripts of Anastasius which contain it. Nevertheless, I am driven to the conjecture that the myth was in the first instance added at the end of some copy of the collection of biographies of the popes which bears the name of Anastasius. For it has long ago been remarked[2] that the life of Benedict III. in this collection is the work of a different author from that of the lives immediately preceding it, especially of the very detailed life of Leo IV. There must, therefore, beyond all doubt, have been copies which came to an end with Leo IV., whose biographer was obviously a contemporary. The notice of Pope Joan might then have been added

---

[1] Gabler's *Kleinere theolog. Schriften*, vol. i., p. 446.

[2] See Bahr, *Geschichte der Rom. Literatur im Karoling. Zeitalter*, p. 269.

at the end by a later hand, and from thence have passed into the manuscripts of Martinus Polonus.

One sees this from the catalogue of manuscripts which Vignoli gives at the beginning of his edition. The Cod. Vatic. 3764 reaches down to Hadrian II., the Cod. Vatic. 5869 only down to Gregory II.; the Cod. 629 to Hadrian I.; others to John VIII., Nicolas I., Leo III., and so forth. In Cod. 3762, which comes down to the year 1142, the fable of the papess is added in later and smaller handwriting underneath in the margin.

This conjecture, one must allow, is by no means easy to prove. But supposing it correct, we have then the simplest of all explanations for the interpolation of Pope Joan between Leo IV. and Benedict III., where she certainly has not the [1] slightest connection with the history of the time. Meanwhile, I find in Martinus himself reasons for this place being assigned to her, and the following two in particular. The first is a mere matter of chance, arising out of the mechanical arrangement; for Martinus did not know

---

[1] **Leo IV. died July 11th, 855.** Benedict was forthwith [the same month] elected; and, after the emperor had given his consent, was consecrated on 29th of September in the same year, the very day after the Emperor Lothair died. It is notorious that contemporaries, such as Prudentius and Hincmar, notice that Benedict was Leo's immediate successor, and a diploma of Benedict's dated as early as October 7th, 855 (Mansi *Concill.* xv., 113) is still extant.

how to fill up the eight lines which he was obliged to devote to the eight years of Leo's pontificate, so that the first lines of the page which contained the second half of the ninth century remained empty. Here, therefore, the interpolation could be managed without the slightest trouble. But there was a further reason in the nature of the story itself. For the extreme improbability that a woman should be promoted to the highest ecclesiastical office, and be chosen by all as pope, was explained in the myth by her great intellectual attainments. She surpassed every one in Rome, so it was said, in learning. Naturally then, as soon as a definite historical place had to be assigned to her (the *popular* form of the myth had not troubled itself with fixed dates), a tolerably early period—at any rate, one anterior to the time of Gregory VII.—had to be chosen for her. For this, however, they were obliged to fall back on a period in which there was only a single instance known of a man being elected to the papacy on account of his preeminent knowledge. Since Gregory the Great there had been no pope who was really very remarkable for learning. In the four centuries between John VI., 701, and Gregory VII., this very Leo IV. is the only one whom Martinus notices in particular as a man who " divinarum scripturarum extitit ferventissimus scrutator," one who already, in the monastery [of St. Martin] to which his parents had sent him **for purposes of study, became** remarkable for his learning **no** less than for **his** mode of life, and on this account also was unanimously [1] elected pope by the Romans after the death **of** Sergius. On that occasion, **then, it** was intellectual attainment which influenced the votes of the Romans ; **and therefore it** might happen **that a woman,** whose **sex was not** known, could **be** chosen as pope by the Romans, because of her intellectual superiority. Now the interpolated Martinus speaks **of** Joan in much the same terms as of Leo ; " in diversis scientiis ita profecit, " **ut** nullus sibi **par** inveniretur ;" and, " quum in urbe " vita et scientia **magnæ** opinionis esset, **in** papam " concorditer eligitur." And hence **in** Martinus Polonus, who speaks in this manner of no **other**[2] **pope in that** century, the place assigned to Pope **Joan was** that immediately after Leo IV., whom she resembled

---

1 [Sergius **died** Jan. 27th. Leo IV. was forthwith elected, and consecrated on April 10th, without waiting even for the leave of the sovereign, not as denying his **authority, but because of** the pressing fear of the Saracens, **who had ventured up** the Tiber, and plundered the Basilica of St. Peter at the end **of 846.** See Baxmann, *Politik der Päpste,* vol. i., p. 352. This **fear of the** Saracens may have had something **to** do with the unanimity **of the electors.**]

2 **For Gerbert** (Sylvester II.) owed **his** promotion, 999-1003, according to Martinus, not to his great learning, but to the devil.

in this particular. And since every one took the work of Martinus as their authority, she retained this position.

It is at the stage when the myth was just beginning to gain circulation, and was still received with suspicion on many sides, that the passages on the subject in the *Historical Mirror* of Van Maerlant and in Tolomeo of Lucca come in. Maerlant's Dutch chronicle is in verse, and is mainly taken from Vincent of Beauvais, but with additions from other sources. Maerlant says moreover (about the year 1283), "I do "not [1] feel clear or certain whether it is fable or fact; "but in the chronicles of the popes it is not usually "found." So also a manuscript list of the popes down to John XXII. (13): "Et [2] in paucis chronicis "invenitur."

One of the first who took the story of Pope Joan from the interpolated Martinus Polonus was Geoffroi de Courlon, a Benedictine of the Abbey of St. Pierre le Vif at Sens, whose chronicle,[3] a somewhat rough compilation, reaches down to 1295.

---

1 *Spiegel Historical*, uitgeg. door de Maatschappij der nederl. letterk. Leyden, 1857, iii., 220.

2 This is appended to the manuscript of the *Otia Imperialia* by Gervasius in Leyden. Wensing, *de Pausin Johanna*, p. 9.

3 *Notices et Extraits*, ii., 16. He adds, moreover, "Unde dicitur "quod Romani in consuetudinem traxerunt probare sexus electi per "foramen cathedræ lapideæ."—See *Hist. Lit. de France*, xxi., 10.

Next comes the Dominican Bernard Guidonis, in his unprinted *Flores Chronicorum*, and also (in the year 1311) in his now printed history [1] of the popes. He inserts Johannes Teutonicus (not Anglicus, therefore, according to him) natione Maguntinus, together with the whole fable about Pope Joan, keeping faithfully to his authority, Martinus Polonus.

About the same period another Dominican, Leo of Orvieto, contributed to the circulation of the fable, by receiving it into his history of the popes and emperors, which reached down to Clement V. [1305]. In his case also, Martinus Polonus is the source from which he draws in this particular, as also in his whole book.[2]

Now follow in the first half of the fourteenth century the Dominican John of Paris, Siffrid of Meissen, Occam the Minorite (who turned the story of Pope Joan to account in his controversy with John XXII.), the Greek Barlaam, the English Benedictine Ranulph Higden, the Augustine Amalrich Augerii, Boccaccio, and Petrarch.[3]

---

[1] Maii *Spicil*. Rom. vi., 202.

[2] In the third volume of Lami's *Deliciæ Eruditorum*, Florent. 1732, p, 143.

[3] *Chronica delle Vite de' Pontefici*, &c., Venetia, 1507, f. LV. He is here called Giovanni d'Anglia, and the dates are advanced two years, so that Benedict III. is placed in the year 857 (instead of

A chronicle of the popes by Aimery of Peyrat, Abbot of Moissac, written in the year 1399, has Johannes Anglicus in the list of popes, with the remark: "Some[1] say that this pope was a woman."

The Dominican Jacobe de Acqui,[2] who wrote about the year 1370, inserts the name without this remark, but with the extraordinary statement that this pontificate lasted *nineteen years*.

Of course people in general regarded the circumstance as to the last degree disgraceful to the Roman See, and, indeed, to the whole Church. The woman-pope had reigned for two years and a half, had performed a vast number of functions, all of which were now null and void; and, added to all this, there was the scandal of her giving birth to a child in the open street. It was scarcely possible to conceive anything more to the dishonor of the chair of the Apostle, or, indeed, of the whole of Christendom. What mockery must not this story excite among the Mohammedans!

As early as the close of the thirteenth, or beginning

855), and Nicolas I. in 859 (instead of 858). [Benedict III. died early in 858—April 7th; so that the difference between that and the end of 859 would not be far short of two years.]

1 *Notices et Extraits* vi., 82.

2 *Monum. Hist. Patriæ, Scriptores*, iii., 1524.

of the fourteenth century, Geoffroi de Courlon introduces the story with the heading *Deceptio Ecclesiæ Romanæ*.

Maerlant[1] says sorrowfully :—

> "Alse die paves Leo was doot—
> Ghesciede der Kerken grote scame."

"Johanne la Papesse," says[2] Jean le Maire, in the year 1511, "fist un grand esclandre à la Papalité."

All state that since that time the popes always avoid that street, so as not to look upon the scene of the scandal.

Now, when we consider that, according to the declaration of the Dominican Tolomeo of Lucca, down to the year 1312, the story was extant nowhere, except in certain copies of Martinus Polonus; that already innumerable lists of the popes, in their chronological order, were in existence, in none of which was there any trace of the female pope to be found,—the eagerness, which suddenly meets us at the close of the thirteenth century, to make the fable

---

1 ["Als der Papst Leo war todt—
Geschah der Kirche grosse Schame—"
After Pope Leo was dead
A great scandal rose in the church.]

2 In the *Traité de la Différence des Schismes et des Conciles de l'Eglise*, part iii., f. 2.

pass muster as history, and to smuggle it into the manuscripts, is certainly very astonishing. The author of the *Histoire Lit. de France* has good reason for saying, "Nous[1] ne saurions nous expliquer comment il "se fait que ce soit précisément dans les rangs de "cette fidèle milice du saint-siège que se rencontrent "les propagateurs les plus naïfs, et peut-être les inven-"teurs, d'une histoire si injurieuse à la papauté." Undoubtedly the thing emanated principally from those otherwise most devoted servants of the Roman See, the Dominicans[2] and the Minorites. It was certainly they, especially the former of the two, who were the first to multiply the copies of Martinus Polonus to such an extent, and thus spread the fable everywhere. The time at which this took place meanwhile solves the enigma. It was in the reign of Boniface VIII., who was not favourably disposed to

---

1 xxi., p. 10.

2 [A serious rupture between Rome and the friars took place under Innocent IV. The University of Paris, alarmed at the hold which the monks were getting, especially on the professorship, decreed that no religious order should hold more than one of the theological chairs. The Dominicans appealed to the pope. Innocent decided against them, and within a few days died. His death was openly attributed to their prayers—"quia impossible erat "multorum preces non audiri." Hence the well-known saying, "From the litanies of the friars, good Lord, deliver us."]

the two orders, and whose whole policy[1] displeased them. We see this in the unfavourable judgments which the Dominican historians formed respecting him, and in the attitude which they assumed at the outbreak of the strife between him and Philip the Fair. We notice that from this time, which was in general a crisis for the waning power of the popes, historians among the monastic orders mention and describe with a sort of relish scandals in the history of the popes.

In the fifteenth century scarcely a doubt is suggested. Quite at the beginning of the century the bust of Pope Joan was placed in the cathedral at Sienna along with the busts of the other popes, and no one took offence at it. The church of Sienna in the time that followed gave three popes to the Roman

---

[1] [This treatment of the English **Franciscans** made this not unnatural. The Franciscans, in direct contradiction to their vow of mendicancy, had gradually become very wealthy. The pope alone could free them from their rule. The English Minorites offered to deposit forty thousand ducats with certain bankers, as the price of permission to hold property. Boniface played with the monks till the money was paid, then absolved the bankers from their obligation to pay back money which mendicants ought never to have owned, and appropriated it as "res nullius" to his own uses. He thus made implacable enemies of the most popular and intellectual order in Europe. When Philip appealed severally to all the monastic orders in France, all the Franciscans, and with them the Dominicans, Hospitallers, and Templars, took their stand by him against the pope.]

See,—Pius II., Pius III., and Marcellus II. Not one of them ever thought of having the scandal removed. It was not till two centuries later, that, at the pressing demand of pope Clement VIII., 1592-1605, Joan was metamorphosed into pope Zacharias.[1] When Huss at the council of Constance supported[2] his doctrine by appealing to the case of Agnes, who became Pope Joan, he met with no contradiction from either side. Even the Chancellor Gerson himself turned to account the circumstance of the woman-pope as a proof that the Church could err[3] in matters of fact. On the other hand the Minorite Johann de Rocha, in a treatise written at the Council of Constance, uses the case of Johannes Maguntinus to show how dangerous it is to make the duty of obedience to the Church depend upon the personal character of the pope.[4]

[1] Lequien, *Oriens Christianus*, iii., 392.

[2] That is to say, he tried to prove that the Church could get on very well for a long time without any pope at all, because during the whole reign of Agnes, namely, two years and a half, it had had no real pope.—L'Enfant, *Histoire du Concile de Constance*, ii., 334. In his work *De Ecclesia* also, Huss comes back with delight to the woman-pope, whose name was Agnes, and who was called Johannes Anglicus. She is to him a striking proof that the Roman Church has in no way remained spotless: "Quomodo ergo illa Romana "Ecclesia, illa Agnes, Johannes Papa cum collegio semper immacu- "lata permansit, qui peperit?"

[3] In the speech which he made at Tarascon before Benedict XIII. in the year 1403. Opera, ed. Dupin, ii., 71.

[4] In Dupin's edition of the writings of Gerson, v. 456.

Heinrich Korner, a Dominican of Lubeck, 1402 to 1437, not only himself received the story about the woman-pope in its usual form into his chronicle, but stated in addition that his predecessor, the Dominican Henry of Herford (about 1350), whom he had often copied, had purposely concealed the circumstance, in order that the laity might not be scandalised by reading that such an error had taken place in the Church, which assuredly, as the clergy taught, was guided by the Holy Spirit.[1]

The matter was now generally set forth as an indubitable fact, and the scholastic theologians endeavoured to accommodate themselves to it, and to arrange their church system and the position of the popes in the Church in accordance with it. Æneas Sylvius, afterwards pope Pius II., had however replied to the Taborites, that the story was nevertheless not certain. But his contemporary, the great upholder of papal despotism, cardinal Torrecremata,[2] accepts it as notorious, that a woman was once regarded by all Catholics as pope, and thence draws the following conclusion: that, whereas God had allowed this to

---

[1] Ap. Eccard., ii., 442

[2] "Quum ergo constet quod aliquando mulier a cunctis Catholicis "putabatur Papa, non est incredibile quod aliquando hæreticus "habeatur pro Papa, licet verus Papa non sit.' —*Summa de Ecclesia,* edit. Venet., p. 394.

happen, without the whole constitution of the Church being thrown into confusion, so it might also come to pass, that a heretic or an infidel should be recognised as pope; and, in comparison with the fact of a female pope, that would be the smaller difficulty of the two.

St. Antoninus, belonging, like Torrecremata, to the middle of the fifteenth century, and like him a Dominican,[1] avails himself of the Apostle's words respecting the inscrutability of the divine counsels in connection with the supposed fact of a female pope, and declares that the Church was even then not without a Head, namely Christ, but that bishops and priests ordained by the woman must certainly be re-ordained.

The Dominican order, whose members chiefly contributed to spread the fable everywhere, possessed in their strict organization and their numerous libraries the means of discovering the truth. The General of the order had merely to command that the copies of Martinus Polonus, and the more ancient lists of the popes, of which there were quantities in existence in the monasteries of the order, should once for all be examined and compared together. But people preferred to believe what was most incredible

---

[1] *Summa Hist.*, lib. 16, p. 2, c. 1, § 7.

and most monstrous. Not one of these men, of course, had **ever seen, or** heard, that a woman had for years been public teacher, priest, and bishop, without being detected, or that the birth of a child had ever taken place in the public street. But that in Rome these two things once took place *together*, in order to disgrace the papal dignity—this people believed with readiness.

Martin le Franc, provost of Lausanne, about 1450, and secretary to the popes Felix V. and Nicholas V., in his great French poem, *Le Champion des Dames*, celebrated Pope Joan at length. First we have his astonishment, that such a thing should have been permitted to take place.

> " Comment endura Dieu, comment
> Que femme ribaulde et prestresse
> Eut l'Eglise en gouvernement?"

It would have been no wonder had **God come down** to judgment, when a woman ruled the world. But now the defender steps forward and makes apology—

> " Or laissons **les** péchés, disans,
> Qu'elle étoit clergesse lettrée,
> Quand devant les plus suffisants
> De **Rome eut l'issue et** l'entrée.
> Encore **te peut être montrée**
> Mainte **Préface que dicta,**
> Bien et saintement **accoustrée**
> Où en la foy point n'hésita."[1]

[1] Ap. Oudin, *Comm. de Ser. Eccl.*, iii. 2466.

She had, therefore, composed many quite orthodox prefaces for the mass.

It was not until the second half of the fifteenth century that the story came into the hands of the Greeks. Welcome as the occurrence of such a thing would have been to a Cerularius and like-minded opponents of the papal chair in Constantinople, no one had as yet mentioned it, until Chalcocondylas, in the history of his time, in which he describes the mode of electing a pope, mentions also the fiction of an examination as to sex, and apropos of that relates the catastrophe of Pope Joan; an occurrence which, as he remarks, could only have taken place in the West, where the clergy do not allow their beard to grow.[1] It is in him that we get the outrageous feature added to the story, that the child was born just as the woman was celebrating High Mass, and was seen by the assembled congregation.[2]

In the fifteenth and sixteenth centuries, says the Roman writer Cancellieri, the romance about Pope

---

[1] *De Rebus Turcicis*, ed. Bekker, Bonn, 1843, p. 303.

[2] Ὡς εἰς τὴν θυσίαν ἀφίκετο, γεννῆσαί τε τὸ παιδίον κατὰ τὴν θυσίαν καὶ ὀφθῆναι ὑπὸ τοῦ λαοῦ.

The cleric, who examines the sex of the newly-elected, cries out with a loud voice: ἄρρην ἡμῖν ἐστὶν ὁ δεσπότης, l. c., p. 303. Barlaam, who had mentioned the fable as early as the fourteenth century, lived in Italy.

Joan circulated widely in all chronicles which were written and copied in Italy, and even under the very eyes of Rome.[1] Thus it appears in print in Ricobaldo's Italian chronicle of the popes, which Filippo de Lignamine dedicated to pope Sixtus IV. in 1474. So also in the history of the popes by the Venetian priest Stella.[2] For a long time, and even as late as 1548 and 1550, it found a place in numerous Roman editions of the *Mirabilia Urbis Romæ*,[3] which was a sort of guide for pilgrims and strangers.

Felix Hemmerlin, Trithemius, Nauclerus, Albert Krantz, Coccius Sabellicus, Raphael of Volterra, Joh. Fr. Pico di Mirandola, the Augustine Foresti of Bergamo, Cardinal Domenico Jacobazzi, Hadrian of Utrecht, afterwards pope Hadrian VI.,—Germans, French, Italians, Spaniards, all appeal to the story, and interweave it with their theological disquisitions; or, like Heinrich Cornelius Agrippa, rejoice that the tenets of the canonists about the inerrancy of the

---

[1] *Storia de' solenni possessi*. Rome, 1802, p. 238.

[2] *Vita Paparum*, R. Basil, 1507, f. E. 2.

[3] Other old editions of this strangers' guide to Rome have the title—*Indulgentiæ Ecclesiarum Urbis Romæ*. The circumstance about the woman-pope is found in all of them; and for well-nigh eighty years no one in Rome ever thought of having the scandal expurgated from a work, which was constantly reprinted, and was put into the hands of every new-comer. [A reprint has lately been published at Berlin, 1869, edited by Parthey.]

Church had come to such glaring shame in the deception of the woman-pope, and that this woman, in the two years and a half of her reign, had ordained priests and bishops, administered sacraments, and performed all the other functions of a pope ; and that all this had, nevertheless, remained as valid in the Church. Even John, Bishop of Chiemsee, introduces Agnes and her catastrophe as a proof that the popes were sometimes under the influence of evil spirits.[1] Platina, who thought the story rather suspicious, nevertheless would not omit it from his history of the popes (about 1460), because nearly every one maintained its truth.[2] Aventin in Germany, and Onufrio Panvinio in Italy, were the first to shake the general infatuation. But still in the year 1575 the Minorite Rioche, in his chronicle, opposes the certainty of the collected Church to the hesitating statements of Platina and Carranza.[3]

In order to arrive at the causes of the origin and development of the myth, let us now proceed to dissect it.

Originally the woman-pope was nameless. The first accounts of her, in Stephen de Bourbon, and

---

[1] *Onus Ecclesiæ*, 1531, cap. 19, § 4.
[2] "Ne obstinate nimium et pertinaciter omisisse videar, quod fere omnes affirmant."
[3] *Chronique.* Paris, 1576, f. 230.

in the *Compilatio Chronologica* in Pistorius' collection, know nothing as yet of a Joan. In the latter authority we read : "fuit et alius pseudo papa, cujus "nomen et anni ignorantur, nam mulier erat." Her *own* name was not discovered till somewhat late— about the end of the fourteenth century. She was called Agnes, under which name she was a very important and useful personage, especially with John Huss ; or Gilberta, [1] as others would have it. For the *pope* a name was found at an early stage ; people took the most common one—John. There had already been seven of this name before 855, and in the period during which the myth was spreading, the number reached one and twenty.

Much the same thing happened as to the *time* at which she was supposed to have lived. The myth while still in its popular form of course did not touch upon this question. But the first authority who relates it at once gives it a date also. The event, says Stephen de Bourbon, took place about the year 1100. He places it therefore (and this is very remarkable) at the very time in which we have the first mention of the use of the pierced chair at the enthronement of the new pope. How people in general came after-

2 [Besides Agnes, Gilberta, or Gerberta and Joanna, she is also called in various authors Margaret, Isabel, Dorothy, and Jutta]

wards to assign the year 855 as her date, has been already explained.

Stephen de Bourbon knows nothing up to his time of England, Mayence, or Athens. The woman is as yet no great scholar or public teacher, but only a clever scribe or secretary (artem notandi edocta), who thus becomes the notary of the Curia, then cardinal, and then pope. A century later, in Amalricus Augerii [1] all this is fantastically enlarged upon and coloured. At Athens she becomes by careful study a very subtle reasoner. While there she hears of the condition and fame of the city of Rome, goes thither and becomes, not a notary, as Stephen says, but a professor, [2] attracts many and noble pupils, lives at the same time in the greatest honour, is celebrated everywhere for her mode of life no less than for her learning, and hence is unanimously elected pope. She continued some time longer in her honourable and pious mode of life; but later on, too much good living made her voluptuous, she

---

[1] Ap. Eccard, ii., 1607.

[2] Even great teachers, says Jakob von Konigshofen (Chronicle, p. 179), were eager to become her pupils, for she had the chief of the schools in Rome. The papal secretary, Dietrich von Niem (about A.D. 1413), professes to give the very school in which she taught, viz., that of the Greeks, in which St. Augustine also taught.

yielded to the temptations of the Evil One, and was seduced by one of her confidants.

Particularly astonishing is the disagreement as to the way in which the catastrophe took place. Three or four versions of it exist. According to the first, as we find it in Stephen de Bourbon, it appears that she was with child at the time of her election to the papacy, and the dénouement took place during the procession as she was going up to the Lateran palace.[1] The Roman tribunal condemned her at once to be tied by the feet to the feet of a horse, and dragged out of the city, whereupon the populace stoned her to death. In this version of the story, however, Stephen stands quite alone. The usual narrative, as it has passed from the interpolated Martinus Polonus into later authors, makes her, after a quiet reign of more than two years, give birth to a child in the street during a procession, die at once, and forthwith be buried on the very spot. Boccaccio is quite different from this again. According to him all takes place tolerably quietly; there is no death, the enthroned priestess merely sheds a few tears, and then retires into private life. "Ex apice pontificatus

---

[1] "Quum ascenderet," i.e., palatium, as we have it in the description of the coronation of Paschal II.;—"ascendensque palatium." Ap. Muràtor. *SS. Ital.* iii., i. 354.

dejecta se in misellam evasisse mulierculam querebatur." And again: " A patribus in tenebras exteriores abjecta cum fletu misella abiit." [1]

The attitude which Boccaccio assumed with regard to the episode of the female pope, which was just the kind of thing to please a man of his turn of mind, is particularly remarkable. In his *Zibaldone*, which he wrote about the year 1350, he included a short chronicle of the popes, which according to his own confession, was entirely borrowed from the *Chronica Martiniana*. In this the female pope is not mentioned; without doubt because he did not find her in his copy of Martinus Polonus. On the other hand, he has inserted her in two later writings, [2] *De casibus virorum et feminarum illustrium*, and *De mulieribus claris*, and has pictured the whole with the enjoyment which was to be expected from the author of the *Decamerone*. His narrative, however, differs essentially from the usual version according to

[1] In the *Fragmentum Hist. Autoris Incerti* in Urstis. P. ii., p. 82, which says that King Theodoric killed "Johanna Papa" at Rome along with Boethius and Symmachus, Johanna is merely a mistake of some copyist for Johanne. [No version of the myth of Pope Joan places her as early as this—524, 525. John I. was pope precisely at this period 523 to 526.]

[2] To speak more exactly, he has related the story twice over in the same work, for the two writings mentioned really make up only one work.

Martinus; and seeing that it agrees with no other known version, it would appear that Boccaccio has taken it directly from popular tradition (where it would naturally assume very various forms), and worked it up. He knows the length of her pontificate with the greatest exactitude: two years, seven months, and a day or two. Her original name he does not know: "Quod proprium fuerit nomen vix cognitum "est. Esto sunt, qui dicant fuisse Gilibertam."

These fourteenth century witnesses are of no very great importance, for they one and all of them merely copied the interpolated passage in Martinus Polonus, often with scarcely the alteration of a word. On the other hand the recently published *Eulogium Historiarum* of a monk of Malmesbury, of the year 1366, has a peculiar form of the story to be found nowhere else, although the author in other places borrows freely from Martinus Polonus. The girl is born in Mayence, and sent by her parents to male teachers to receive instruction in the sciences. With one of these, who was a very learned man, she falls in love, and goes with him in man's attire to Rome. Here, because she surpassed every one in knowledge, she was made cardinal by pope Leo. When, as pope, she gives birth to a child during the procession, she is merely deposed. This version, therefore, would come nearest to the description given by Boccaccio. It knows nothing of the journey to Athens.[1]

The catastrophe appears somewhat further spun out in a manuscript chronicle of the abbots of Kempten. There we are told that "the Evil Spirit "came to this Pope John, who was a woman, and "afterwards was with child, and said, 'Thou pope, "'who wouldest be a Father with the other Fathers "'here, thou shalt show publicly when thou bringest "'forth that thou art a woman-pope; therefore will I "'take thee body and soul to myself and to my com- "'pany.'"[2]

Another less severe and uncompromising finale was however attempted. By a revelation or an angel she was allowed to choose, whether she would suffer shame on earth or eternal damnation hereafter. She chose the former, and the birth of her child and her own death in the open street was the consequence.[3]

The story of the papess once believed, many other fables attached themselves to it. It was through the special aid of the devil, we are told, that she rose to

[1] *Eulogium, Chronicon ab orbe condito usque ad annum* 1366; edited by Frank Scott Haydon. Lond. 1858, t. I.

[2] Ap. Wolf, *Lection. Memorab.*, ed. 1671, p. 177.

[3] So in the *Urbis Romæ Mirabilia*, a work frequently printed in Rome during the fifteenth and sixteenth centuries. Then in Hemmerlin, pp. 1597, f. 99, and in a German chronicle of Cologne.

the dignity of pope, and thereupon wrote a book on necromancy.[1] Formerly there was a greater number of Prefaces in the missal. The reduction in number which took place afterwards with regard to those whose author and purpose were unknown, was explained by the supposition, that Pope Joan had composed those which were struck out.[2]

Now, how is the first origin of the myth to be explained? Four circumstances have contributed to the production and elaboration of the fable:—1. The use of a pierced seat at the institution of a newly elected pope. 2. A stone with an inscription on it, which people supposed to be a tombstone. 3. A statue found on the same spot, in long robes, which were supposed to be those of a woman. 4. The custom of making a circuit in processions, whereby a street which was directly in the way was avoided.

In one street in Rome stood two objects, which were very naturally supposed to be connected,—a statue with the figure of a child or small boy, and a monumental stone with an inscription. In addition

---

[1] Tiraquell, *de Leg. Matrim. ed. Basil.*, 1561, p. 298.

[2] Thus, in an Oxford manuscript of Martinus Polonus we read:—" Hic (Johannes Anglicus) primus post Ambrosium multas præ-" fationes missarum dicitur composuisse, quæ modo omnes sunt " interdictæ." Ap. Maresium, *Johanna Papissa Restit.*, p. 19. So also the above-mentioned Martin le Franc.

to this came the circumstance, that solemn and state processions made a circuit round this street. The statue is said to have had masculine rather than feminine features; but certain information on this point is wanting, for Sixtus V. had it removed. The figure carried a palm-branch, and was supposed to represent a priest with a serving boy, or some heathen divinity. But the long robes and the addition of the figure of the boy to the group, created a notion among the people that it was a mother with her child. The inscription was then made use of to explain the statue, and the statue to explain the inscription, the pierced chair and the avoiding of the street served to confirm the explanation. This piece of sculpture was not (as has been maintained) first mentioned by Dietrich von Niem in the fifteenth century; but Mærlant says, as early as 1283, i. e., at the time of the first circulation of the myth :—

> ".En daer leget soe, als wyt lesen
> Noch also up ten Steen ghehouwen,
> Dat men ane daer mag scouwen."

The myth now sought, and soon found, further circumstances with which to connect itself. The enigmatical inscription on a monumental stone which stood on the spot, and which hitherto no one had been able to interpret, became all at once clear to the

Romans. It referred to the female pope and the catastrophe of the dénouement.

The stone was set up by one of those priests of Mithras who bore the title "Pater Patrum," apparently as a memorial of some specially solemn sacrifice; for the worship of Mithras from the third century of the Christian era onwards was a very favourite one in Rome and very prevalent, until in the year 378 the worship was forbidden and the grotto of Mithras destroyed.

The earliest notice of the stone with the inscription, which was supposed to be the tombstone of the female pope, is to be found in Stephen de Bourbon. According to him the inscription ran thus,—

"Parce Pater Patrum papissæ prodere partum."

Now without doubt it did not stand so in as many words. But "Pap." or "Parc. Pater Patrum" followed by "P. P. P." was certainly the reading; an abbreviation for "propria pecunia posuit."

"Pater Patrum" appears constantly on monuments as the title of a priest of the Mithras[1] mysteries. In this case, probably, the name of the priest of

---

[1] Conf. Orelli, *Inscriptionum Latinarum Ampl. Coll.* 1848, 1933, 2343, 2344, 2352.

Mithras was **Papirius**.[1] The remaining letters may have become illegible.

The problem therefore now was to interpret the three "P's."

One reading was,

"Parce Pater Patrum papissæ prodere **partum**;"[2]

or as others supposed,

"**Papa** Pater Patrum papissæ pandito partum;"

or, according to another explanation still better,

"**Papa Pater Patrum** peperit papissa papellum."

Thus was the riddle of the inscription solved, and the myth confirmed in connection with the statue and the pierced chair. The stone had turned out to be the tombstone of the unhappy Pope Joan.[3]

The verse, however, especially in its first and second form, was altogether a most extraordinary one for an epitaph. There must be something more to account for it, and, accordingly, the myth was soon

---

[1] For several inscriptions with the abbreviation P. a P., see Orelli, ii., 25.

[2] This is the oldest interpretation as given by Stephen de Bourbon; see Echard, S. Thomæ Summa suo Auctori Vindicata, p. 568.

[3] Hence the most ancient witness, Stephen de Bourbon, says expressly: "Ubi fuit mortua, ibi fuit sepulta, et super lapidem super ea positum scriptus est versiculus, etc."—Ap. Echard., l c., p. 568.

enlarged. It was reported that Satan, who of course knew the secret of the papess, had addressed her in the words of the verse in a full consistory.[1] That, however, did not seem a very satisfactory explanation; and so the supposed epitaph was altered and enlarged, —and the story at last ran thus:—that the papess, while exorcising a man possessed by a devil, had asked him when the unclean spirit that dwelt in him would leave him, and it had mockingly answered—

" Papa Pater Patrum papissæ pandito partum,
Et tibi nunc edam (or dicam) de corpore quando recedam."[2]

Other instances have occurred of an unintelligible inscription being explained by a story [3] being attached to it. Thus the chronicles, since the time of Beda, declare that an inscription had been found at Rome with the six letters:—

"R. R. R. F. F. F."

According to other instances of abbreviations in inscriptions, this can at any rate mean—

" Ruderibus rejectis Rufus Festus fieri fecit."

---

[1] So the *Chronica S. Ægidii*, ap. Leibnitz SS. Brunsvic., iii., 530. The Chronicon of Engelhusius (Leibnitz, ii., 1065) makes the evil spirit in the air shout out the verse at the birth of the child during the procession.

[2] So, for instance, the Chronicle of Hermannus Gygas, p. 94.

[3] [Compare the famous verse about Pope Sylvester II.— " Scandit " ab R. Gerbertus in R, post papa viget R," p. 268.]

But people constructed out of it the prophecy of an ancient Sibyl respecting the destruction of Rome, and interpreted—

"Roma Ruet Romuli Ferro Flammaque **Fameque.**"

While the inscription on the stone occupied more especially the clergy and the more educated among the laity, and stimulated them to attempt explanations of it, the imaginative powers of the populace were chiefly excited by the seat which stood in a public place, and was always to be seen by every one, on which every newly-elected pope, in accordance with traditional custom, took his seat.

From the time of Paschal II. in the year 1099, we find mention of the custom that, at the solemn procession to the Lateran palace, the new pope should sit down on two ancient pierced seats made of stone. They were called "*porphyreticæ*," because the stone of which they were made was of a bright red kind. They dated from the times of ancient Rome, and had formerly, it appears, stood in one of the public baths; and had thence come into the oratory of S. Sylvester near the Lateran.[1] Here then it was usual for the pope first to sit on the right-hand seat, while a girdle from which hung seven keys and seven seals was put round

---

[1] Montfaucon, *Diar. Ital.*, p. 137.

him.[1] At the same time a staff was placed in his hand, which he then, sitting on the left-hand seat, placed along with the keys in the hands of the prior of St. Lawrence. Hereupon another ornamented garb, made after the pattern of the Jewish ephod, was placed on him. This sitting down was meant to symbolise taking possession; for Pandulf goes on to say: "per cetera Palatii loca solis Pontificibus "destinata, jam dominus vel sedens vel transiens "electionis modum implevit."

It was therefore a mere matter of accident that these stone seats were pierced. They had been selected on account of their antique form and the beautiful colour of the stone. Every stranger who visited Rome could not fail to be struck with their unusual shape. That they had formerly been intended to be used in a bath had passed out of every one's knowledge; and the idea of such a use would be one of the last to occur to people in the middle ages. They were aware that the new pope sat, and on this occasion only in his whole life, on this seat, and this was the only use to which the seat was ever

---

[1] "Ascendens palatium," we read in the Roman sub-deacon, Pandulfus Pisanus, "ad duas curules devenit. Hic baltheo suc- "cingitur, cum septem ex eo pendentibus clavibus septemque "sigillis. Et locatus in utrisque curulibus data sibi ferula in "manu, etc."—Ap. Murator. *SS. Ital.,* P. iii., P. i., p. 354.

put. The symbolical meaning of the act and of the ceremonies connected with it was unknown and foreign to the popular mind. It accordingly invented an explanation of its own, just such a one as popular fancy is wont to give. The seat is hollow and pierced, they said, because they wanted to make sure that the pope was a man. The further question, what need there was to make sure of this, produced the explanation :—because, in one instance certainly, a woman was made pope. Here at once a field was opened for the development of a myth. The deception, the catastrophe of the discovery ; all that was forthwith sketched out in popular talk. Myth delights in the most glaring contrasts. Hence we have the highest sacerdotal office, and together with it its most shameful prostitution by sudden travail during a solemn procession, followed by childbirth in the open street. This done, the woman-pope has fulfilled her mission. The myth accordingly at once withdraws her from the scene. She dies in childbirth on the spot ; or, according to an older version, is stoned to death by the enraged populace.

The story that the newly-elected pope sat down on the pierced seat in order to give a proof of his sex is first found in the Visions of the Dominican, Robert d'Usez,[1] who died in Metz in the year 1296. He relates that in the year 1291, while he was staying at Orange, he was taken in the spirit to Rome, to the Lateran palace, and placed before the porphyry seat, "ubi dicitur probari papa an sit homo."[2] After him Jacobo d'Agnolo di Scarperia in the year 1405 declares respecting it, in a letter to the celebrated Greek, Emanuel Chrysoloras, in which he describes the enthronisation of Gregory XII. as an eye-witness, that it is a senseless popular fable.[3] It is consequently not correct to say, what has been frequently maintained, that the English writer, William Brevin,[4] about 1470, was the first to make mention of the supposed investigation as to the sex of the pope.[5]

1 *Hist. Litt. de France*, xx. 501.

2 *Liber trium Virorum et trium Spirit. Virginum*, ed. Lefebre, Paris, 1513, f. 25.

3 Juxta hoc (sacellum Sylvestri) geminæ sunt fixæ sedes porphiretico incisæ lapide, in quibus, quod perforatæ sint, insanam loquitur vulgus fabulam, quod Pontifex attractetur, an vir sit. Ap. Cancellieri, p. 37.

4 In a work *De Septem Principalibus Ecclesiis Urbis Romæ*.

5 According to Hemmerlin (*Dialog. de Nobil. et Rusticis*), the investigation was made by two of the clergy : " et dum invenirentur "illæsi (testiculi), clamabant tangentes alta voce ; testiculos habet. "Et reclamabant clerus et populus : Deo gratias." According to Chalcocondylas the words were : — ἄρρην ἡμῖν ἐστὶν ὁ δεσπότης. [De rebus Turcicis, ed. Bekker, Bonn., 1843, p. 303.] How readily the popular story was believed is shown by Bernardino Corio, of Milan, who describes in his historical work the coronation of pope

Of later witnesses it is worth mentioning, that the Swede Lawrence Banck, who minutely described the solemnities which accompanied the elevation of Innocent X. to the papacy [Sept. 1644], declares, with all earnestness, that it certainly was the case, that an investigation into the sex of the pope was the object of the ceremony.[1] At that time, however, the custom of sitting on the two stone seats, along with several other ceremonies, had long since disappeared, namely, since the death of Leo X. And, moreover, Banck does not state that he himself had seen the ceremony,[2] but only that he had often seen the *seat*, and by way of proof that it took place, and with this particular object, *appeals to writers of the fifteenth and sixteenth centuries*. Cancellieri, therefore, had good reason for expressing astonishment at the shamelessness of a man, who speaks on other things as an eye-witness, and who had only to inquire of Alexander VI. in the year 1492, when Corio himself was in Rome. There we read, "Finalmente essendo finite lo solite solemnitati in *Sancta Sanctorum* et dimesticamente toccatogli li testiculi, ritorno al palacio." *Patria Historia*, P. vii., fol. Riv. Milano, 1503. In the later editions the passage is omitted. Corio, however, says himself, that he was not in the church where it took place, but was standing outside.

[1] In the book *Roma Triumphans*, Franecker, 1645, Cancellieri has quoted his long account entire.

[2] Cancellieri, p. 236.

any educated Roman to learn that the custom in question had been given up for more than a hundred years.

But the strongest case of all is that of Giampetro Valeriano Bolzani, one of the literary courtiers of Leo X., and loaded with benefices,[1] according to the immoral custom of the time. This man, in a speech addressed to cardinal Hippolytus dei Medici, printed at Rome with papal privilege, did not scruple to decorate the fiction about the investigation into the sex of each newly-elected pope with new and fabulous circumstances. The ceremony takes places, he declares, quite openly in the gallery of the Lateran church before the eyes of the assembled multitude, and is then most unnecessarily proclaimed by one of the clergy and entered in the register.[2] Thus the wanton frivolity of Italian literati, and the stupid indifference of ecclesiastical dignitaries, worked together to spread this delusion, damaging as it was to the otherwise jealously guarded authority of the papal see, right through the whole mass of the populace. At the same

---

[1] For the long list of his benefices, see Marini, *Archiatri Pontificij*, i., 291.

[2] Resque ipsa sacri præconis voce palam promulgata in acta mox refertur, legitimumque tum demum Pontificem nos habere arbitramur, quum habere illum quod habere decet oculata fide fuerit contestatum.

time one could hardly have a more striking instance of the irresistible power which a universally-circulated story exercises over men, even over those of superior intellect. Any one could learn without trouble from a cardinal, or from one of the clergy taking part in the ceremony, what really took place there. But people never asked, or else imagined that the answer meant no more than a refusal to vouch for the fact. They heard this examination of the newly-elected pope spoken of everywhere, in the streets and in private houses, as a notorious fact.

Did, then, the meaning assigned to the pierced seat influence the explanation of the inscription and of the statue; or did, contrariwise, these two objects give origin to the myth about the ceremonies connected with the seat? That point it is now, of course, out of our power to determine. We can only see that the explanation of the three objects is as old as the myth about the woman-pope.

A further confirmation of the whole was soon found in a circumstance of no importance in itself, and for which a perfectly natural explanation was ready at hand. It was remarked that the popes in processions between the Lateran and the Vatican did not enter a street which lay in the way, but made a circuit through other streets. The reason was simply the narrowness of the street. But in Rome, where the papess was already haunting the imagination of the masses, it was now discovered that this was done to remind men how the woman had given birth to a child as she was going through this street, and to express horror at the catastrophe which had taken place just at that spot. In the first version of the fable, as we find it in the interpolated Martinus Polonus, it is said: "*creditur omnino a quibusdam,* "*quod ob detestationem facti hoc faciat.*" With [1] later writers the thing is thoroughly established as a notorious fact.

It may now be worth while to show by a few examples, how easily a popular myth, or a mythical explanation, may be called into existence by a circumstance, so soon as anything is perceived in it, which seems in the eyes of the people to be astonishing, or which excites their imagination.

The bigamy of the Count of Gleichen plays an important part in our literature, and is still believed to be true by numberless people. A count of Gleichen

---

[1] The chroniclers copy one from another to such a slavish extent in this narrative, that the incorrect expression of the interpolater, "Dominus Papa, quum vadit ad Lateranum, eandem viam semper "*obliquat*" (instead of *declinat*) has been retained by all his followers. The avoided street was, moreover, pulled down by Sixtus V., on *account of its narrowness.* [The spot where the catastrophe was said to have taken place is between the Colosseum and St. Clement's.]

is said to have gone to Palestine in the year 1227, in company with the Landgrave of Thuringia, and there to have been captured by the Saracens and thrown into prison. Through the daughter of the Sultan he obtained his liberty; and the story goes that, although his wife was living, he obtained a dispensation from pope Gregory IX. in the year 1240 or 1241, and married the princess; and the three lived together in undisturbed peace for many years afterwards. It is a well-known fact that the very bed itself (an unusually broad one) of the count and his two wives, was shown for a long time afterwards.

This story is told for the first time in the year 1584, that is to say, three centuries and a half later.[1] But from that time onwards it is related in numerous writings, and in the next century became a matter of popular belief, so that henceforth it was printed in all histories of Thuringia, and is to be found in particular in Jovius, Sagittarius, Olearius, Packenstein, etc. In this case, also, it was a *tombstone* which gave occasion to the story. On it was represented a knight with two [2] female figures, one of whom had a peculiar

---

[1] In Dresseri *Rhetorica*, Lips., p. 76, squ.

[2] It is, as Placidus Muth, of Erfurt, has conjectured with much probability, the monument of a count of Gleichen, who died in 1494, and his two wives.

head dress decorated with a star. No sooner had the myth which fastened on to this figure begun to weave its web, than relics and signs began to multiply. Not only was the bedstead shown, but a jewel which the pope had presented to the Turkish princess, and which she wore in her turban; a " Turk's road," was pointed out, leading to the castle, and a " Turk's room " within it. And not a word about all this until the seventeenth century. In earlier times no one had ever heard a syllable about the story or the relics.[1]

Another instance is afforded by the Püstrich at Sondershausen, a bronze figure, hollow inside, with an opening in the head. It was found in the year 1550, in a subterranean chapel of the castle of Rothenburg, near Nordhausen, and was brought to Sondershausen in the year 1576, where it still exists in the cabinet of curiosities. Thirty or forty years had scarcely passed before a legend had grown up, which quite harmonised with a time immediately succeeding the great religious contest of the Reformation, and with a country in which the old religion was vanquished. The Püstrich was said to have stood in a niche in a pilgrimage church, and by monkish jugglery to have been filled with water, and made to vomit flames of fire, in order to terrify the people, and induce them to make large offerings. Frederick

---

[1] See *Hallesche Encycl*. Bd. 69.

Succus, preacher in the cathedral of Magdeburg, from 1567 to 1576, relates all this, with many details as to the way in which the deception was managed, adding the remark, "that no one could do the like "now-a-days, so as to make the image vomit flames, "and that many thought it was perhaps brought "about by magic and witchcraft." [1]

Again, every one knows the story of Archbishop Hatto, of Mayence, who had a strong tower built in the middle of the Rhine, in order to protect himself from the mice; but in spite of that was devoured by them. This event, which would have fallen within the year 970, had it happened *at all*, is mentioned for the first time at the beginning of the fourteenth century, in Siffrid's chronicle. Before that there is not a trace of it. The Mäusethurm, or Muusthurm [2] (that is, Arsenal), as Bodmann explains, was not built till the beginning of the thirteenth [3] century.

---

[1] Rabe, *Der Püstrich zu Sondershausen*, Berlin, 1852, p. 58. He shows how absurd the story is, although repeated in the seventeenth century by Walther, Titus, and Röser. Even in the year 1782 Galetti, and in 1830 the preacher Quehl, related the ridiculous story. Rabe conjectures with probability that the Püstrich is nothing more than the support of a font. [Others have supposed it to be an idol of the Sorbic-Wends.]

[2] Ap. Pistor. SS., Germ., i., 10.

[3] [By a bishop named Siegfried, together with the opposite castle of Ehrenfels, as a watch tower and toll-house for collecting duties on all goods which passed up or down the river. Maus is possibly only another form of Mauth, toll or excise. Archbishop Hatto died in 970.]

Its name with the people slipped from Muusthurm to Mäusethurm, and thus, according to all appearance, gave rise to the whole story. In all that is historically known of Hatto II. there is not a feature with which the legend could connect itself. The story of a prince or great man, who tried to save himself from the pursuit of mice in a tower surrounded by water, is to be found in several other places. It appears in the mountains of Bavaria; it occurs among the myths of primitive Polish history. In [1] the latter case King Popiel, his wife, and two sons, are followed and killed by mice in a tower in the Goplosee, which to this day bears the name of Mouse-tower. Wherever a tower on an island was to be seen, the object of which could no longer be explained, there sprang up the story of the blood-thirsty mice. [2]

---

[1] Ropell's *Geschichte Polens*, i., 74. [See Appendix C.]

[2] Liebrecht's explanation in Wolf's *Zeitschrift für deutsche Mythologie*, ii., 408, seems to be erroneous. He says, that "at the "root of legends on this subject lies the primitive custom of "hanging the chiefs of the nation as an offering to appease the "gods, on the occurrence of any national calamity, such as famine "through the ravages of mice, for instance." In the first place, human sacrifice by means of hanging is almost, if not quite, unknown; secondly, it is not usually a tree, but a tower on an island, to which the legend attaches itself; and, lastly, the legend places the event, as in the case of Hatto, very much later—quite in Christian times. [But may we not give up the hanging, and even the tree, and still retain the idea of propitiatory sacrifice?]

If an unusual hollow was remarked in a stone, a hole of extraordinary shape, anything which the imagination could take for the impress of a hand or a foot, there at once a myth found lodgment. A stone in the wall of a church at Schlottau in Saxony, which is thought to look like the face of a monk without ever having been carved by the hand of man, has given occasion to a legend of attempted sacrilege, and marvellous punishment. [1]

On the Riesenthor (Giant-Porch) of St. Stephen's Cathedral at Vienna, a youth is introduced in the carving of the upper part, who appears to rest a wounded foot on the other knee. A legend has been spun out of that. The architect, Pilgram,[2] is said to have thrown his pupil, Puchsprunn, from the scaffolding, out of jealousy, because the execution of the second tower had been transferred to the latter while still under Pilgram.[3]

The fable of the papess belongs to the local myths

---

[1] See Grasse's *Sagenscha'z des Konigreichs Sachsn.* Dresden, 1855.

[2] [Pilgram was one of the later architects, successor of Jörg Œchsel about 1510. The church was founded in 1144. The Riesenthor seems to belong to a period subsequent to the fire of 1258; but it and the Heidenthürme are almost the oldest parts of the present building, and therefore existed long before Pilgram's time.]

[3] Hormayr. *Wien, seine Geschichte, u s. w.*, 27, 46.

of Rome, of which a whole cycle existed in the Middle Ages. Hence it may be worth while to compare the birth of such a myth with a Roman example. The legend about the origin of the house of Colonna, whose power and greatness afforded material for the imagination of the people, is so far similar in its origin to that about Pope Joan, as it was a piece of sculpture, viz., the arms of the house with a column, which the legend endeavoured to explain. Just as the lozenge of Saxony, the wheel of Mayence, and the virgin of the Osnabruck arms, have called forth legends of their own to explain them.

A smith in Rome notices that his cow, every day, goes of her own accord in the same direction. He follows her, creeps after her through a narrow opening, and finds a meadow with a building in it. In the building stands a stone column, and on the top of it a brazen vessel full of money. He is about to take some of the money, when a voice calls out to him, "It is not thine; take three denarii, and "thou wilt find on the Forum to whom the money "belongs." The smith does so, and flings the three pieces of money to three different parts of the Forum. A poor neglected lad finds them all three, becomes the smith's son-in-law, buys great possessions with the money on the column, and so founds the house of Colonna.[1]

This, perhaps, is sufficient illustration of the way in which the legend of Pope Joan arose. Two circumstances, however, require special discussion, the statements that the woman came from Mayence, and that she had studied in Athens.

The first mention that we find respecting the original home of the female pope, namely, in the passage interpolated into Martinus Polonus, combines two contradictory statements. It makes her **an Englishwoman,** and, at the same time, a native **of Mayence: "Johannes Anglus, natione** Mogun- **"tinus."** Probably two stories were extant, of which **one made** the impostor come from the British Isles, the other from Germany. The reason for one story making her a native of England may have been this. It was a common thing for Englishwomen to go **on** pilgrimages to Rome: we find St. Boniface even in his day complaining of the number of them, and **their** dubious character. Or it may have been that the birth, and first spreading of the myth, fell just within that long period of the violent struggle between Innocent III. and king John, while England

---

[1] Fr. Jacobi de Acqui *Chronicon Imaginis Mundi*, in the *Monumenta Hist. Patriæ, Script.*, Vol. iii., p. 1603.

was accounted in Rome as the power which above all others was hostile to the Roman see. For, from the very beginning, the fictitious event was considered as a deep disgrace, a heavy blow struck at the authority of the Roman see; and the myth expressed that by making a country which was considered as hostile to Rome, to be the home of the papess, a woman-pope. In like manner the **mythical** king Popiel, who was devoured by mice, on account of the wrong done to his father's brothers, is represented in the Polish myth as having married the daughter of a German prince, in order that the guilt of instigating him to the crime might fall on a woman of a foreign nation, and one always hostile to the Sclaves.[1]

It is not difficult to explain how the other version of the story, which became the prevalent one, came to assign Mayence as the native place of the papess.

The rise of the myth falls into the period of the great contest between the papacy and the empire, a time when the Germans often appeared in arms before Rome, and in Rome broke down the walls of the city, took the popes prisoners, or compelled them to take to flight. "Omne malum ab Aquilone," was the feeling at that time in Rome. Germany had then no special capital; no recognised royal or

---

[1] Röpell, *Geschichte Polens*, p. 77.

imperial place of residence. No city but Mayence could be called the most important city in the realm. It was the seat of the first prince of the empire, [1] and the centre of government. "Moguntia, ubi maxima "vis regni esse noscitur," says Otto of Freysingen. [2] In the *Ligurinus* of the Pseudo-Gunther, it is said of Mayence: "Pene fuit toto sedes notissima regno."

In the cycle of myths which cluster round Charlemagne, and which Italy also appropriated (e.g. in the *Reali di Francia*, which was extant as early as the fourteenth century, and in other productions belonging to the same cycle of myths), Roman aversion to the German metropolis, Mayence, is glaringly prominent. Mayence is the seat and home of the malicious scheme of treachery against Charles the Great and his house. Ganelo, the arch-traitor, is count of Mayence. All his party, and his associates in treachery, are called "Maganzesi." They and Ganelo, or the men of Mayence, represent the treacherous usurpation of the empire by the Germans, in violation of the birthright of Rome.

[1] [The electoral archbishops of Mayence were the premier princes of the empire; they presided at diets, and at the election of the emperor. Even in Roman times the Castellum Moguntiacum was the most important of the chain of fortresses which Drusus built along the Rhine, and which in like manner became the germs of large towns.]

[2] *De Gestis Friderici I.*, c. 12.

So again in Pulci's *Morgante,* and in Ariosto's *Cinque Canti* or *Ganeloni.* The poem, *Doolin of Mayence,* is, to a certain extent, a German rejoinder to the polemics of Rome, as shown in the Carolingian myths. Here Doolin, son of Guido, count of Mayence, steps forward as the rival of Charlemagne, first fights with him, then after an indecisive battle is reconciled to him, with him goes to Vauclere, the city of Aubigeant (Wittekind), king of Saxony, marries Flandrine, the daughter of the latter, and ends by joining with Charles in the subjugation of Saxony.

Ganelo of Mayence, the treacherous founder of the first German kingdom by separation from the West Frank kingdom, is supplemented in the Italian myth (which thus represents the great contest and opposition between Guelf and Ghibelline) by another native of Mayence, Ghibello. The story is to be found in Bogardo's Italian version of the *Pomarium* of Riccobaldo of Ferrara.[1] King Conrad II. (it is Conrad III. who is meant) nominates Gibello Maguntino to be administrator of the kingdom in Lombardy in opposition to Welfo, whom the Church had set up as regent of Lombardy. Gibello is of noble but poor family, had studied for awhile in

[1] In Muratori, *SS.* Ital ix , 360, 57.

Italy, acquires then great eminence in his native city, Mayence, becomes chancellor of Bohemia, but is publicly convicted of " baratteria," **i.e., of** political fraud or treason. He and Welfo now have a contest together, which ends in Gibello dying at Bergamo, and Welfo at Milan. Gibello of Maganza is, as one sees, a repetition of Gano or Ganelo of Maganza. But it is also evident why Johannes or Johanna must be made to come from Mayence, and why " Magun- " tinus" or " Magantinus" must be called " Margan- " tinus." [1]

In later times the story, now romancing with an object, endeavoured to harmonise the two statements,

[1] Both in manuscripts and printed copies we repeatedly find Marguntinus instead of Marguntinus. It would appear that Margan, a famous abbey in Glamorganshire, is here indicated, where the *Annales de Margan*, with which the second volume of Gale's *Historiæ Anglic. Scriptores* commences, were composed. People could not reconcile the appellation Anglicus with the distinctive **name** Maguntinus, and accordingly changed the German birthplace **into** an English one. Bernard Guidonis came to the **rescue in a different** way; instead of Anglicus, he wrote Johannes **Teutonicus natione** Maguntinus. *Vitæ Pontificum*, ap. Maii *Spicil*. **Rom. vi., 202.** Among the amusing attempts which have been made **to reconcile the two adjectives** Anglicus and Maguntinus, may be **mentioned the version of** Amalricus Augerii (*Historia Pontificum*, ap. Eccard, **ii., 1706).** Here the woman-pope is called Johannes, Anglicus natione, dictus *Magnanimus* (instead of Maguntinus). The author would intimate that the boldness and strength of character, without which such a course of life, involving the concealment of her sex for so many years, **would not have been possible,** had won for her the **distinctive title of** " magnanimous."

that the female pope was "Anglicus," and also "natione Maguntinus." The parents of Joan were made to migrate from England to Mayence; or she was called "Anglicus," it was said, because an English monk in Fulda had been her paramour.[1]

In Germany, however, people began now to be ashamed of the German origin of Pope Joan. She was thrown in the teeth of the Germans, we are told in the chronicle of the bishops of Verden, because she is said to have come from Mayence.[2] Indeed some went so far as to say that this circumstance of the German woman-pope was the reason why no more Germans were elected popes, as Werner Rolevink mentions, adding at the same time that this was not the true reason.[3] In order to conceal the circumstance, we find in the German manuscripts of Martinus Polonus "Margantinus" constantly instead of "Magantinus;" and the *Compilatio Chronica* in Leibnitz [4] knows only of Johannes Anglicus. This feeling that the nationality of the papess was a thing

---

[1] Compare Maresii *Johanna Papissa Restituta*, p. 19.

[2] Ap. Leibnitz, *SS. Brunsvic.*, ii., 212.

[3] *Fascic. Temp. æt.* vi., f. 66. So also in the Dutch *Divisie-Chronyk*, printed at Leyden in the year 1517. "Om dat dese Paeus "wt duytslant rus van ments opten ryn, so menen sommige, dat dit "die sake is, dat men genen geboren duytsche meer tat paeus "settet."

[4] *SS. Brunsvic.*, ii., 63.

of which Germany must be ashamed even produced a new romance, the object of which was manifestly nothing else than to transfer the home of the female pope and her paramour from Germany to Greece.[1]

The other feature in the myth, that the woman studied in Athens, and then came and turned her knowledge to account in Rome as a teacher of great repute, is thoroughly in accordance with the spirit of mediæval legends. As a matter of fact, no one for a thousand years had gone from the West to Athens for purposes of study; for the very best of reasons, because there was nothing more to be found there. But that was no obstacle to the myth, according to which Athens in ancient times (that means perhaps before the rise of the University of Paris) was accounted as the one great seat of education and learning. For that there was, and ought to be, only one "Studium," just as there was, and ought to be, only one Empire and one Popedom, was the prevailing sentiment of that age. "The Church has "need of three powers or institutions," we read in the *Chronica Jordanis*, "the Priesthood, the Empire, and "the University. And as the Priesthood has only

---

[4] It is to be found in a manuscript from Tergernsee, now in the royal library at Munich, of the fifteenth century, *Codex lat. Tegerns.*, 781. [See Appendix A.]

"one seat, namely Rome, so the University has and
"needs only one seat, namely Paris. Of the three
"leading nations each possesses one of these in-
"stitutions. The Romans or Italians have the
"Priesthood, the Germans have the Empire, and the
"French have the University." [1]

This University was originally in Athens, thence it was transported to Rome, and from Rome Charlemagne (or his son) transplanted it to Paris. The very year of this transfer was stated. Thus we find in the *Chronicon Tielense*,[2] "Anno D. 830, Romanum "studium, quod prius Athenis exstitit, est translatum "Parisios."

Hence in ancient times, according to the prevalent notion, the University was at Athens; and whoever would rise to great eminence in the sphere of knowledge must go there. There were only two ways in which a foreign adventurer could attain to the highest office in the Church—piety, or learning. The legend could not make the girl from Mayence become eminent through piety; this would not agree with

---

[1] In Schard. *De Jurisd. Imperiali ac Potest. Eccles. Variorum Authorum Scripta.*, Basil., 1566, p. 307.

[2] Ed. van Leeuwen, Trajecti, 1789, p. 37. So also Gobelinus Persona. The anonymous writer in Vincent of Beauvais had previously stated, "Alcuinus studium de Roma Parisios transtulit, "quod illuc a Græcia translatum fuerat a Romanis."

her subsequent seduction and the birth of the child in the open street. Therefore it was through her learning that she won for herself universal admiration, and, at the election to the papacy, a unanimous vote. And this learning she could only have attained in Athens. For the University, as **Amalricus** Augerii says, was at that time in Greece.[1]

1 See Eccard, ii., 1707.

[For additional matter on the general subject of the Papess, see Appendix B.]

II. POPE CYRIACUS.

Pope Cyriacus was foisted into the Roman list of popes about the same time as Pope Joan, and like her, maintained his usurped position for a long time. Here intentional imposture, visionary fancy and groundless credulity conspired together to create a pope as unreal and as purely invented as Pope Joan.

In the middle of the twelfth century the nun Elizabeth, in the monastery of Schönau, in the diocese of Treves, stood far and wide in high repute. Her visions were inexhaustible; and as often as a grave was opened, and the bones and remains of some nameless corpse were found, the name and history of the unknown dead were revealed to her, as she said, by an angel or a saint. This worked with inspiriting effect on those who wanted new relics of saints for a church or a chapel to attract the stream of population thither. Elizabeth had already been busy with the myth of St. Ursula [1] and her maidens;

[They are said to have been martyred in 237; the sixteenth centenary of the event was celebrated in 1837. Yet it was the Huns returning from their defeat at Chalons, in 451, who put the maidens to death! St. Ursula's name appears in no martyrology earlier than the tenth century. Mr. Baring-Gould considers her as "no other than the Swabian goddess Ursel or Horsel transformed "into a saint of the Christian calendar."—*Curious Myths of the Middle Ages*, 1869, p. 331].

and since 1155 thousands of corpses had been dug up in the fields near Cologne, all of which were said to have belonged to St. Ursula's company. At last, however, the corpses of *men* also came to light. Tombstones with inscriptions were discovered there, or rather were forthwith invented. They spoke of an Archbishop Simplicius, of Ravenna, Marinus, bishop of Milan, Pantulus, of Basle, and several cardinals and priests. There was, moreover, a stone with the inscription—" St. Cyriacus Papa Romanus qui cum " gaudio suscepit sacras virgines et cum iisdem re- " versus martyrium suscepit et St. Alina V." These epitaphs were sent by the abbot Gerlach to Elizabeth. By the visions which she saw in her states of magnetic clairvoyance she was to decide whether these tablets were to be believed.[1] For he himself, as he said, entertained a suspicion that the stones might have been secretly buried there with a view to gain. Her[2] unwillingness to act as judge was overcome, and now the following history came to light. At the

[1] The inscriptions and the narration of St. Elizabeth are to be found, *Acta Sanctorum* Octbr. ix., 86-88. The finding of the tombstones was set on foot, it seems, to explain the appearance of so many bones of males in the field (ager Ursulanus), where people had been accustomed to expect only the bones of the pretended virgins, and in order to vindicate the honour of the maidens.

[2] " Diutina postulatione me multum resistentem compulerunt," are her words.

time when Ursula and her maidens came to Rome, Cyriacus had already reigned a year and eleven weeks as the **nineteenth pope.** In the night he received the command of heaven to renounce his office, and go forth with the maidens, for a martyr's death awaited him and them. He accordingly resigned his authority into the hands of the cardinals, and caused Antherus to be raised to the papacy in his place. The Roman clergy, however, were so indignant at the abdication of Cyriacus that they struck his name out of the list of the popes.

Accordingly, every objection created by previously-existing authorities was forthwith quashed, and the chroniclers of the thirteenth century determined without further thought that the newly discovered pope must be inserted between **Pontianus and Anteros (238).** The first to do this was the Premonstratensian monk, Robert Abolant at Auxerre, who in the first part of this century composed a general chronicle. The Dominicans, Vincent of Beauvais and Thomas of Chantinpré, followed, and after them the Cistercian Alberich. Martinus Polonus was in this case also the decisive authority and source of information for the times subsequent to himself. In him the reason why Cyriacus was not found in the *Catalogus Pontificum* is given with more particularity: " Credebant enim "plerique cum non propter devotionem, sed propter "oblectamenta virginum Papatum dimisisse." And on this point Leo of Orvieto has followed him. Aimery du Peyrat[1] also, and Bernard Guidonis[2] contend for Cyriacus, while Amalrich Augerii passes him over. The oldest chronicle in the German language (about 1330) says of him : " Want er lies daz babes-"thum und die würdikeit wider der Cardinal willen, " und fur mit den XI. tusing megden gen Colen, und " wart gemartert, darumb tilketen die cardinal sinen " namen abe der bebiste buche."[3] The *Eulogium historiarum*, compiled by a monk of Malmesbury about the year 1366, introduces him with the remark, " Hic cessit de papatu contra voluntatem cleri."[4] In the fifteenth century Cyriacus, as was to be expected, appeared in all the better known historical works ; in Antonius, Philip of Bergamo, Nauklerus, etc., and

1 *Notices et Extraits*, vi., 77.

2 Maii *Spicil*, vi., 29.

3 ["Since, against the will of the Cardinals, he gave up the papacy and the honor, and went with the eleven thousand maidens to Cologne, and was martyred, on this account the Cardinals expunged his name from the Popes' Book."] *Oberrheinische Chronik*, edited by S. A. Grieshaber, 1850, p. 5.

4 Ed. Scott Haydon, Lond., 1858, i., 180. [Huic successit Siriacus papa qui sedit anno uno, mensibus iii.; hic cessit de papatu contra voluntatem cleri, sequendo xi m. virgines quas baptizaverat, et substituendo Anaclerum, et ideo non apponitur in catalogo paparum.]

hence passed even into the older editions of the Roman breviary.¹

But as early as the last year of the thirteenth century the story of Cyriacus had become of no small practical importance, and the lawyers had appropriated it for their purposes.

The resignation of Cœlestine V., and the consequent elevation of Boniface VIII. to the papacy, created very great commotion. Many were of opinion that it was utterly impossible for a pope to resign, for he had no ecclesiastical superior who could release him from his sacred obligations, and no one can release himself. The numerous opponents of Boniface pounced upon this question, and it was now of importance to discover instances of popes resigning. Accordingly the author of the Glossa Ordinaria to the decree, in which Boniface VIII. affirmed the right of popes to resign, appealed to the undoubted instance of Cyriacus;² and thenceforward nearly all

---

1 Berti, in the *Raccolta di Dissertazion* of Zaccaria, ii., 10, remarks that he finds the fabulous acts of St. Ursula even in the breviary of 1526; and, according to Launoi, they are still found in the breviary of 1550.

2 "Datur autem certum exemplum de Cyriaco Papa, de quo "legitur, quod cum Ursula et undecim millibus virginum martyr-"izatus est." Then follows the narrative as given by Martinus Polonus. Thus it stands in the older editions of the Lib . vi. *Decretal.*, cap. Renunciat., Lugdun. 1520, 1550, 1553. In the later editions the passage is omitted.

canonists availed themselves of the same pretended authority, and not only they, but theologians also, as, for example, Ægidius Colonna [1] and Sylvester Prieras. It was usual to quote three popes in primitive times as instances of abdication, Clement, Marcellinus, and Cyriacus; [2] so that it really was a most strange mishap that all three cases should be invention.

The supposed resignation of Clement was invented merely to harmonise the discrepancy between the statements, according to which he was sometimes said to have come immediately after St. Peter, sometimes not till after Linus and Anacletus.

---

[1] *De Renunciatione Papæ*, in Rocaberti *Biblioth. Maz. Pontif.*, ii., 61.

[2] So, for instance, Augustinus de Ancona, *Summa*, quest. 4, art. 8: "Respondes dicendum, quod Canones et gesta Pontificum qua-"tuor Summos Pontifices narrant renunciasse Pontificatui, Clemen-"tem, Cyriacum, Marcellinum et Cælestinum." So too, Albericus de Rosate, Dominicus a S. Geminiano, Johannes Turrecremata, Antonius Cucchus Bartholomæus Fumus, and others.

III. MARCELLINUS.

The fable about Pope Marcellinus is far more ancient than the fiction of Pope Cyriacus. For nearly a thousand years it passed for truth along with the equally imaginary synod of Sinuessa, and has been much used by theologians and lawyers in support of their theories.[1]

At the beginning of the persecution under Diocletian (this is the fable in substance), the pontifex of the Capitol represented to Marcellinus, who was then pope, that he might without scruple offer incense to the gods, for the three wise men from the East had done so before Christ. Both agreed to let the point be decided by Diocletian, who was at that time in Persia, and he naturally ordered that the pope should offer incense. Accordingly Marcellinus is conducted to the temple of Vesta, and there offers

---

[1] [It is well known that this fable has been admitted into the Roman breviary. The interpolation seems to have been made in the first half of the sixteenth century. "A la fête de Saint Marcellin, "le 16 Avril, l'ancien bréviaire romain de 1520 se borne au récit du "martyre de ce Pape. Mais voici un autre bréviaire romain de 1536 "(Bibl. Sainte Geneviève, No. B B 70), et un autre de 1542 (Ibid. "No. B B 67) où l'on introduit la fable odieuse et ridicule du "prétendu concile de Sinuesse."—A. Gratry, *Première lettre à Mgr.* "*Deschamps*, p. 58.]

sacrifices, in the presence of a crowd of Christian spectators, to Hercules, Jupiter, and Saturn. At the news of this three [1] hundred bishops leave their sees, and gather together to hold a council, first in a cavern near Sinuessa, but, as this would not hold more than fifty, afterwards in the town itself. Along with them were thirty Roman priests. Several priests and deacons are deposed, merely because they had gone away when they saw the pope enter the temple. Marcellinus, on the other hand, neither may nor can be judged, being supreme head of the church,—this conviction pervades the whole synod,—the [2] pope can only be judged by himself. At first he attempts to palliate his act; but seventy-two witnesses make accusation against him. Thereupon he [3] acknowledges his guilt, and himself pronounces his own deposition on the 23rd of August, 303. After this the bishops remain quietly together in Sinuessa, until Diocletian, upon receiving intelligence of this synod

---

1 [A number quite impossible for that country, especially in a time of persecution.]

2 [The bishops say to him, "Tu eris judex; ex te enim damnaberis, et ex te justificaberis, tamen in nostra præsentia. Prima Sedes non judicabitur a quoquam."]

3 [He denied his guilt the first two days; but on the third day, being adjured in God's name to speak the truth, he throws himself on the ground, covers his head with ashes, and repeatedly acknowledges his guilt, adding that he had been bribed to offer sacrifice.]

in Persia, sends an order for the execution of many of the three hundred, and this is carried into effect.

Since the time of Baronius not a single historian worth mentioning has renewed the attempt to maintain the authenticity of this synod of Sinuessa and its acts, this clumsy structure of absurdities and impossibilities.[1] Whether any residuum of truth, any actual lapse on the part of Marcellinus in the persecution, lies at the bottom of the fabrication, cannot now be stated with certainty. Contemporary writers say nothing on the subject. Later on the Donatists alone, in the time of Augustine, professed to know that Marcellinus, and with him his successors, Melchiades, Marcellus, and Sylvester, who were at that time priests, had [delivered up the Scriptures, and had] offered incense to the gods in the persecution. The bishop of Hippo treats it as a fabrication. Theodoret maintains that Marcellinus was conspicuous at the time of the persecution (of course for

---

[1] [Hefele (*Conciliengeschichte*, III., iii., § 10, note 2) gives the main authorities against the fable. Augustine, *De unico Baptismo contra Petilianum*, c. 16; Theodoret, *Hist., Eccl.*, lib. i., c. 2. Among commentators, Pagi, *Crit. in Annales Baronii.* ad ann. 302, n. 18; Papebroch, in the *Acta Sanct. in Propyl. Mag*, vol. viii.; Natalis Alexander, *Hist. Eccl.* sæc. iii., diss. xx., vol. iv., p. 135, ed. Venet., 1778; Remi Ceillier, *Hist. des auteurs sacrés*, vol. iii., p. 681. Among Protestant authors, Bower, *Hist. of the Popes*, vol i , p. 68 ff.; Walch, *Hist. d. Papste*, p. 68 ff.; *Hist. der Kirchenvers.*, p. 126]

his constancy). However, it has lately come to light that a fiction, composed about the same time, and perhaps by the same hand, as that about the synod of Sinuessa, was connected with events which really took place in Rome. This was the *Constitutum Silvestri*. And hence it is possible that a circumstance, at that time still known in Rome, may have afforded the first material for the fabrication respecting Marcellinus also.

But however that may be, of a synod at Sinuessa at this time there is not a trace anywhere else to be found. The Acts of the pretended synod are evidently fabricated in order to manufacture an historical support for the principle, *that a pope can be judged by no man*. This incessantly-repeated sentence is the red thread which runs through the whole; the rest is mere appendage. By this means it is to be inculcated on the laity that they must not venture to come forward as accusers of the clergy, and on the inferior clergy that they must not do the like against their superiors. The date and occasion of the fabrication can be stated with tolerable certainty. The older list of the popes, which comes down to the death of Felix III. in 530, and can scarcely have been made later than the seventh century, has already accepted the fable about the apostasy of Marcellinus.

On the other hand, the language of the document is so barbarous that it can hardly have been written before the close of the fifth century. And thus we are directed to those troubled sixteen years (498-514), in which the pontificate of Symmachus ran its course. At that time the two parties of Laurentius and Symmachus stood opposed to one another in Rome as foes. People, senate, and clergy were divided; they fought and murdered in the streets, and Laurentius maintained himself for several years in possession of part of the churches. Symmachus was accused by his opponents of grave offences. He had to answer for himself before a synod, which King Theodoric summoned; if he should be found guilty he must be deposed, cried the one party; while the other party maintained that for a pope there was no earthly tribunal.[1] This was the time at which Eunodius wrote his apology for Symmachus, and this accordingly was also the time at which the synod of Sinuessa, as well as the *Constitutum* of Sylvester, was

---

[1] "Hos (his, viz., nonnullis episcopis et senatoribus) palam pro "ejus defensione clamantibus, quod a nullo possit Romanus Ponti- "fex, etiamsi talis sit, qualis accusatur, audiri." *Vita Symmachi* in Muratori, *SS Ital.*, iii., II., 46. ["In sacerdotibus cæteris potest si "quid forte nutaverit, reformari : at si papa urbis vocatur in dubium, "episcopatus videbitur, non jam episcopus, vacillare."—*Avitus ad Seratt.* apud Labbe, p. 1365.
He adds further on, "Non est gregis pastorem terrere, sed judicis."]

fabricated. The hostile party were numerous and influential, their opposition was tenacious and unremitting, their demand for an inquiry and examination of witnesses seemed natural and fair; and therefore the adherents of Symmachus caught at this means of showing that the inviolability of the pope had been long since recognised as a fact, and enounced as a rule.

A third fabrication, the *Gesta de Xysti purgatione et Polychronii Ierosolymitani episcopi accusatione*, was produced by the same hand, and for the same purpose.[1] As in the Apology of Eunodius, so also in the *Constitutum* and the *Gesta*, the principle is inculcated that a pope has no earthly judge over him. If he lies under grave suspicion, or if charges are brought against him, he must himself declare his own guilt, himself pronounce his own deposition, as Marcellinus, or he must clear himself by the simple asseveration of his own innocence, as Xystus III., according to the *Gesta*, is said to have done, when a charge of unchastity was brought against him by Bassus. Besides all this, the prosecution of a bishop for anything whatever was rendered difficult or impossible according to the three fictitious documents;

[1] They are all to be found in the Appendix to Constant's edition of the *Epistolæ Pontificum Rom.*

for seventy-two (or, according to the *Gesta*, at any rate forty) witnesses were to be required in such cases.

In later times the fable was made use of for altogether different purposes. Pope Nicolas I. quoted it in his letter to the Greek emperor [1] Michael [A.D. 862], because it showed that the deposition of Ignatius was contrary to ecclesiastical discipline, since he had been sentenced by his inferiors.

Gerson [2] made use of it, on the other hand, together with the lapse of Liberius, in order, by means of these instances of *heresy* in popes (this word, as is well known, was specially used at that time in the wider sense of *a denial of the faith*), to prove the legitimacy of a council assembled either *without* or *against* the authority of the pope. Gerbert also appealed to it with a similar object.

1 In Harduin, *Conc. Coll.*, v., 155.
2 *Serm. coram Alex.* v. II., 136, ed. Dupin.

IV. CONSTANTINE AND SYLVESTER.

IF the mere number of witnesses could make a statement credible, there would be no fact more certain or irrefutable than that the Emperor Constantine, more than twenty years before his death, was baptized at Rome by pope Sylvester, and at the same time cured of leprosy. For nearly eight hundred years the whole of western Europe had no other belief, and for just as long a period people laboured in vain to explain the fact how, nevertheless, the sources from which every one acquired his knowledge of the fourth century on other points, viz., the *Historia Tripartita*, the Chronicle of Jerome, and the Chronicle of Isidore, could be unanimous in stating that Constantine was baptized, not in Rome, but in a castle near Nicomedia, not by the pope, but by the Arian bishop Eusebius, not immediately on his conversion from heathenism, but only just before his death.

It cannot be denied that according to the mode of thought and historic sentiment of the Middle Ages, the real facts must have appeared inconceivable, while the fabulous version, on the other hand, seemed perfectly natural and intelligible. The most important and decisive event of antiquity, the transition of the ruler of the world from heathenism to Christianity, —where else could this take place but in the capital of the world? It must have been the Head of the Church who opened the doors of the Church to the Head of earthly sovereigns. And that the pious Constantine, the son of the sainted Helena, the founder of the Christian empire of Rome, should of his own accord have remained all his life long unbaptized, not receiving the sacraments, and in reality having no claim even to the name of Christian,—that was a thing which it was utterly impossible to believe.

A baptistery which bore the name of Constantine at a very early period, possibly because it was really built by his order, and at his cost, may have given the first occasion to the myth, in that people thought that it was so called because Constantine was baptized in it. For in later times it was considered as an irrefragable and monumental witness to the truth of a circumstance which all were eager to believe.

The legend of Sylvester, manifestly fabricated in order to attest the fact of Constantine's having been baptized in Rome, cannot have been composed later than the close of the fifth century. It is all of one casting, and bears no traces of later additions. The Greek[1] text in which it is contained is evidently a translation from the Latin, which no doubt was written in Rome.[2] In the whole document there is not one historical trait to be found. Constantine is, to begin with, the enemy of the Christians, and causes many of them—along with them his own wife—to be executed, because they will not offer sacrifice to idols, so that Sylvester flies to Mount Soracte. The emperor, struck with leprosy, is told that to be cured he must bathe in a pool filled with boys' blood newly shed; but overcome by the tears of the mothers of these boys he rejects the horrible remedy, and is directed in a heavenly vision to apply to Sylvester. Sylvester heals him of his disease by means of Christian baptism; whereupon the whole of Rome, senate and people, believe in Christ. Two episodes are interwoven with the story; the first respecting an enormous snake living under the Tarpeian Rock, and slaying thousands with its pestiferous breath, until Sylvester closes the entrance of its hole; and secondly, a long disputation with the Jews

---

[1] Edited by Combefis in his *Illustr. Chr. Martyrum lecti Triumphi*, Paris 1660.

[2] This is shown by a passage quite at the beginning, in which it is said of Eusebius: τῇ ἑλληνίκῃ συνεγράψατο γλώσσῃ. Of course no Greek would have made such a remark.

(brought about by Helena), in which Sylvester comes off victorius.

The author is acquainted with the ecclesiastical history of Eusebius. He intends (as he says at the outset) to complete the narrative of Eusebius; but he either was not acquainted with the biography of Constantine, which gives an account of the baptism of the emperor, or at any rate he presupposed that his readers were not acquainted with it. And he actually did succeed in making his fable current, in spite of the decisive and unanimous witnesses of the fourth century. Even the Chronicle of Jerome, which people otherwise followed with unqualified assent in matters of history, was at last on this point superseded.

The legend of Sylvester is mentioned for the first time in the decretal of Pope Gelasius (492–496), *De Libris Recipiendis et non Recipiendis*. There it is said, "the name or the author is indeed unknown,[1] but it "has been said that it was read by many Catholics "in the city of Rome, and many churches imitated "this ancient custom."[2] It is manifest that these

---

[1] Cf. the double text in Fontanini *De Antiquitatibus Hortæ.* Rome, 1723, p. 322, and Credner's edition.

[2] "Pro antiquo usu," which means the ancient custom of introducing the writings used in Rome into other churches also. In another manuscript the reading is "et pro hoc quoque usu multæ "hæc imitantur ecclesiæ."—See Credner, *Zur Geschichte des Kanons*, 1847, p. 210.

are not the words of Gelasius himself, and were not written in Rome, but elsewhere. The whole is a subsequent addition; one of the many which gradually crept into the document in the period between A.D. 500 and 800. Nevertheless, the invention of the legend must fall either within the time of Gelasius, or more probably soon after him, within the time of Symmachus, 498-514. For in the fictions which belong to the time of Symmachus, and which were called into existence by the circumstances relating to this pope, especially in the *Constitutum Sylvestri* and the *Gesta Liberii Papæ*, the baptism of Constantine at Rome, and his cleansing from leprosy, are mentioned with unmistakeable reference to the legend. And moreover, this is done so designedly and unnaturally as to betray the fact, that the legend of Sylvester excited the very gravest doubts, and therefore must be supported and confirmed. Above all, it was intended to weaken the strength of such weighty evidence as that which Jerome, Ambrose, Prosper, and others afforded for the baptism of Constantine in the palace of Acyron, near Nicomedia; and therefore in the *Gesta Liberii* an emperor is invented, who is supposed to be the nephew of Constantine, and who is called in turn Constantine, Constantius, and Constans. Then, without any further occasion or any closer connection with the contents of the document, it is asserted of this personage that he was baptized by Eusebius of Nicomedia in Nicomedia, at the Villa Aquilo. Here everything is taken into account: the change of name, as well as the transformation of the son into a nephew of Constantine. This nephew takes it as a grievous affront that Liberius should say that his uncle was baptized by Sylvester, and thereby cleansed from his leprosy; and he threatens that when he comes to Rome he will give the flesh of Liberius to the birds and beasts of prey. Hence it is the more probable—nay, certain, that the legend of Sylvester and the fiction of the baptism of Constantine at Rome became extant contemporaneously with the fables which were invented in the interests of Symmachus and the Roman clergy of that time, that is to say, in the first few years of the sixth century.

There was, however, still a considerable interval before the story passed into the chronicles, and from them into ecclesiastical literature generally. Isidore adhered to the historical version of the matter, and Fredegar also (A.D. 658) remained still true to the genuine account. Gregory[1] of Tours (died A.D. 598)

---

[1] [In two of his three accounts of the baptism of Clovis by St. Remigius, e.g.: "Procedit novus Constantinus ad lavacrum, deleturus leprae veteris morbum," &c. In the magnificent new edition of the *Recueil des Historiens des Gaules et de la France* (Palmé, Paris,

already alludes to the fable, and Bede (in the year 729) is, properly speaking, the first who, by means of his chronicle, prepared the way for the introduction of the story of Constantine's baptism in Rome into the annals of the West;[1] nevertheless he did not succeed for some time longer. Frekulf (about the year 840), who holds fast to good authorities in his *Universal History*, abides by a baptism in Nicomedia at the end of the emperor's life. Even the painstaking Hermann the Lame of Reichenau (about A.D. 1050) seems to know nothing of the fable, and his contemporary, Marianus Scotus, who follows Jerome as an authority, has still the correct version.[2]

1869) there is the following interesting note, *in loco:* "Colb. ad " Marginem hæc habet, ab annis circ. 400 addita., *Ecce iste Historio-* ' *graphus concordat cum Historia St. Sylvestri de leprâ Constantini* " *mundatâ in fonte baptismi.* Et quidem certum videtur ex hoc loco, " ubi etiam Chlodoveus **Constantino et sanctus Remigius beato** " Sylvestro comparantur, tunc temporis jam invaluisse opinionem de " baptizato Romæ Constantino per beatum Sylvestrum, lepráque ejus " mundatâ." But in cod. Reg. this passage is left blank.]

[1] Venerabilis **Bedæ Opera** Historica Minora, ed. Stephenson, London, 1841, p. 81. [Bede does not dwell on the supposed event; he mentions it merely in passing. "**Constantinus fecit** *Romæ, ubi* " *baptizatus est,* basilicam beati Joannis Baptistæ, quæ appellata est "**Constantiniana:** item basilicam beato Petro in templo Apollinis, "nec non et beato Paulo, corpus utriusque ære Cyprio circumdans v " pedes grosso," &c.]

[2] The reading "rebaptizatus" instead of "baptizatus" in a manuscript of Gemblours, on which Schelstrate lays great stress, is manifestly the correction of a copyist who believed in the baptism at Rome.

CONSTANTINE AND SYLVESTER.

For the majority, however, the authority of the *Liber Pontificalis*, the Roman biographies of the popes, was irresistible. The fable of the baptism in Rome had already passed into the oldest list of the popes, one reaching back to the sixth century and in like manner into the enlarged collection which was based upon this one, the so-called Anastasius. In like manner Ado (died A.D. 875) inserts in his universal chronicle, which is based upon Bede, the fable of Constantine having been baptized in Rome, being misled by Bede, and by the *Liber Pontificalis*. He betrays the latter source by the long list of ecclesiastical donations and buildings, which Constantine is said to have ordered in Rome, and which Ado borrowed from that Roman chronicle of the popes. On the other hand, Ordericus Vitalis (about A. D. 1107), and Hugo of Fleury (in the year 1109), who in their ecclesiastical works narrate the whole fable,—leprosy, bath of children's blood and all—have drawn directly or indirectly from the legend of Sylvester; while Otto of Freysing, though he declares these details to be apocryphal, nevertheless holds fast to the baptism in Rome by Sylvester, "in accordance with the Roman " tradition," as he says.

The first critical attempt to remove the contradiction between the old and new versions of the story was made about the year 1100 by Eccard, a monk in the monastery of Michaelsberg, and from 1108 onwards abbot of the monastery of Aurach. The means which he employed were these. He transferred the outrageous cruelty of Constantine, the execution of his nephew, of his son, his wife, and many friends, to the earlier part of the emperor's reign, after his victory over Licinus. Thereupon the Cæsar is struck by God with leprosy, but baptized by Sylvester. He says, in conclusion: "Some persons " maintain that Constantine fell into the Arian heresy, " and was rebaptized by Eusebius of Nicomedia. The " church histories, however (that of Eusebius, namely, " of which Eccard made much use), do not state this, " but that he died in great sanctity." Eccard, therefore, understood the version of Jerome to relate to a second baptism, by means of which Constantine got himself received into the sect of the Arians,—a means of getting out of the difficulty at which many since Eccard have caught. Nevertheless the author of the Magdeburg [1] Annals (written in the year 1175), a monk in the monastery of Bergen, near Magdeburg, does not allow himself to be misled by the authority of Eccard, whom he otherwise uses as his basis. He

---

[1] Formerly known as *Chronographus Saxo;* now as *Annales Magdeburg.*, in Pertz's collection, **xvi.**, p. 119.

remains true to the version of the *Ecclesiastical History* (the *Tripartita*), that Constantine put off his baptism till the end of his life.

Another variation is tried by the Italians, under the leadership of Bonizo, bishop of Sutri, and subsequently of Piacenza (died A.D. 1089), an authority not used by the Germans. In his history of the popes,[2] Bonizo had to choose between three accounts of Constantine's baptism. That is to say, besides the two ordinary accounts, he had also before him the one contained in a spurious decretal of pope Eusebius, now no longer extant, stating that this pope (and therefore in the year 310[3]) had already instructed, and baptized the emperor. The decretal was, of course, pure intention, in order that, by changing the Nicomedian into the Roman Eusebius, support might be got for the theory of Constantine's baptism in Rome, a theory of immense importance to the Romans. Bonizo will only allow the first half of the statement, considers the "baptizatum," as a *vitium scriptorum*, and gives it as his opinion, that after the instruction which he had received in Rome, Constantine postponed baptism on account of the dis-

---

2 It is found in the fourth book of his *Libri Decreti*, whence Mai gives it in the *Nova Bibliotheca Patrum*, vii., P. 3, p. 39.

3 [The papacy of Eusebius falls wholly within the year 310.]

tracting cares of government, receiving it at the hands of Sylvester, and not before. But he wholly denies the statement in the *Tripartita Historia*, that he was not baptized until the end of his life, and then into the Arian faith. None but a maniac could believe that, after the council of Nicæa, and after the circumstances of Arius' death, of which the emperor had been a witness, he still could have lapsed into Arianism. Bonizo goes so far as to claim the authority of the whole Church in favour of his opinion. " That Constantine was baptized by " Sylvester," he says, " is the undoubting belief of " the Catholic Church." And the Italian chroniclers of the twelfth and thirteenth centuries, Sicard [1], bishop of Cremona, and Romnald, [2] of Salerno, have copied him in this, the latter word for word. On the other hand, Gotfried of Viterbo, in his *Pantheon*, undismayed by the "mente captus" of Bonizo, avails himself of the hypothesis of an Arian re-baptism in Nicomedia. In this bishop Anselm of Havelberg (about the year 1187) had already preceded him in his dialogues against the Greeks.[3] Anselm was misled by another apocryphal writing, viz., a spurious *History of Pope* [4] *Sylvester*, forged under the name

---

[1] Muratori, *SS.*, vii., 555.   [2] Ibid., vii., 78.
[3] In D'Archery's *Spicilegium*, nov. edit., i, 207.
[4] It exists in manuscript, according to D'Achery, in the library

of Eusebius of Cæsarea, and differing from the legend.

Of great influence in the matter was the additional fact, that the popes also themselves made use of the apocryphal legend of Sylvester, and maintained Constantine's baptism at Rome as historical. Hadrian I., in the letter which was read at the second council of Nicæa, A.D. 787, quoted a long passage out of the legend as evidence of the primitive use of images.[1] Nicolas I. (858-867) cited a supposed passage from a pseudo-Isidorian letter which bore the name of Sylvester, with the distinctive title "Magni Constantini baptizator."[2] Leo IX., also, in the controversy with the Patriarch Cærularius, laid stress on

---

of St. Germain. Ratramnus (in D'Achery, l. c., p. 100) quotes a passage from it. It seems to have been forged, in order to defend Roman claims and customs against the objections of the Greeks.

[1] In Harduin, iv., 82 [The gist of it is this. The apostles Peter and Paul appear to Constantine, and tell him to abandon the idea of the bath of blood, and seek out Sylvester in his exile on Mt. Soracte; he will cure the emperor of his leprosy. Constantine goes to Sylvester, who produces images of SS. Peter and Paul, in order to prove to the emperor that the two who appeared to him in the vision were not gods, but these two apostles. Constantine recognises the likeness, is convinced and baptized, and proceeds to build and restore churches, which he takes care to adorn with images. Compare the curious and very different version of the story given in the *Urbis Romæ Mirabilia*, reprinted from the Vatican manuscripts by Gustav Parthey, Berlin, 1869.]

[2] Ibid., v., 144.

the fact that Constantine was the spiritual son of Sylvester by baptism.[1]

Among the Greeks, Johannes Malalas, at Antioch, is the first who accepted the Roman baptism of Constantine.[2] He lived at the end of the sixth century, and was certainly one of the least intelligent, and most prolific in fables, of all the Byzantine annalists. His authority may possibly have been the Greek translation of the legend of Sylvester, which had recently been made. It is true that he did not accomplish much in the way of introducing the fable, because his own work was not very widely disseminated. But seeing that Constantine was honored in the Greek Church as a saint, and that his festival was yearly celebrated on the 21st of May, with the greatest[3] solemnity, especially in Constantinople, it gradually came to appear quite inconceivable to the Greeks, that he should, of his own accord, have remained all his life outside the pale of the Church, and should not have received baptism till he was on his death-bed.[4] Accordingly we find an author as

---

[1] Harduin, vi., 933

[2] Ed Dindorf, p. 317

[3] Bolland, ad 21 Mai, p. 13, 14.

[4] [In Constantine's own age it was probably too common a case to provoke either surprise or censure. A century later we find St. Ambrose and St. Augustine postponing the reception of baptism

early as the abbot Theophanes (died A.D. 817) setting the Anatolian theory of the baptism in Nicomedia, by Eusebius, in opposition to the Roman theory of the baptism of Sylvester, but forthwith declaring that he considered the Roman account as the more correct; for, of course, Constantine, if **unbaptized**, could not have taken his seat with the fathers at Nicæa, and could not have taken part in the sacred mysteries: to assert or suppose that he could, was to the last degree absurd.[1] Accordingly, if even the Byzantines, as early as the ninth century, had become so unfamiliar with the circumstances and true history of the fourth century, it cannot excite wonder that the later Greek historians should have considered the incorrect account as an established fact. And this is the case with the lately published Theodosius Melitenus,[2] Cedrenus, also Zonaras, Georgius Hamartolus, Glycas, and Nicephorus Callistus.

Seeing, then, that all the chronicles of the popes subsequent to the *Liber Pontificalis*, and based upon it, relate the baptism of Constantine at Rome, and that Martinus Polonus, with his predilection for what

till they were over thirty years of age, long after they were convinced of the truth of Christianity. Stanley's *Eastern Church*. Lect. vi., sub fin.]

1 Ed. Classen, i., 25.
2 *Chronographia*, ed. Tafel., Monachii, 1859, p. 61.

is fantastic and distorted, has imported the *Gesta Silvestri* with its whole tissue of fables into his standard work, the fable maintained itself in unquestioned sovereignty throughout the Middle Ages; until, with the re-awakening of the knowledge of the Greek language and literature, and of the critical historic sense, the two most advanced spirits of their age, Æneas Sylvius and Nicolas of Cusa, recognised the truth.[1] Nevertheless it needed still two centuries and more, before the powerful authorities which gave support to the fable were demolished. All the canonists kept fast to the theory of a Roman baptism for some time longer, for in the collections of canons by Anselm and Deusdedit, and, above all, in the *Decretum* of Gratian (here indeed marked as "*palea*," that is, as a later insertion), bits out of the *Gesta Silvestri* found a place, and these presupposed the truth of the statement respecting the emperor's baptism. Hence the Cardinals Jacobazzi, Reginald Pole, Baronius, Bellarmine, and in later times even Ciampini himself, and Schelstrate, still continued to defend the theory of a baptism in Rome, sometimes again taking refuge in the desperate resource of an Arian re-baptism. It was the profound erudition

---

[1] Opera, Basil., 1551, p. 338.

and historical criticism of French theologians which first enabled truth to win a complete victory.

Besides all this, the legend of Sylvester was welcome material for the poetry of the Middle Ages. The venomous dragon, the disputation with the Jews, the slain ox, the emperor's leprosy, and its healing—all this is picturesquely described in the *Kaiserchronik*, but with the greatest elaboration in the poem *Sylvester*, by Conrad of Würzburg. The *Lackenspieghel* of Jan de Clerc, and the versified legends of the saints, avail themselves of it in like manner; and even Wolfram of Eschenbach alludes in the *Parzival* to the miracle of the ox raised to life again.

[The exploded falsehood still lives on in that museum of exploded falsehoods—Rome. On the base of the ancient obelisk which adorns the piazza of St. John Lateran, an inscription in large capitals still states—

CONSTANTINVS
PER CRVCEM VICTOR
A S. SILVESTRO HIC
BAPTIZATVS
CRVCIS GLORIAM
PROPAGAVIT;

and the *custode* of the Baptistery is still allowed to tell all visitors, that in that building pope Sylvester baptized the emperor.]

V. THE DONATION OF CONSTANTINE.

THE *Liber Pontificalis* enumerates a quantity of houses and pieces of land in various places, which Constantine is said to have given to the Church of Rome. The source alone renders these donations suspicious, one which has made such abundant use of the fictions of the age of Symmachus. And the suspicion increases when one remarks that so enormous a number of donations are attributed to Constantine alone, while the book does not mention a single other donation of any of the emperors who follow, until Justin and Justinian in the sixth century; and they are said to have given nothing more than cups and vessels. In addition to this there is the silence of all contemporary writers, and the circumstance that Constantine, liberal as he proved himself towards the Church, nevertheless, according to all accounts, never gave lands, but only made over to it rents or sums of money. Accordingly the author of the *Vita Silvestri* in the *Liber Pontificalis* appears to have attributed the whole amount of property, which had been gradually inherited or occupied, just as it existed in his own day (that is in the seventh or eighth century), exclusively to donations of Constantine. Indeed Assemani says that Hadrian I. certainly had documents of the donation of Constantine before him, for in his letter to Charlemagne in the year 775 he appeals to such as existing in the archives of the Vatican. However, if one looks closer, Hadrian is speaking of donations in Tuscany, Spoleto, etc., which various emperors, patricians, and other pious persons had made to St. Peter and the Roman Church, but which the Lombards had taken away from it; respecting these there are several documents[1] still extant. Christian Lupus already remarks that Ammianus Marcellinus, up to the year 370, knows only of one source of papal property, viz., the offerings of matrons; and that, accordingly, the Roman Church at that time was not yet in possession of large and rich patrimonies.[2]

Until the middle of the eighth century there is not a trace to be found of the Donation which has since become so famous, by virtue of which Constantine, immediately after his baptism, and to show his gratitude for the cure wrought by Sylvester, gave to

[1] *Ital. Historiæ Scriptores Illustr.*, iii., 228. The statement of Gfrörer is misleading (*Gregor VII.*, vol. v., p. 6). He says that Baronius has "published several documents, by means of which Constantine conferred houses, lands, &c., on the three chief basilicas of Rome." What Baronius did was merely to print the passages from the *Liber Pontificalis*.

[2] *Synodorum Gener. Decreta*, &c., Bruxell, 1671. iv., 397.

this pope and his successors, a number of the most comprehensive ecclesiastical and civil rights, and to the Roman clergy many honourable privileges, and, moreover, made over Rome and Italy to the pope.

Here, then, at the outset we have these two questions to answer. *Where* and *when* was this document forged?

We have it both in Latin [1] and in Greek. It does

---

[1] ["There is one old Latin text of it, but four Greek texts. See F. A. Biener, *De collectionibus cann. Ecclesiæ Græcæ*, Berol., 1827, 8, p. 72, ss. The first alone is of historical importance, being found in the pseudo-Isidorian decretals under the title of *Edictum domini Constantini Imp.*, and extracts from it in the *Decret. Gratiani dis'*., xcvi., c. 13." Gieseler, *Church History*, ii, 117, 246, 356; New York edition. In the first letter of Hadrian I. to Charles the Great, A.D. 777 (*Cod Carol*, No. 49), occurs the following: " Et sicut temporibus b. " Sylvestri Rom Pont. a sanctæ recordationis piissimo Constantino " M. Imperatore per ejus largitatem sancta Dei catholica et apostolica " Romana ecclesia elevata atque exaltata est, *et potestatem in his* " *Hesperiæ partibus largiri dignatus. est;* ita et in his vestris " felicissimis temporibus, atque nostris S. Dei Ecclesia, i.e., b. " Petri Apostoli, germinet atque exultet : quia ecce novus christianis- " simus Dei Constantinus Imperator his temporibus surrexit, per " quem omnia Deus sanctæ suæ Ecclesiæ bb. Apostolorum principis " Petri largiri dignatus est. Sed et cuncta alia, quæ per diversos " Imperatores, Patricios etiam et alios Deum timentes, pro eorum " animæ mercede et venia delictorum—b. Petro Apostolo—concessa " sunt, et per nefandam gentem Langobardorum per annorum " spatia, abstracta atque ablata sunt, vestris temporibus restituantur. " Unde et plures donationes in sacro nostro scrinio Lateranensi " reconditas habemus," &c. Some think that we have here an allusion to the donation of Constantine, e.g. de Marca (*De Conc. Sac.*, iii., 12), according to whom the Donation was forged, A.D. 767,

not exist in the more ancient manuscripts of the legend of Sylvester, nor in the more ancient copies of the *Liber Pontificalis*; later on, however, it has been inserted into both. But it is certainly to be found as early as the most ancient manuscripts of the pseudo-Isidore collection, and was therefore at any rate composed before the year 850.

That the Donation was a fiction of the Greeks, composed in Greek, and brought from the East to Rome, was indeed long ago maintained by Baronius. Next Bianchi [1] undertook to defend this view, on no better grounds, however, than the weak allegation, that is to be found in Balsamon; and, lately, Richter [2] also has given as his opinion that it probably originated in Greece. But from the Greek text, as well as from the contents of the document itself, the very opposite of this can be demonstrated to a certainty.

At the very beginning of it Constantine speaks of

"jussu Romanorum Pontiff: pia quadam industria." Cenni, on the contrary, shows (*Monum. Domin. Pontiff.*, i., 304) that Hadrian has in view only the *Acta Silvestri*, to which he also refers in his letter to Constantine and Irene, and which in part suggested the later donation of Constantine. The words "potestatem in his Hesperiæ partibus largiri dignatus est" are especially remarkable in this connexion. Gieseler, vol. ii., ch. 2 § 5.]

1 *Della podestà e polizia della chiesa*, v., p. 1, 209.
2 *Krchenrecht*, fifth edition, p. 77.

his "satraps," whom he places before the senate and the "archons" (optimates). This expression does not occur in the Byzantines, but was of common use in Rome and with western writers; for. instance in the letter of pope Paul I. to Pepin [1] [A.D., 757], and in a document of king Ethelred, for Ealdorman. Moreover, the Greek translator has either read incorrectly or not understood the expression in the Latin, that "the "emperor had chosen St. Peter and his successors as "sure 'patroni' before God;" that is to say, he turns "firmos apud Deum patronos" into "primos "apud Deum patres," for he absurdly translates "πρώτους πρὸς τὸν Θεὸν πατέρας." [2]

Again, if a Greek had composed the document, he would certainly, in mentioning the four Oriental

[1] "Ducem Spoletinum cum ejus Satrapibus.' In Cenni, *Monumenta*, i., 154. In like manner King Luitprand sends, "Duces et Satrapas suos." *Lib. Pontif.* ed. Vignoli, ii, 63. [Not Paul's first letter to Pepin, in which he announces his election to the papacy as successor to his brother Stephen (for the election had been contested in favour of the Archdeacon Theophylact), but the second, in which he complains that the promised territory has not been ceded to the papal see. Ealdorman, i.e., governor of a county, later earl. The history of the word is a curious one, supplanted in its honourable meaning by the Danish "earl," living on itself as the less honourable "aldermen"]

[2] From the addition καὶ δεφενσόρας we may be tolerably certain that, in the Latin original used by the translator, "patronos *et* "*defensores*" was the reading.

"Thrones," have placed Constantinople not last, but first. Nowhere but in Rome would Constantinople have been mentioned last, for there, down to the time of Innocent III., recognition was persistently refused to the canons of the second and fourth general councils which settle the order of precedence for the patriarchates. On the other hand, the Byzantine tendencies of the translator are shown in that, though he retains the expression about the Lateran *palace*, "that it surpasses all palaces in the "whole world," he nevertheless omits the distinction given to the Lateran *church*, that it is accounted "caput et vertex omnium ecclesiarum in universo "orbe terrarum." Equally characteristic is it that the passage about the possessions in Judæa, Asia, Greece, Africa, &c., which Constantine gives "pro con- "cinnatione luminarium" in the Roman churches, is left out in the Greek version, and the words "summus Pontifex et universalis urbis Romæ Papa," are merely rendered "τῷ μεγάλῳ ἐπισκόπῳ καὶ καθολικῷ πάπᾳ." Thus the title οἰκουμενικός, which had been assumed by the patriarchs of Constantinople, and which would correspond far better than καθολικός to *universalis*, is avoided no doubt intentionally, so that the whole title, according to the language in use in the Oriental Church, might have been applied equally well to the bishop of **Alexandria**, who was also called πάπα,[1] as to the bishop of Rome.

Further on we meet with a word never used by any Greek author with whom I am acquainted, κοίνσουλοι for consuls, with the usual word ὕπατοι merely inserted alongside as explanatory. This can only be explained on the supposition that the text is a translation. And here the Greek text itself affords palpable evidence of a distorting of the original in a way which betrays the unlearned translator. The original ordains that

[1] [παπας or παπα, Papa, was originally a general name for **all Greek presbyters and Latin bishops; but from an** early age it was the special address which, long before the name of a patriarch or archbishop, was given to the bishop of Alexandria. "Pope of Alex-"andria" was a **well-known dignity centuries** before the bishops of **Rome claimed an** exclusive **right to** the title of pope. This was **first done** by Gregory VII., **in** a Council held at Rome in 1076. Stanley (*Eastern Church*, p. 113) gives the following curious explanation **of** the name : " Down to Heraclas (A.D. 230), the bishop of "Alexandria, being the sole Egyptian bishop, was called ' **Abba**' "(father), and his **clergy ' Elders.'** From his time more **bishops** "were created, who then received the name of ' Abba,' and **con-** "sequently the name of 'Papa' (*ab-aba*, pater patrum, grandfather) "was appropriated to the Primate. The Roman account (inconsistent "with facts) is that the name was first given to Cyril, as represent- "ing the bishop **of** Rome in the council of Ephesus (Suicer, *in* "*voce*) " He then adds other fantastic explanations : " 1 *Poppœa*, "from the short life of each pope ; 2. *Pa*, for Pater ; 3. *Pap*, suck ; "4. *Pap*, breast; 5. *Pa* (Paul), *Pe* (Peter) ; 6. παπαῖ! (admiration); "7. *Papas*, keeper (Oscan); 8. *Pappas*, **chief** slave ; 9. *Pa*(ter) "*Pa*(triæ) ; 10. *Pa*, sound of a father's kiss. See Abraham "Echellensis, *De Origine Nom. Papæ*, **60**. **It** is a little difficult to believe that all **of these** are serious."

the Roman clergy shall have the same privileges as the imperial senate, namely, that its members become patricians and consuls, and so can attain to the very highest honours which the Byzantine kingdom has to bestow. Instead of this object, which expresses a wish of the Roman clergy, quite natural and not unattainable under the circumstances of the time, the Greek text represents **the emperor as making an** enactment, the realisation of **which no one could have** seriously expected, namely, that **to the** Roman clergy generally should be attributed that pre-eminence **and** greatness, which the great senate, *or* the patricians, consuls, and other dignitaries possessed. Last of all comes the story that Constantine, holding the reins of Sylvester's horse, had performed the office of groom to Sylvester (στράτωρος ὀφφίκιον ἐποιήσαμεν), a story which, both in its wording and circumstances, **is unmistakeably** of western growth, alike **foreign to oriental** customs and oriental sentiment. This thing **occurs** for the first time in the year 754, when Pepin showed this mark of **respect** to Stephen III., who had come to visit him.[1] This act caused such great satisfaction in Rome, that it was forthwith transferred to Constantine, and made into **a** pattern and rule for kings and emperors.

[1] "Vice stratoris usque in aliquantum loci juxta ejus sellarem "properavit."—*Vita Steph.* in Vignoli, ii., 104.

The **chief passage in the** document, the cession **of Rome** and Italy *or* of the western regions to the pope, is correctly rendered in the text as given by Balsamon. On the other hand, **it** is wanting in other Greek recensions, especially in the one by Matthew Blastares[1] (about 1335), and in others given by Boulanger and Fabricius,[2] from a Parisian manuscript.

This is not hard to explain. The fictitious Donation has acquired a high canonical authority among the Greeks. Since Balsamon's time it has taken its place among a mass of manuscripts respecting Greek ecclesiastical rights;[3] **and** Greek eyes, usually so keensighted for the discovery of Latin forgeries, were **in this case so** blinded, that they readily accepted the palpable forgery, and set to work to make capital out of it in practice. Blastares quite goes into raptures over it. " Nothing more pious or more worthy of

---

[1] Beveridge, *Pandectæ Canonum*, i., p. 2, p. **117**. **But the** Latin translator has made a laughable perversion of the sense, **making** the emperor say, " Placuit ut Papa ab urbe Roma et occidentalibus " omnibus provinciis et urbibus exiret."

[2] *Biblioth.* **Gr**. ed. nov. vi., 699.

[3] They are for the most part enumerated in Biener *De Collectionibus Canonum Eccles. Græcæ*, 1827, p. 79. In the Vienna Codex, which Lambecius describes *Comment.*, lib. viii., p. 1019. nov. ed., the remark is added παρεξεβλήθη ἀπὸ τοῦ ἁγιωτάτου πατριάρχου κωνσταντινουπόλεως κυροῦ φωτίου ταῦτα. A man so well read as Photius **in literature and history, of course perceived** not only the unauthenticity of the document, but also the object of the fiction.

"reverence is to be seen anywhere," he says, "nothing which better deserves to be proclaimed far and wide." This satisfaction rested on a very simple calculation. The canon of the second œcumenical synod of 381, that palladium of the Byzantine Church, enacts that the bishop of Constantinople shall have the privileges of the bishop of Rome, and (as was further concluded) that the clergy of new Rome shall have, in like manner, all the rights of the clergy of old Rome. Therefore, says Balsamon, and this was the opinion of the clergy of the capital, all in the way of honors, dignity, and privileges, which Constantine had showered on the clergy of old Rome with so prodigal a hand, holds good also for the clergy and patriarch of new Rome. Another and later imperial enactment, also cited by Balsamon,[2] serves to confirm this, viz., that Constantinople shall enjoy, not merely the privileges of Italy, but those of Rome itself. The emperors themselves accepted the objects at which this document was aimed, at any rate those which had reference to the relations between ecclesiastical and civil dignities. Thus Michael Palæologus, in the year 1270, wrote to direct the patriarch, that whereas he, the emperor, had appointed the deacon Theodore Skutariotes to the office of Dikæophylax (supreme

---

[1] Cf. tit. 1, c. 36, p. 38, then tit. 8, c. 1, pp. 85, 89, ed. Paris, 1620.

judge or *custos justitiæ*), the said deacon should also be invested with an equivalent ecclesiastical dignity, namely, that of an exokatakoilos (that is an assessor of the patriarch with the right of precedence of the bishops) according to the terms of Constantine's rescript to Sylvester.[1]

Moreover, the Donation was acknowledged in the West centuries before it was known and noticed by the Greeks. The lately-published Georgius Hamartolus[2] (about the year 842) recounts the fables connected with the legend of Sylvester in considerable detail, but does not say a single word about the Donation. On the contrary, he represents the emperor as giving up the West to his sons Constantius and Constans, and to his nephew Dalmatius, intending to make Byzantium his own place of residence. The first Byzantine who mentions and makes use of the Donation is Balsamon, who died patriarch of Antioch in the year 1180, that is at a period when the Greeks had long since lost every foot of territory in Italy, and the giving away of Italy to the papal chair was a matter perfectly harmless so far as they at least were concerned. But at that time the Latins had for long

---

[1] *Novellæ Constitutiones Imperatorum post Justinianum*, ed. Zachariæ, 1857, p. 592.

[2] *Chronicon* ed. E. de Muralto, Petropoli, 1859, p. 399.

been paramount in Syria, and it was from them probably that Balsamon got the document.

The Donation of Constantine, therefore beyond all doubt was composed in the West,[1] in Italy, in Rome, and by a Roman ecclesiastic. The time of its appearance points to the same conclusion.

The date at which the Donation of Constantine was composed may be placed with overwhelming

[1] [The author of *Der Papst und das Concil* entirely concurs in this conclusion, placing the date of it a little before 754, it having been obviously composed with a view to being shown to Pepin. "There can be no doubt as to the Roman origin of the 'Donation.' "The Jesuit Cantel has rightly recognised this in his *Hist. Metrop.* "*Urb.*, p. 195. He thinks that a Roman subdeacon, John, was the "author. The document had a threefold object—against the "Lombards, who were threatening Rome, against the Greeks who "would acknowledge no imperium of the Roman see over their "church, and also with a view to the Franks. The attempt of the "Jesuits in the *Civiltà* to make a Frank the author merely because "Æneas of Paris and Ado of Vienna mention the Donation in the "ninth century, is scarcely worth serious discussion; it condemns "itself. The closest agreement in style and thought exists between "the Donation and contemporary Roman documents, especially the "*Constitutum Pauli* i. (Harduin *Concil* iii., 1999 ff.), and the *Epistola* "*S. Petri*, composed in 753 or 754, about the same time as the "Donation. The expression 'Concinnatio luminarium,' which "occurs in papal letters of that age, in the *Constitutum Pauli* and "the *Donatio*, and nowhere else, betrays at once a Roman hand. So "do the form of imprecation and threat of hell-torments, exactly as "in the *Constitutum* and the *Epistola S. Petri*; and the term "'Satrapæ' wholly foreign to the West, and occurring only in the "Donation and contemporary papal letters. See Cenni, *Monum.* "*Dominat. Pontif.*, i., 154." Janus, iii., note 103]

probability in those years which extend from the time when the power of the Lombard kingdom began to decline, i. e., from about A.D. 752,[1] to the year 777, in which pope Hadrian first makes mention of the gift of Constantine. Earlier than that the author could not well expect any result from his invention. What he aimed at was a great kingdom embracing the whole of Italy under the rule of the pope, instead of an Italy divided between the Lombards and the Greeks, in which Rome was perpetually exposed to the attacks of the one and the maltreatment of the other. In Rome the rule of the Greeks, however oppressive it might be at times, was always preferred to that of the Lombards. The latter dominion was considered as the greatest of all evils, while the emperor and exarch of Ravenna received, on the whole, willing obedience in Rome. The popes were far from wishing to overthrow the Byzantine dominion in Italy, even when its yoke seemed intolerable, as for example, under the two iconoclasts Leo and Constantine Copronymus. Even when the opportunity presented itself, they still did not wish to overthrow it. At any rate, between 685 and 741, we see ten popes

[1] [The year of Pepin's accession; in 755 he was besieging the Lombards in their own capital. Astolph yielded at once, and ceded the whole of the contested territory to Pepin and the Pope. Cf Milman, *Latin Christianity* bk. IV., chap. XI.]

follow one another, **all of** whom, with one exception, were either Syrians (John V., Sergius, Sisin**ius**, Constantine, and Gregory **III.**), **or** Greeks (Conon, **John VI.,** John **VII., and** Zacharias). This fact alone is sufficient to show that Byzantine influence in Rome was still quite predominant.[1] And **the one** Roman amongst them, Gregory **II., did all that** lay **in his** power to keep down the Italians (who were embittered by Leo's tyrannical persecution **of** image-worship, **and**

[1] ["Noch völlig überwiegend war." Some might **think** this expression rather too strong of the period between 716 and 741. Gregory II. (716–713) begins a new era in the papacy. His immediate predecessor Constantine "was the last pope who was the "humble subject of the Eastern Emperor." Gregory's opposition to Leo the Isaurian on the subject of iconoclasm is quite uncompromising. His letters to the emperor on the question are arrogant and defiant, almost brutal in tone. "Neque judicium Dei reformi-"dasti, quum scandala in hominum corda, non fidelium modo, sed "et infidelium, ingruerent." "Tu mundum totum scandalizasti, "ut qui mortem nolis subire, et infelicem rationem reddere." "Ingredere rursum ad veritatem, unde exivisti; excute spiritus "elatos, et pertinaciam tolle; atque ad omnes scribe quoquoversum; "eosque quibus offendiculo fuisti, erige, quosque excæcasti; tametsi "præ nimiâ tuâ stupiditate illud pro nihilo habes." "Scripsisti ut "concilium universale cogeretur; et nobis inutilis ea res visa est "Tu persecutor es imaginum, et hostis contumeliosus et eversor. "Cessa, nobis hoc largire ut taceas: tum mundus pace perfruetur, "et scandala cessabunt." Gregory concludes this long and offensive letter with a prayer that God will drive out from the Emperor's heart the evil beings which dwell there. Harduin *Acta Concil.*, IV., 1. The second letter is also strong in language. Gregory III. during his briefer pontificate (731–741) maintained the inflexible opposition of his predecessor.]

had already begun to think of electing a Roman emperor of their own), under the yoke of subjection. He caused a rebellion which had broken out against Byzantium to be put down by Roman troops, and had the head of the ringleader of the rebels sent to Constantinople. The **popes always** regarded as a calamity every conquest which the **Lombards** made in Italy at the expense of Greek dominion; a calamity which they zealously strove to avert by prayers and remonstrances, as well as by personal intercession with the Lombard kings. They had clearly and fully recognized the fact, that when the possession of the exarchate should have strengthened Lombard power and Lombard craving for the possession of the whole peninsula, then the decree for their own subjection, and that of Rome, under this detested dominion, would be already sealed.

How powerful the fear of the **Lombards** and the aversion to them must have been in Rome, may be seen from the fact that Byzantine dominion was always considered preferable there; although, assuredly, neither the popes nor the Roman clergy had had so much to endure at the hands of the Lombards as at the hands of the Greeks. True, they had to bear heavy exactions, owing to the avarice of the exarchs, to one of whom even the sacred vessels belonging to St. Peter's had to be given as **pledges** (about the year 700). True, that if ever the emperor's suspicions were excited in Byzantium, the popes must submit to be summoned thither to answer for themselves; as Sergius is said to have been brought thither at the command of Justinian II., and pope Constantine, in the year 709, was compelled to obey the summons of the emperor to Nicomedia in Asia, while the exarch John caused four leading ecclesiastics to be executed [1] in Rome. For all that the antipathy to the Lombards was paramount. The reason for this hatred was, as it seems, mainly the Lombards' [2] barbarous mode of warfare, the perpetual ravaging, firing, and burning, which threatened to change the beautiful peninsula at last into an unproductive uninhabited wilderness. Not until the incapacity or disinclination of the Greeks to protect the provinces of Italy against the Lombards compelled the Italians to renounce the hopes and wishes they had hitherto entertained, did they throw themselves into the strong arms of the Franks. But even as late as 752 Stephen

1 *Vita Constantini*, ed. Vignoli, ii, p. 9.

2 [The Lombard host contained various wild Teutonic or Sclavonian hordes. Their wars with the Franks kept them somewhat in check, otherwise they might have devasted Italy still more. Compare the story of Alboin pledging his adulterous queen Rosmunda in a cup made of her father's skull, and the tragical end of both.]

IV. had made another appeal to the Greek emperor, imploring him to appear with an army for the defence of Italy against the Lombards.

After the year 728 Gregory II. made an attempt to form a confederation of cities, which was to maintain itself independently alike of the Greeks and of the Lombards; the head and centre of it was to be the papal chair.[1] The plan came to nothing. In Rome, however, the idea ripened more and more, that the power of the pope might come forward in Italy and take the place of the decaying power of the Greeks, and the reluctantly tolerated power of the Lombards; and hence this document of the Donation was forged, to represent this as the normal condition of things, planned long ago by the first Christian emperor. Whether this was before the donation of Pepin or after it, can now no more be decided; but at any rate it was before the founding of the Frankish kingdom of Italy, and therefore before 774. For after this was established all prospect of realising a union of Italian states fell to the ground, and then the fiction of the Donation would have ceased to have any object. But it may very well have been composed soon after

[1] [This statement somewhat qualifies what is said in Essay VIII. of Gregory being well aware that Italian states could not stand without Byzantine support; and, least of all, the Roman.]

the giving up of the exarchate through Pepin, in order to prepare the way for claims to the whole of Italy, and to give them an historical basis against the day when the internal weakness of the Lombard kingdom should end in complete disintegration. And so, not long after this, in the time of Charlemagne,[1] a document was forged, in which, in very wild, and in some places scarcely intelligible Latin, a detailed narrative is put into the mouth of king Pepin of all that had taken place between him, the Greeks, the Lombards, and pope Stephen; and it then makes Pepin give nearly the whole of Italy (Venetia and Istria included) to the pope, either there and then, or (as in the case of Beneventum and Naples) by promising them when they should be conquered.[2]

The pseudo-Isidore, as has been noticed already,

---

[1] In Fantuzzi; *Documenti Ravennati*, VI., 265.

[2] Instead of the emperor Constantine, Pepin talks of the emperor Leo (the Isaurian is intended), saying that Leo's ambassador, Marinus, had come to him. Here there is a confusion of the presbyter, Marinus, sent from Rome to Pepin, and that Spatharius Marinus, whom Leo had sent to Italy with the commission to put pope Gregory II. out of the way. The document, moreover, makes the Greek emperor give the pope formal leave to choose out a protector, with whom he could then decide as seemed best respecting the Roman duchy and the exarchate. It is manifestly invented with a double object, first, by supplying the consent of the Byzantine court to do away with a legal objection; and, secondly, to bring about an enlargement of the donation of Charles the Great.

incorporated the Donation of Constantine into his collection as an ancient document; and it certainly is found in all known manuscripts. The pseudo-Isidore, undoubtedly, did not compose it himself, although this has lately been supposed by Gregorovius.[1] The contents and purpose of the fiction were altogether alien to the West-Frankish author of the False Decretals. The language also is different from his. But it is equally untenable, on the other hand, that it did not come into existence till the tenth century, as the Oratorian Morin attempted to show. His main argument is, that Otho III., in his deed of gift of the year 999, mentions a deacon John with the sobriquet "Digitorum mutius," (i.e. mutilus, *mozzo*,) as the man who wrote the document in golden letters in Constantine's name. This John the deacon, Morin supposes, is the man whom John XII. first used as his tool, and then, in the year 974, caused his right hand to be cut off.[2] A mistaken idea; for a man who had lost his right hand would not have been called "with mutilated fingers," as a sobriquet. Moreover, the Donation of Constantine may very well have been extant at an

---

[1] *Geschichte der Stadt Rom.*, iii., 400. Cenni had anticipated him in maintaining this, and that "plaudentibus nostri ævi eruditis," as he thinks. *Monum.*, i., 305.

[2] According to Luitprand, *Hist. Ottonis*, in Pertz, v., 346, and *Contin. Reginon.*, ad a. 964.

earlier period, before John the deacon, of whom the draughtsman of Otho's document makes mention, wrote it out in golden letters, in order to invest it with greater dignity.

An analysis and closer consideration of the contents of the document will give a still higher degree of certainty to the supposition that it originated in Rome between 750 and 774.

The following are among the grants made in the Donation to the popes and the Roman clergy:—

1. Constantine desires to promote the Chair of Peter over the empire and its seat on earth, by bestowing on it imperial power and honour.

2. The Chair of Peter shall have supreme authority over the patriarchal Chairs of Alexandria, Antioch, Jerusalem, and Constantinople, and over all churches in the world.[1]

3 It shall be judge in all that concerns the service of God and the Christian Faith.[2]

---

[1] ["Ut principatum teneat tam super quatuor sedes, Alexandrinam, Antiochenam, Hierosolymitanam ac Constantinopolitanam, quamque etiam super omnes in universo orbe terrarum ecclesias." As cited by Leo IX., Harduin, VI., 935.] The Greeks have omitted this article in the recension in Blastares, and in that of the Parisian manuscript.

[2] This article also is wanting in both the above-mentioned texts. [Leo IX., of course, retains it, "et ejus judicio quæque ad cultum "Dei vel fidei Christianorum stabilitatem procuranda fuerint, dis-"ponantur."]

4. Instead of the diadem, which the emperor **wished to place on** the pope's head, but which the pope refused, Constantine has given to him **and to his successors the** phrygium [1] (that is the tiara) and the lorum which adorned the emperor's neck, as well as **the** other gorgeous robes and insignia of the imperial dignity.

5. The Roman clergy shall enjoy the high privileges of the imperial senate, being eligible **to the dignity of** patrician or consul, and having **the right to** wear the decoration worn by the **(optimates or)** nobles in office under the empire. [1]

6. The offices of cubicularii, ostiarii, and **excubitæ, shall** belong to the Roman Church.

7. The Roman clergy shall ride on horses decked with white coverlets, and, like the senate, wear white sandals.

---

1 [Leo **IX.** says, at **first,** *both* the diadem and **the phrygium:** "deinde diadema, videlicet coronam capitis nostri, simulque "**phrygium, necnon** et superhumerale, videlicet lorum quod imperiale "circumdare assolet collum." But later on, after mentioning Sylvester's refusal of the gold crown, "phrygium autem candido nitore, "splendidam resurrectionem Dominicam designans, ejus sacrat-"issimo vertici manibus nostris imposuimus, et tenentes frenum "equi ipsius, pro reverentia beati Petri, &c."]

2 Imperialis militia, στρατία, which Münch (*On the Donation of Constantine,* p. **22**) translates as "the imperial army," remarking that the Roman clergy had been desirous of wearing military decorations. A glance at Duncange's *Glossary* would have told him what "militia" or "στρατία" meant at that time [viz., court officials].

THE DONATION OF CONSTANTINE. 125

8. If a member of the senate shall wish to take orders, and the pope consents, no one shall hinder him.[1]

9. Constantine gives up the remaining sovereignty over Rome, the provinces, cities, and towns of the whole of Italy *or* of the western regions, to pope Sylvester and his successors.

Judging from the detailed and careful manner in which each single clause is treated, we may conclude that the author, who beyond all doubt was a Roman ecclesiastic, had the articles and colour of the dress proper to the pope and clergy, with their titles and insignia of rank, far more at heart than the ninth clause which, tacked on at the end and expressed in few words, was so pregnant with consequences, *the Donation of Rome and Italy*. And here one must at the same time remember, that the composer intended Italy alone, and not almost the whole of the West which belonged to the kingdom of Rome at the time of Constantine, that is to say, Gaul, Spain, Britain, etc., to be comprehended in the Donation as well as Italy. In all probability he knew nothing of the real extent of the empire at the time of Constantine, but had only

---

[1] So the Greek text. The Latin reading " nullus ex omnibus " præsumat superbe agere " makes no kind of sense with the context just preceding.

the circumstances of the eighth century before his eyes, for he says "Italy *or* the western regions," doubtless merely to define more closely the geographical expression "Italy," and to include Istria, Corsica, and Sardinia. Not until a later age was the "*or*" changed into "*and*." And for long the matter was so understood. The popes [1] Hadrian I. and Leo IX, the emperor Otho III. and cardinal Peter Damiani found in the document merely the donation of Italy.

If one considers the remaining clauses, that is to say, the demands and wishes of Roman ecclesiastics clad in the form of supposed concessions, one sees that they altogether have reference to the state of affairs in Rome and Italy about the middle of the eighth century. The author naturally has not so much the arrangement and relations of rank in Constantinople before his eyes, as those of that part of Italy which at that time was still Byzantine. The *senate*, with which the clergy in Rome wished to be placed on an equality in certain privileges, was no

---

1 ["Et sicut temporibus beati Sylvestri Romani Pontificis, a sanctæ "recordationis piisimo Constantino Imperatore, per ejus largitatem "sancta Dei Catholica et Apostolica Romana Ecclesia 'elevata atque "exaltata est, et potestatem in his Hesperiæ partibus largiri dignatus est, &c., &c." Letter of Hadrian I. to Charles the Great.— *Recueil des Historiens des Gaules et de la France*, ap. Palmé, Paris, 1869, v., 550, c.]

longer the old Roman senate. That had perished in the sixth century, during the wars with the Goths and the Lombards. The senate is never mentioned [1] in the period from the end of the sixth to the middle of the eighth century, but reappears first in the year 757 as the collective body of the Roman optimates. [2] After that time we have mention made of a special place for the senators [senatorium] in the two chief churches in Rome. Those who sat there received the holy communion from the hands of the pope himself. [3] It was, in fact, a new official nobility which was formed, partly out of the military aristocracy of citizens, partly out of ecclesiastical dignitaries; and the latter were also to have their share—this was one of the objects which the author of the fiction had in view—in the highest titles of honour which the emperors granted to certain pre-eminent members of the civil, or rather military aristocracy.

The ranks of *patrician* and *consul*, for instance, which were to be made accessible to the Roman

[1] Savigny's assertions (*Geschichte des Röm. Rechts*, i., 367) are on this point too strong; that in all centuries, as he says, are to be found undeniable traces of the real continuance of the Roman senato is, at any rate, without foundation as regards the period between 660 and 750.

[2] "Salutant vos et cunctus procerum senatus, atque diversi "populi congregatio." Cenni, ii., 146.

[3] Mabillon, *Mus. Ital.*, ii., xliv., lix., 10.

clergy, were at that time the highest at which ambition [1] could aim. A patrician, [2] or member of the imperial Privy Council, was promoted to his rank by being solemnly invested with an embroidered robe of state ; and even governors of provinces felt themselves raised in dignity by the addition of this title, the highest in the empire. From the year 754 onwards the pope, in the name of the Roman republic (which still continued to be considered as always virtually existing), and with the acquiescence of the Roman people, claimed to have the power of conferring the title of "patrician of Rome ;" and gave it, as is well known, in the first instance to king Pepin and king Carloman. [3] Thus the highest temporal dignity

1 In the *Vita Agathonis*, Vignoli, i., 279, we have the high dignitaries thus reckoned : "Patricii, Hypati cum omni Syncleto." In the year 701 Theophylact was Cubicularius, Patricius, **Exarchus Italiæ**, ibid., i., 315.

2 [This new **rank of patrician** was created at Constantinople, and was not conferred on old Roman **families**. It was a personal, not an hereditary dignity, and became **extinct with the** death **of the** holder. A patrician family at **this period meant one, of** which the head was a patrician. The patricians were the highest of the *illustres* ; consuls alone ranked higher. A patrician was distinguished by such titles as Magnificentia, **Celsitudo**, Eminentia, and Magnitudo. **The** new dignity was not confined to subjects of the empire, but was sometimes given to foreigners, such as Odoacer. Other sovereigns imitated the emperors and popes in conferring this title on eminent subjects, but such patricians ranked far below Roman patricians. Smith's *Dictionary of Antiquities*, "Patricii," sub fin.]

3 ["In the meantime the right of conquest, and the indefinite

in Rome, after that of emperor or a Cæsar, was to be in the pope's gift, and that without any theoretical infringement of the imperial prerogative. When the Greek dominion perished in north and central Italy, the patriciate, as a dignity conferred on particular governors, vanished along with it, and there remained only the one Roman patriciate, the chief dignity among the inhabitants of the city of Rome.

The consuls also, as Savigny[1] has remarked, were first mentioned in the middle of the eighth century, and constituted the rank next to the patricians. The chief city magistrates bore this title, one, however, which thenceforward occurs merely as a title of honour. One such consul (and *dux*) was Theodatus, the tutor of Hadrian I., and afterwards primicerius of the Roman Church. His contemporary Leoninus, in like manner, was at the same time both consul and dux, afterwards a monk.[2]

Further use of Constantine's name was made to obtain for the popes the right of having gentlemen of the bed-chamber, door-keepers, and a body-guard

title of patrician, assigned by the pope (Stephen), acting in behalf, and with the consent of the Roman republic, to Pepin—a title which might be merely honorary, or might justify any authority which he might have power to exercise—gave a kind of supremacy to the king of the Franks in Rome."—Milman, *Lat. Chr.*, iv., c. xi.]

[1] A., a., O., p. 370. He quotes Fantuzzi, *Mon. Rav.*, i., 15.
[2] *Vita Hadr.*, in Vignoli, ii., 162, 210.

(cubicularii, ostiarii, excubitores). Here again the date fits exactly. Formerly in Italy there were only *imperial* cubicularii. Not until the time of Stephen IV. and Hadrian I. do we find an instance of a *papal cubicularius*, viz., Paul **Afiarta**,[1] who at the same time was *superista*, that is, overseer of the palace. In [2] the first *Ordo Romanus* in Mabillon, who describes the Roman ceremonial at the end of the eighth and beginning of the ninth century, the cubicularius tonsuratus, who had to carry the papal robes, is mentioned for the first time.

In the Roman *Ordo* of Cencius (twelfth century) the *portarii* or *ostiarii pro custodiendo palatio* were placed in the second rank under the Roman scholæ or guilds of the papal court servants, and described according to their duties.[3] Lastly, the *excubitores* are unmistakeably the so-called *adextratores* of a later age, a guard of honour,[4] which escorted the pope in processions and visits to churches.

The author of the Donation manifestly attached great importance to the point, that the Roman

---

[1] That he was cubicularius of the **pope**, and not of the emperor, is plain from the *Vita Hadr.*, in Vignoli, ii., 164 and 166; for in other instances the *Liber Pontificalis* adds *imperialis*, as in the case of Theodore Pellarius, ib. i., 263.

[2] *Mus. Ital.*, ii., 6.

[3] l. c., p. 194, 96.

[4] l. c., p. 196.

clergy should have the privilege of decking their horses with white coverings,—altogether in harmony with the spirit of the time and place, where this was considered as a thing of extraordinary importance, and as a precious privilege of the Roman clergy surpassing all others. Hence Gregory the Great had before this notified the archbishop of Ravenna, that the Roman clergy would on no account concede that the use of horse-coverlets (*mappulæ*) should be allowed to the clergy of Ravenna.[1] The Roman biographer finds great fault with pope Conon, because (about A.D. 687) he had allowed the deacon Constantine of Syracuse, whom he had nominated rector of the patrimony there, to make use of such a coverlet.[2]

Lastly, the object attributed to Constantine is altogether in accordance with the sentiments of the eighth century, viz., that he endowed the Roman Church with possessions in the East and West, in order that the lamps and tapers which burnt in the churches and at the tombs of the Apostles St. Peter and St. Paul might be kept up by the revenues. And thus pope Paul I. writes to Pepin, in the year 761, saying that the contest which the king had under-

---

[1] Greg. M. *Opera*, ii., 6., ed. Paris, cf. Gratian. *Decrœ.*, dist. 93, c. 22.

[2] *Vit. Conon.* ap. Vignoli, i., 3.

taken against **the Lombards** was waged by him for the restoration of the lamps of St. Peter.[1]

Both internal and external evidence, therefore, conducts us to the period between **750 and 775** as the time when the Donation of Constantine came into existence. The supposition of Natalis Alexander and of his follower Cenni,[2] that it was **not** known in Rome before the middle of the ninth century, is certainly incorrect. Hadrian **I. undeniably alludes** to it in the words that Constantine had "given **the** dominion in these regions **of the West**" to the Romish Church. These are the "occidentalium regionum provinciæ (*δυσμῶν χωρῶν ἐπαρχίαι*)" of which the Donation speaks. Nevertheless, it is quite certain that at first no pains were taken to make it generally known. From Hadrian I. to Leo IX. (**776 to 105**3) there is no trace of it to be found in the **letters** of **popes ; in the** older manuscripts of **the** *Liber Pontificalis* there is no mention of it; but by means **of** the pseudo-Isidore (that **is from 840** onwards), **it** began **to be** known outside Italy, **and** indeed **perhaps more** in France than in Italy itself. For **though** Luitprand, bishop of Cremona, as imperial ambassador at Byzantium

---

[3] Cenni, i., 185: "**Pro** cujus restituendis luminariis decertatis." So also the pseudo-Constantine, "Quibus pro concinnatione luminariuum possessiones **coutulimus.**"

[4] *Monum.*, i., 304.

THE DONATION OF CONSTANTINE. 133

boasted of the large donations which Constantine had given to the Roman Church, in Persia, Mesopotamia, and Babylonia; yet he knew nothing of the contents of the forged document, or at any rate, gave no hint of it; while, on the other hand, two men who for their age were so learned and so well read in ecclesiastical history and literature as Æneas, bishop of Paris, and Hincmar, bishop of Rheims, readily accepted it. The former of them (about the year 868) represents to the Greeks that Constantine had declared that two emperors, the one of the realm, the other of the Church, could not rule in common in one city. He had therefore removed his residence to Byzantium, but had placed the Roman territory, "and a vast "number of various provinces," under the rule of the Apostolic chair, and had conferred royal power [1] on the pope. Hincmar expresses himself with more reserve. He and his contemporary bishop Ado, of Vienne, in his chronicle (about 860), know only of Constantine's having given up the city of Rome to the pope. [2]

Pope Leo IX. recounted nearly the whole text of the Donation to the patriarch Michael Cerularius in the year 1054, openly and confidently, without

---

[1] *Liber adversus Græcos*, in D'Achery, *Spicil.*, vii., iii.
[2] Epist. 3, c. 13.

having (as it would seem) a single misgiving as to the weakness of his document. He wished the patriarch to convince himself "of the earthly and heavenly "imperium, of the royal priesthood of the Roman "Chair," and retain no trace of the suspicion that this chair "wished to usurp power by the help of "foolish [1] and old wives' fables." He is, however, the only one of all the popes who has brought the document expressly before the eyes of the world, and formally challenged criticism. In remarkable contrast to him, his guide and adviser and successor, Gregory VII., never made use of it, in not one of his numerous letters even mentions it,—a most expressive silence, when one considers how strong the temptation must have been to him to avail himself of this weapon against his numerous and overpowering enemies. Not so his friend, cardinal Peter Damiani. He holds up the privilege granted by Constantine as an impenetrable shield against the Greeks, who supported the cause of the imperial anti-pope Caladous, and does not forget to add that the emperor had also given

---

[1] Harduin, *Conc.*, vi., 934. ["Sed ne forte adhuc de terrena ipsius "dominatione aliquis vobis dubietatis supersit scrupulus, neve leviter "suspicemini ineptis et anilibus fabulis sanctam Romanam sedem "velle sibi inconcussum honorem vindicare et defensare aliqua- "tenus," &c., &c.]

over the kingdom of Italy to the rule of the popes.[1]

The use and meaning of the forged Donation entered, to a certain extent, a new stage when Urban II., in the year 1091, used it to support the claim of the Roman Church to the possession of Corsica. He deduced the right of Constantine to give away islands, from the strange principle that all islands were legally *juris publici*, and therefore state domain. It cannot but excite surprise that Urban did not prefer to appeal to the donation of Charlemagne, or rather does not once mention it. For not only is Corsica enumerated among the donations which Charlemagne is said to have made, but Leo III. says this distinctly in a letter to Charlemagne in the year 808.[2] The Church at that time, however, having no fleet, was not in a position to maintain a possession which was perpetually threatened by the Saracens; and so Leo was obliged to beg the emperor to take the island to himself, and protect it with his "strong arm;" and (as the Corsican historian Limperani[3] remarks) the

---

[1] Harduin, 1. c., 1122. [As "defensor Romanæ ecclesiæ," he argues that Constantine had abdicated, as regards Rome and Italy, in favour of the pope. If, then, the emperor had no authority in Rome, how could he have a voice in the election of the pope?]

[2] Cenni, li., 60.

[3] *Istoria della Corsica*, Roma, 1760, li., 2.

Roman **Chair for** 189 years abstained from exercising any **dominion in Corsica.** Not until the year 1077 do we find Gregory VII.[1] saying, that the Corsicans are ready to return under the supremacy of the pope; and from the letter of Urban II. to bishop Daibert, of Pisa, it appears that this actually took place at that time, or not long afterwards.

On this notion, that it was the islands especially that Constantine had given to the popes, they proceeded to build, although nothing had been said about them in the original document; and with a bold leap the Donation of Constantine was transferred from Corsica to the farthest West, viz., to Ireland; and **the** Papal Chair claimed possession of an island, **which** the Romans themselves had never possessed, and had scarcely known. This was done by Hadrian IV. (1154-1159),[2] an Englishman by birth; "Anglicana

---

[1] Lib. 6, epist. 12.

[2] [Nicolas Breakspeare, the poor English scholar, yielded to none of his predecessors, Hildebrand not excepted, **in** the assertion of the papal authority. " He was surpassed by few in the boldness "and courage with which he maintained **it.** English pride might " mingle with sacerdotal ambition **in his boon** of a new kingdom to " his native sovereign. The language **of** the grant developed " principles as yet **unheard** of in Christendom The popes had " assumed the feudal sovereignity of Naples and Sicily, **as in some** " vague way the successors to the power of Imperial Rome. But " Hadrian declared that Ireland, and all islands converted to Christianity, belonged to the special jurisdiction of St. Peter. The pro-

affectione," as the Irish chieftains declared somewhat later (1316) in a letter to John XXII.[1] At the desire of the English king, Henry II., the pope conferred on him the dominion over the island of Ireland (1155), which, "like all Christian islands, undoubtedly "belonged of right to St. Peter and the Roman "Church." The king thus received a dominion which, it must be owned, he had first to win with the sword; and, indeed, it was not till after a contest of five hundred years, and for the most part only by colonization from outside, that it was completely won. It did not help the English much to say to the Irish, "Your island belonged in former times to the pope, "and since he has given it to king Henry, it is your "duty to submit yourselves to English rule." The Irish, who were not altogether ignorant of the history of their native land, knew quite well that neither the Roman emperors nor the popes had ever possessed a foot's breadth of their country, and could not therefore

"phetic ambition of Hadrian might seem to have anticipated the "time, when on such principles the popes should assume the power "of granting away new worlds."—Milman, *Lat. Christ.*, viii., c. vii.]

1 In M'Geoghegan's *Histoire de l'Irlande*, ii., 106 sq. They state that up to 1170 they had sixty-one kings, "nullum in temporalibus "recognoscentes superiorem." Hadrian had acted "indebite, ordine "juris omisso omnino." [For this famous letter of Hadrian to Henry II., see Appendix D.]

exactly understand how pope Hadrian had the power to make a present of it to England.

Hadrian does not mention the Donation of Constantine in his Bull; but his friend and confidant, John of Salisbury, the one who,[1] according to his own confession, induced him to take this step so pregnant with consequences, quotes the Donation of the first believing emperor as the ground of this "right of St. Peter" over all islands.[2]

---

[1] "Ad preces meas illustri regi Anglorum, Henrico II., concessit "et dedit Hiberniam jure hæreditario possidendam, sicut literæ "ipsius testantur in hodiernum diem. Nam omnes insulæ, de jure "antiquo, ex donatione Constantini, qui eam fundavit et dotavit, "dicuntur ad Romanam Ecclesiam pertinere."—*Metalog.* 4, 42, opp. ed. Giles, v., 206. The embarrassment of Irish writers in later times, as regards the Bull, was, as one might expect, considerable. Stephen White (*Apologia pro Hibernia*, ed. Kelly, Dublin, 1849, p. 184), and Lynch, or Grantianus Lucius (*Cambrensis eversus*, Dubl., 1856, ii., 434 sq.), struggle in vain to prove it a bungling forgery. Lanigan, on the other hand (*Eccles. History of Ireland*, iv., 160), admits its genuineness, and gives vent to some sharp criticisms on the pope and his Bull. M'Geoghehan (*Histoire de l'Irlande*, Paris, 1758, i., 462) foregoes the appeal to the Donation of Constantine, and contents himself with saying, "Le Pape, qui était né son sujet, lui accorda "sans peine sa demande; et la liberté d'une nation entière fut sacrifiée "à l'ambition de l'un par la complaisance de l'autre."

[2] The Abbé Gosselin (*Pouvoir du Pape sur les Souverains*, ii., 247, ed. de Louvain) has attempted to show that pope Hadrian, properly speaking, did not in the least intend to dispose of Ireland in his Bull; that he claimed nothing but a purely spiritual jurisdiction in Ireland, merely the right to demand the payment of Peter's pence. His reasons for this view are very weak, and he omits to notice evidence which is quite decisive. He omits to notice that Hadrian

THE DONATION OF CONSTANTINE. 139

The Roman clergy with their Donation of Constantine had, on the whole, obtained their object very successfully; attempts were now made in Naples to advance the interests of the clergy there by similar means. In a chronicle of the church of St. Maria del Principio, it is stated that Constantine gave the whole of the kingdom of Sicily on both sides of the straits, along with other possessions, to pope Sylvester; the town of Naples was the only thing which he reserved as imperial property. Accordingly the two, Constantine and Sylvester, came to Naples together, and, seeing that Constantine very often heard mass here in the Episcopal Church, he attached fourteen prebendaries to it, and endowed these with landed and other property, and founded the dignity of a cimeliarch.[1]

says, "that the people of Ireland are to accept and honour the king "(who up to this time had not had the most remote right to the "island) as their lord and master (sicut Dominum veneretur)." He omits all notice of the statement of John of Salisbury, who was better informed than any other man respecting the whole circumstance, and respecting the meaning of the Bull, which had been introduced by himself. Lastly, he omits to notice the fact that Hadrian formally invested king Henry with the rights of a suzerain by means of a ring which he sent him. The words, that all islands belong "ad jus beati Petri et SS. Rom. Ecclesiæ," Gosselin persists in understanding of the spiritual jurisdiction of the pope, quite in defiance of the use of words in the language of that time.

[1] Parascandolo, *Memorie stor. crit diplomatiche della chiesa di Napoli*, 1847, p. 212. The chronicle appears to belong to the end of the twelfth or beginning of the thirteenth century. [Cimeliarch, κειμηλιαρχης, treasurer.]

Meanwhile, in Italy at this time the Roman story of Constantine's Donation was rejected without scruple, so soon as it clashed with maintained rights or with political plans. In Rome, in the year 1105, the monks of the monastery Farfa, which had been endowed with great privileges by the emperors, contended with some of the Roman nobility for the possession of a certain castle. The latter upheld the title of the Roman Church (on which their own title was supposed to depend) to the disputed property, and traced back this title to the Donation of Constantine. Thereupon the monks, without directly denying the genuineness of the document, **brought** forward a detailed historical **proof** that the document could not possibly mean a **Donation of** Italy, for the emperors who had succeeded Constantine **had** always possessed **and** exercised **in full** their dominion over Italy. Accordingly, Constantine **could only** have given spiritual rights to the popes in Italy.[1] In Rome itself at that time (under Paschal II, 1099-1118,) the pope was so far from being recognised as the temporal sovereign of a distinct territory, that the monks with their abbot felt able, without contradiction, to state before the Roman judges as a recognised fact—that temporal power and government did not befit the pope, for it

---

[1] *Historiæ Farfenses*, in Pertz *Monum.*, xiii., 571.

was not the keys of an earthly kingdom, but only the keys of the kingdom of Heaven that he had received from God.

About forty years later commenced the great political and religious movements in Italy generally, and the efforts of the Arnoldists, in **Rome in** particular, which aimed [1] at placing **the** control **of the** imperial dignity in the hands of a rabble in Rome— a town populace constantly augmented by the influx of people from the country, but which was supposed to represent the true Romans and heirs of the old Roman empire. Thence began the first misunderstandings between the Hohenstaufen, Frederick I., and the Papal Chair. It was inevitable that the Donation of Constantine should again play an important part. When a Roman faction, stirred up by Arnold of Brescia, was purposing to arrogate to itself the control of the city, the papal party in Rome had appealed to the Donation, according to which it appeared that Rome belonged to the pope. In opposition to this Wetzel, an Arnoldist, maintained in his letter to Frederick, in the year 1152, **that** " that lie " and heretical fable of Constantine's having conceded

---

1 [That to Arnold of Brescia himself much higher aims, and a much nobler policy, must be attributed than are here allowed to his followers, would perhaps scarcely be denied.]

"the imperial rights in the city to pope Sylvester,
"was now so thoroughly exposed, that even day
"labourers and women were able to confute the most
"learned on the point, and the pope and his cardinals
"would not venture to show themselves for shame."[1]
And in fact, Eugenius III. had been obliged to
leave Rome[2] (for the second time) in the beginning
of the year 1150, and remained until December of
1152 in Segni and Ferentino. It is, however, remarkable that the arguments with which the Arnoldist
and his Roman day labourers and housewives knew
so well how to demolish the lie about the Donation of
Constantine, themselves in their turn rested upon
errors and fictions. Constantine, says Wetzel, was a
Christian already, and therefore had been baptized
before the time of Sylvester, consequently the whole
story of the Donation to Sylvester is untrue. As
proof of this a passage is quoted out of an apocryphal[3] letter of pope Melchiades, which is found in

[1] Ap. Martene, *ampl. coll.*, ii., 556.

[2] [On the first occasion (March, 1146) Eugenius retired first to Viterbo, and thence to Sienna; then, after a year's delay, to France, where he became little more than the mouthpiece of St. Bernard. He returned to Italy towards the end of 1148, but to Viterbo and Tusculum, not to Rome. It was not till the end of 1149 that he once more entered the capital, and then only as its bishop, not as its sovereign.]

[3] A document much used, sometimes under the title *Libellus de Munificentia Constantini.*

the pseudo-Isidorian collection, and is also made use of by Gratian; and it is proved from the *Historia tripartita* (of Cassiodore) that Constantine was a Christian before his entry into Rome.[1]

In spite of this contradiction in Rome itself, the Donation was made the basis of higher and constantly increasing claims at this time, and, indeed, as early as the close of the eleventh century. Already in the time of Gregory VII., or immediately after him under Urban II., the inclusion of the Donation in the new collection of rights and title-deeds showed clearly an intention of making an extensive use of it. This was now done by Anselm of Lucca, cardinal Deusdedit, and the compiler of the collection which is known under the name of Ivo of Chartres.[2] On the other hand, Burchard of Worms, in his collection, which was made between 1012 and 1023, has not yet included it. Specially surprising is the change which is made in Anselm's work of the "*or*" into a most significant and comprehensive "*and*." He has, "quod

---

[3] Wetzel does not appeal, as one would have expected him to have done, to the baptism in Nicomedia at the end of the emperor's life, as related in the Tripertita from Eusebius. No doubt the idea of the baptism in Rome was too deeply rooted in the minds of the Romans to allow him to make such an appeal.

[1] More exact references in Antonius Augustinus, *De Emend. Grat. Opp.*, ed. Lucens, iii., 41, in the notes.

"Const. Imp. Papæ concessit coronam et omnem "regiam dignitatem in urbe Romana, et Italia, *et in* "*partibus occidentalibus.*" What practical meaning Roman ecclesiastics intended to give to these last words, appears from a statement made by Otto of Freisingen. In his chronicle, which was composed between 1143 and 1146, he asserts the authenticity [1] of the Donation, and relates how Constantine, after conferring the imperial insignia on the pope, went to Byzantium, adding that "for this reason the "Roman Church maintains that the western king- "doms have been given over to her possession by "Constantine, and demands tribute from them to "this day, with the exception of the two kingdoms of "the Franks" (that is, the French and the German one). The defenders of the empire, however, objected "that in each transaction Constantine had not con- "ferred the empire on the popes, but had merely "chosen them as spiritual fathers."

To the best of my knowledge there are no papal documents extant, with the exception of the one about Ireland, in which the payment of tribute is demanded of the whole realm on the strength of the Donation of Constantine. Just the very pope who went the greatest lengths in such demands, Gregory

---

[1] Chron. 3, 3 ap., Urstis. i., 80.

VII., never appealed to the Donation in making them, but to feudal rights of the **Roman** See dating **from an** earlier period; and he **attempted** [1] (without result, however), to exact tribute from France. And yet, **as** appears from his letters,[2] **Gregory had** had the archives thoroughly searched, in **order to discover** documents, **from which** a feudal **dependence of the** several kingdoms **and** countries **upon the Roman** Chair might **be claimed.**

However, **the ninth** canon **in the** *Dictatus,* which, though not proceeding from Hildebrand himself, **are,** nevertheless, the work of his time, is unmistakeably borrowed from the Donation; "**the pope** alone may "make use of the imperial insignia." Serious stress was never laid on this point. **The** popes did not assume the sceptre, sword, and **ball.** Boniface **VIII.** is the only **pope who,** according **to one account, is** said to have done so at once at the celebration **of the** Jubilee in the year 1300. But if Constantine had really ceded Italy and the West to the pope, **it** appeared to follow naturally and fairly that **the empire in** its whole extent of territory **was a present,** a free gift of **the popes,.and** therefore **(according to** the then **prevalent ideas and** policy) a fief of the Roman Chair,

---

[1] Cf. Muratori, *Antichità Ital.*, **Firenze**, 1833, x. 126 sq.
[2] *Epist* 23, lib. 8.

the emperor being vassal and the pope suzerain. And
then, if not the kingdom of Germany, at any rate that
of Italy with the Lombard crown would be reckoned
as a papal fief. Certainly, since A.D. 800, since the
first founding of the Western empire, a broad way
had been made towards this end. At that time the
pope prostrated himself to the ground before the
newly-crowned emperor, and did obeisance to him in
the form of homage paid to the old emperors. [1]
Now, however, a picture was placed in the Lateran
palace which represented the emperor Lothair doing
homage to the pope,[2] with verses, in which it was
stated in so many words that the king had first
confirmed the rights of the city before the gates of
Rome, and had then become the vassal (homo) of the
pope, whereupon he received the crown as a gift [3]
from the latter. At the same time many Romans
declared that the German kings had possessed the
Roman empire,[4] no less than the Italian kingdom,

[1] *Annales Laurissenses* in Pertz, I, 138; "Et post laudes ab "Apostolico more antiquorum principum adoratus est."

[2] [Compare the gross misrepresentations of the circumstances of the council of Florence in the *bassi relievi* on the gates of St Peter's at Rome.—Marriott's *Testimony of the Catacombs*, London, 1870, p. 104, etc.]

[4] Radevic., i., 10; Murat., vi., 748.

[2] Imperium Urbis. The imperial dignity itself the pope could not confer on the strength of the Donation of Constantine, which contained nothing about it, but only (as the Romans said) as the

merely as a present from the popes. From this arose that storm of dissatisfaction which broke out in Germany in the year 1157, when a letter from Hadrian to Frederick Barbarossa spoke of "beneficia" which he had granted to the emperor, or could still grant, and expressly called the imperial crown itself such a beneficium, i. e., a feod, as it was understood at the imperial court. Hadrian could easily justify himself, by saying that he had used the word in its ordinary, not in its technical and political sense; that he had intended to say nothing more than that it was he who had placed the crown on the emperor's head.[1] But, in Germany, men mistrusted the Roman clergy, and the bitter feeling remained, as we find provost Gerloh of Reigersburg expressing it at the time in sharp words, a man otherwise thoroughly devoted to the

organ of the Roman republic and in their name, for they considered themselves as the heirs of the old populus Romanus; or else, as the defenders of the Donation supposed, as the supreme Head of the city of Rome, to which the right of electing the emperor, originally inherent in the Roman republic, came as a matter of course. Hence, although the *empire* itself was no fief of the Roman Chair (for which reason it was never actually given away), nevertheless it was possible to maintain in Rome, that the *imperium urbis* and the *kingdom of Italy* belonged to the pope alone to confer, seeing that he had received both from Constantine, and that he would confer them only as fiefs, reserving his own supremacy; but that without these two things there was no empire.

[1] "Per hoc vocabulum 'contulimus' nil aliud intelleximus quam 'imposuimus.'"

Papal See. He says that the custom (which of course rested for support on the Donation of Constantine) of the emperor holding the pope's stirrup had prompted the Romans to paint these offensive pictures, in which kings or emperors were represented as vassals of the popes; from which they gained nothing, excepting the embittered feelings and hard words of temporal princes.[1] If the popes, by allowing such pictures, claimed to be emperors and lords of emperors, making the emperors their vassals, this was nothing else than to destroy the power ordained of God and to go against the divine order.

However, whatever meaning and extent of application the Roman clergy might give to the supposed Donation; whatever new collections of laws might contain on the subject, the historians of this and the following period are wont, when they mention the Donation at all, cautiously to confine it within tolerably narrow limits. Sicard of Cremona gives a very detailed account of the fabulous baptism of Constantine,[2] but quotes nothing more than this from the Donation, that the emperor gave Sylvester regal privileges, and ordained that all bishops should be

---

[2] Treatise of the provost Gerhoh of Reigersburg, *De Investigatione Antichristi*, edited by Stulz, Vienna, 1858, pp. 54, 56.

[3] In Muratori, vii., 554.

subject to the pope; **but** he does not go on to explain the nature of these regal privileges. Romuald of Salerno knows and mentions merely this ecclesiastical supremacy.[1] Robert Abolant confines himself to mentioning a privilege bequeathed by Constantine to the popes, without any **farther statement**.[2] A hundred years later, an historian so entirely devoted to papal interests as Tolomeo of Lucca quotes nothing beyond this from the Donation, that the emperor **had** conferred on certain Roman ecclesiastics (the cardinals of a later age) the rights and prerogatives of the Roman senate.[3] And while of the papal biographers Bernard Guidonis is entirely silent about the Donation, the dominion over the city of Rome, and the conferring of the imperial insignia, is all that Amalrich Augerii quotes from it.[4] On the other hand the Spaniard, Lucas B. of Tuy (about A.D. 1236), represents the dominion over Italy (regnum Italiæ) as having been conferred on the pope.[5] His contemporary, the Belgian Balduin, monk in the Monastery Ninnove, restricts Constantine's gift once more to the dominion **over** Rome.[6]

[1] Muratori, vii., 79.
[2] *Chronologia*, Trecis, 1609, p. 49.
[3] *Hist. Eccl.*, 5, 3, 4, in Muratori, XI., 825.
[4] Ap. Eccard, ii., 1665.
[5] *Corpus Chronicorum Flandriæ*, ed. de Smet, ii, 613.
[6] *Chronicon Mundi*, ap. Schotti *Hisp. Illustr.*, iv., 36.

All the more remarkable on this account is the discussion in which, at the close of the twelfth century, a man who, in a certain sense, belonged to both nations, engaged. Gottfried, a German, educated in Bamberg, chaplain and secretary to the three Hohenstaufen sovereigns—Conrad, Frederick, and Henry VI.,—who ended his days as a canon at Viterbo, states in his *Pantheon*,[1] which he dedicated to pope Urban III., A.D. 1186, that, in order to secure greater peace to the Church, Constantine had withdrawn with all his pomp to the Greeks, to Byzantium, and had given the pope regal privileges, and, on the strength of them, as it would appear, Rome, Italy, and Gaul. (This is the first time that *Gaul* is expressly mentioned as included in the Donation.) Thereupon he makes the "supporters of the empire," and the "defenders of "the Church," state their *pros* and *cons*. The former point to the historical fact, that Constantine divided his kingdom between his sons, and to the well-known texts in the Bible. The latter, however, answer, that the will of God is declared in the very fact of the Donation; that God would allow His Church to have fallen into the error of a possession to which it had no right, was not to be supposed. Gottfried himself, however, does not venture to decide; he leaves the solution of this question to the powers that be.

[1]. Ap. Pistori, ii., 208.

In the *Otia Imperiala* (leisure hours), which Gervasius of Tilbury wrote for the emperor Otho IV. about the year 1211, it is stated that Constantine had conferred royal power over the countries of the West on Sylvester, without intending to transfer to him along with it either the kingdom itself or the empire, which he reserved for himself. But the giver is superior to the receiver, and the royal and imperial power is derived immediately from God. God, he says, is the creator of the empire, but the emperor is the creator of the papal supremacy.[1]

On the whole, however, the authority of the Donation from the close of the twelfth century onwards was in the ascendant; and belief in it, and in the wide extent of territory which Constantine included in it, grew stronger. Gratian himself did not include it, but it was soon inserted as "palea,"[2] and thus found an entry into all schools of canonical jurisprudence, so that from this time forth the lawyers were the most influential publishers and defenders of the fiction. The language of the popes also was henceforward more confident. "Omne regnum Oc-"cidentis ei (Silvestro) tradidit et dimisit,"[3] says

---

1 Ap. Leibnit, *SS. Brunsvic.*, i., 882.
2 But with the more moderate expression, "Italiam *seu* occi-"dentales regiones," not with the unlimited "*et*" of Anselm.
3 *Sermo de S. Silvestro*, *Opera*, Venetiis, 1578, i., 97.

Innocent III. (1198-1216). Gregory IX. (1214-1227) followed this out to its consequences in a way surpassing anything that had been done before, when he represented to the emperor Frederick II., the ablest and most formidable opponent who had yet sustained the lists against the Roman See, that Constantine had, along with the imperial insignia, given over Rome with the duchy *and the imperium* to the care of the popes for ever. Whereupon the popes, without diminishing in any degree whatever the substance of their jurisdiction, established the tribunal of the empire, transferred it to the Germans, and are wont to concede the power of the sword to the emperors at their coronation.[1]

This was as much as to say that the imperial authority had its sole origin in the popes, could be enlarged or narrowed at their good pleasure, and that the pope could call each emperor to account for the use of the power entrusted to him. But the highest rung of the ladder was as yet not reached. This was first achieved by Gregory's successor, Innocent IV., when the synod of Lyons resulted in the deposition of Frederick; in which act this pope went beyond all his predecessors in the increase of his claim, and the extension of the authority of Rome. It is an error,

[1] Ap. Raynald., ad annum 1236, 24, p. 481, ed. Rom.

THE DONATION OF CONSTANTINE. 153

Innocent declares, in the year 1245, to suppose that Constantine was the first to confer temporal power on the Roman See; rather Christ Himself entrusted to Peter and his successors *both* powers, the sacerdotal and the royal, and the reign of both kingdoms, the earthly and the heavenly. Constantine, therefore, had merely resigned an unlawfully possessed power into the hands of its legitimate possessor, the Church, and had received it back again from the Church.[1]

Another half century, however, elapsed before theologians were found to reduce this new doctrine to a formal shape, and to furnish it with the usual scholastic, and in such cases very elastic apparatus. Under the influence of circumstances which took place towards the end of the thirteenth century, and of the spirit in which a Martin IV. and a Boniface VIII. ruled, the use which had been made of the Donation of Constantine assumed a different form. The Dominican, Tolomeo of Lucca, author of the

---

[1] *Cod Epist. Vatican.*, 4957, 49; *Codex Vindobon Philol.*, 61, f. 70—305, f. 83. In Raumer, *Geschichte der Hohenstaufen*, iv, 178 (first edition), who quotes the Latin text. The document was not known in the centuries immediately following, though the fact of Innocent IV. having taken up such a position was well known, for Alvaro Pelayo says (*De Planctu Ecclesiæ*, i., 43, about the year 1350), "Collatio autem Constantini potius fuit cessio quam collatio; sic "etiam fertur Innocentius IV. dixisse imperatori Frederico, quem "deposuit."

two last books of the work *De Regimine Principum*, the first two books of which are by Thomas Aquinas, goes beyond [1] his predecessors, and explains the Donation as a formal abdication of Constantine in favour of Sylvester; [2] and connecting with this other historical circumstances which are either inventions or misconceptions, he thence draws the conclusion that the power of all temporal princes derives its strength and efficacy solely from the spiritual power of the popes. There was no halting half way; and immediately afterwards, in the contest of Boniface VIII. with Philip of France, the Augustinian monk, [3]

---

[1] These last two books were written subsequent to 1298; for the putting to death of Adolf of Nassau, by Albert, is mentioned as an event which had already taken place.

[2] "Primo quidem de Constantino apparet, qui Silvestro in imperio "cessit."—*De Regimine Principum*, 3, 10. *Opuscula Th mæ Aquin.*, Lugd., 1562, p. 232.

[3] If the treatise *De Utraque Potestate* (which is found in Goldast, *Monarchia*, ii.) were from the pen of Ægidius, he must have professed the very opposite principles in the interest of king Philip. But, seeing that Ægidius, as archbishop of Bourges, is found among those prelates who went to Rome against Philip's will to the council summoned by Boniface, and thereupon was punished with confiscation, one may be quite certain that the writing in question was not composed by him. In his genuine and still unprinted work, the substance of which is given by Charles Jourdain, *Un Ouvrage Inédit de Gilles de Rome*, Paris, 1858, Ægidius says bluntly enough, "Patet quod omnia temporalia sunt sub domino Ecclesiæ "collocata, et si non de facto, quoniam multi forte huic juri "rebellantur, de jure tamen et ex debito temporalia summo pontifici

Aegidius Colonna of Rome, whom the pope had nominated to the archbishopric of Bourges, drew the natural conclusions without the slightest disguise in a work which he dedicated to his patron. Towards the middle of the century two theologians of the papal court, Agostino Trionfo and Alvaro Pelayo, the one an Italian, the other a Spanish minorite, took the same line of argument. This theory, reduced to its simplest terms, runs thus: Christ is Lord of the whole world; at His departure He left this dominion to His representatives, Peter and his successors; therefore the fullness of all spiritual and temporal power and dominion, the union of all rights and privileges, lies in the hands of the pope. Every monarch, even the most powerful, possesses only so much power and territory as the pope has transferred to him, or finds good to allow him. Trionfo says without reservation, that if an emperor, like Constantine, has given temporal possessions to Sylvester, this is merely a restitution of what had been stolen in an unjust and tyrannical way.[a]

This theory, utterly unknown to the earlier popes and to the whole of Christendom, was invented in the

---

[a] "sunt subjecta, a quo jure et a quo debito nullatenus possunt absolvi," p. 13.

[1] *Summa de Ecclesia*, 94, 1.

first instance in order to meet the objections to the Donation of Constantine. For there were not wanting persons who declared that Constantine had no power to make such a suicidal Donation, so ruinous to the empire. An emperor could not tear in pieces the empire, for this was in direct contradiction to his office.[1]

The French advocate, Peter Dubois, at Coutances declared, in his opinion about the Bull of Boniface VIII. to Philip, that the Donation was from the first legally null and void; all lawyers were unanimous in maintaining this, only the very long prescription conferred on it at the present time a legal validity.[2]

Contemporaneously with him the Dominican, John Quidort of Paris, magister of the theological faculty there (died A.D. 1306), in his book *On the Regal and Papal Power*, contended against the Donation of Constantine, for, as all lawyers maintained, the emperor,

---

[1] Brought out more in detail by Dante, for example, in the *De Monarchia*, 3, 10; *Opere Minori*, ed. di Fraticelli, Firenze, 1857, ii., 460. ["Ergo scindere Imperium, Imperatori non licet. Si ergo "aliquæ dignitates per Constantinum essent alienatæ (ut dicunt) "ab Imperio," &c. Here the sceptical "ut dicunt" shows that Dante doubted the *fact* as well as the rightfulness of the Donation. So also "*Dicunt quidam* adhuc, quod Constantinus Imperator, "mundatus a leprâ intercessione Sylvestri, tunc summi pontificis, "imperii sedem, scilicet Romam, donavit ecclesiæ, cum multis aliis "imperii dignitatibus."]

[2] In Dupuy, *Histoire des Différentes Preuves*, p. 46.

as semper Augustus, could only enlarge, not diminish the empire; on the contrary, such a mutilation of the empire, of which he was only the administrator, might be set aside by each of his successors as null and void.[1]

From the time that the harmonious relations between the empire and the papacy were destroyed, and one conflict after another between the two powers arose with a sort of inherent necessity, and the transfer of the papacy into French hands made the restoration of due relations impossible (that is to say, from the death of Frederick II. to the death of Lewis the Bavarian, 1250-1346), the Donation of Constantine was perpetually mentioned in the various memorials, opinions, and apologies, which had reference to the contest. The defenders of the imperial cause, appealing to the prevailing view of the civil jurists, usually without circumlocution pronounced the Donation null and void or obsolete.[2] One of the ablest and acutest contenders for the imperial power, the Minorite Marsiglio of Padua, does not quite know how he stands towards it.

[2] Fratris Johannis de Parisiis Tract. *de Potestate Reg. et Pap.*, in Schardii *Coll. de Jurisdictione Imp.*, p. 208 sq.

[1] So the author of the inquiry, *Whether the pope had power to enforce an armistice on the Emperor, Henry VII.*, in Doenniges, *Acta Henrici* VII., ii., 158.

"Some say that Constantine conferred the privilege on the pope," is the expression he uses; but he then goes on to say that those in the papal interest, either because the document was not clear and comprehensive enough, or had become obsolete, or had never been legally valid, had invented this entirely new theory of a universal, spiritual, and temporal power derived immediately from Christ the God-man.[1] But even this Marsiglio found the Donation of Constantine a welcome weapon against the primacy of the Roman See in general, for from it it was very easy to draw the conclusion that even the ecclesiastical supremacy of the pope over all other churches and bishops rested merely on the grant of the emperor, and therefore on a purely human, perishable, and in such things properly invalid right.[2] Marsiglio knew well how to turn this weak spot to good account.

In the thirteenth and fourteenth centuries the same amount of uncertainty and arbitrariness as before continued to prevail in the definitions respecting the real extent of the Donation. In the decretal of pope Nicholas III. merely the cession of Rome to the popes by Constantine is mentioned, in accordance with the

[1] *Defensor Pacis*, Heidelberg, 1599, p. 101.
[2] l. c., p. 203.

special object of this document.[1] In the form of oath which the emperor, Henry VII., had to take before his coronation, Clement V. made this monarch swear that he would protect and uphold all the rights which the emperors, and Constantine of course first of all, had granted to the Roman Church, without however going on to state in what these rights consisted.[2] John XXII., in his refutation of Marsiglio of Padua, in the year 1327, merely mentions in passing the fact that Constantine had given up the imperial city to Sylvester, quoting the words of the Donation.[3] The oldest, or second oldest commentator on Dante, the compiler of the *Ottimo Commento*, who wrote in the year 1333, contents himself with the indefinite statement that Constantine had given Sylvester "all the dignity of the empire."[4]

The author of the commentary on Dante, which was written in the year 1375, states quite simply that Constantine gave to the pope and the Church exactly what the pope possesses to this day;[5] in opposition

---

[1] In 6 to, 1, 6, 17.
[2] Clementin, 9 de jur. ej.
[3] In Raynald, a. 1327, 31.
[4] *L'Ottimo Commento della divina Commedia*, Pisa, 1827, 1355, Peter Aureoli says very much the same (about the year 1316): "Honor imperii translatus est in personam Silvestri et in Rom. ecclesiam."—*Aurea Scripturæ Elucidatio*, Venetiis, s., a. f. 89.
[5] *Chiose sopra Dante, testo inedito*, Firenze, 1846, p. 161.

to which a later commentator, Guiniforto delli Bargigi, is convinced that only "the patrimony in Tuscany, in "the neighbourhood of Rome," is included in the Donation.[1]

Rudolf or Pandulf Colonna,[2] canon of Sienna, and probably a Roman by birth (fourteenth century), gives the Donation once more the widest extent of meaning, including "Rome, Italy, and all western "kingdoms."[3] Nicolas of Clamenge himself says without any hesitation, that Constantine conferred the western empire on the Roman Church, and intended the cardinals to be senators of it.[4]

In France efforts were made to secure the country

---

[1] *Lo Inferno, col comento di G. d. B.*, pubbl. da G. Zacheroni, Firenze, 1838, p. 456.

[2] Not Raoul de Coloumelle, canon of Chartres, as the *His'oire littéraire de la France*, xxi, 151, represents him. The *His'oire* itself notices that the author in two manuscripts of his small work is called "Canonicus Senensis,' and only in one "Canonicus Carno-"tensis." A Frenchman would have expressed himself differently respecting the "translatio imperii a Francis ad Germanos," and would not have contented himself with saying merely, "Regnum "mundi translatum est ad Germanos vel Teutonicos," p. 2𝑢7. The whole historical view is taken from the standpoint of a Roman ecclesiastic; and the author gives one pretty clearly to understand that he is a Roman ecclesiastic by noticing that pope Hadrian was by birth "de regione Viæ latæ," p. 292. Moreover, Radulf has copied Marsilius of Padua, or the latter has copied him, as one can see by comparing them in Schardius, p. 287 and p. 226.

[3] *De Translatione Imperii*, in Schardius, p. 287.

[4] *De Annatis non Solvendis, Opera*, ed. Lyndius, p. 92.

against the consequences which were drawn, or might be drawn, from the extent of a Donation which embraced the whole of the West. The Parisian theologian, Jacob Almain, contends therefore that Constantine had no power whatever to transfer the empire to the pope without the consent of the people;[1] and in the second place, that the kingdom of Gaul at any rate could not have been included, for the Romans had never been masters of Gaul, and the people of Gaul had never of their own accord voted for submitting to Roman rule. He seems to have had no misgivings as to the extent to which the Celtic population of Gaul had allowed themselves to become Romanized. Almain maintains moreover that it is the common opinion of doctors generally, that as a matter of fact Constantine did not resign the empire.[2]

Lupold of Babenberg in the fourteenth century, in his treatise *On the Roman Empire*, dedicated to Baldwin, archbishop of Tréves (1307–1354), discusses

[1] "Contradicente populo occidentali." In Gerson, Opp. ii., **971**, cf p. 1063.

[2] "Quod resignaverit imperium occidentale, nunquam legitur." It is remarkable how uncertain people were even at this late date (Almain wrote about the year 1510) respecting a fact so unmistakeable. If one considers to what a high degree of historical discernment some writers attained even as early as the twelfth century, one might almost say, that in this direction, and in all that relates to a rational understanding of history, the movement for three whole centuries was a retrogression rather than an advance.

the Donation very thoroughly while investigating the question whether the king of Rome had to take the oath of a vassal to the Roman See.[1] The discussion with him means nothing less than the decision of the still wider question, whether the pope is really the suzerain of the German empire and possessor of the dominium directum, so that in all countries of the empire all that accrues to the emperor is the dominium utile. Hence we once more meet with the most different opinions as to the validity or nullity of the Donation; whereupon Lupold remarks that all canonists are wont to maintain that the Donation is legally valid and irrevocable. But then the other kingdoms of the West must have stood in the same relation of vassaldom to the pope. Lupold, however, is keen-sighted enough to see through the unhistorical character of the whole fiction. He knows that the emperors ruled over the West just as much after Constantine's time as before it; and he himself had found passages in the ecclesiastical law-books which speak merely of giving up the city of Rome to the pope. In the end, however (belief in the Donation was at that time still so powerful), he does not venture to come to a decision, but prefers to leave the settlement of the matter to higher powers.

[1] In Schard, p. 391.

THE DONATION OF CONSTANTINE. 163

From a legal point of view the matter remained just as debatable as ever. It was not, however, easy to explain how Constantine, as elective emperor (and the old Roman emperors were supposed to have been elective like the German ones), could have given away half the empire. In a treatise which, so far as I am aware, has never been printed, and which seems to have been written in the time of Lewis of Bavaria in reference to his contests,[1] the question is discussed, whether in virtue of his election the emperor can forthwith and immediately exercise control over the whole realm, or whether he needs to be empowered by the pope to do so. In consequence of the Donation of Constantine, says the author, the whole jurisdiction of the emperor became dependent on confirmation by the pope; but, on the other hand, it must be admitted that the rights and constituent parts of the realm could not be alienated so arbitrarily, without the consent of the princes, barons, and high officials.[2]

[1] *Brevis Tractatus de Jurisdictione Imperii et Auctoritate Summi Pontificis circa Imperium.* Cod. Lat. 5832 in the National Library at Munich, f 121, ff.

[2] "Sed contra hoc est, quod jura imperii alienari non possunt "quum sint bona republicæ, quæ sine publicis officialibus "dispensari non possunt, ut sunt principes et barones et quorum "interest assistere ministerio imperiali aulæ diversorum apicum." f. 123.

On the other hand the Donation is defended towards the end of the fifteenth century by the Strasburg parish priest, John Hug of Schlettstadt, in his *Wagenfuhr der h. Kirche und des Römischen Reichs*, which he dedicated to cardinal Raymond of Gurk (1493-1505). Accursius, he says, has declared the gift to be invalid on account of its extravagance, but John Teutonicus, the annotator of the *Decretum* (of Gratian), has proved its immutable validity from the Clementines,[1] which inserted the Donation into the imperial oath.

The German law-books gave the Donation of Constantine a remarkable extension, inasmuch as they maintained that Constantine gave to Sylvester the civil or king's bann to the amount of sixty schillings, "in order to compel all those who will not reform "themselves by corporal punishment, to be compelled "to do so by means of fines."[2] This is a specific German invention, utterly unknown to the Latin nations. The sense is as follows: in consequence of the wide and indefinite sphere of the ecclesiastical [3]

---

[1] [The *Constitutiones Clementinæ* are that part of the *Corpus Juris Canonici* which contains the decrees of the council of Vienne (A.D. 1311), together with decrees of Clement V.; published in 1313.]

[2] *Sachsenspiegel*, von Homeyer, i., 238 (3, 63). *Das Rechtsbuch nach Distinctionen*, edited by Ortloff, p. 325 (6, 16). *Schwabenspiegel*, in Senckenberg, *Corp. Jur. Germ.*, ii., 10.

[3] [These ecclesiastical courts (Send-gerichte, synodus) were held

courts, it became a custom in Germany that the ecclesiastical judges should impose fines, levying them themselves, for various crimes, some of which belonged entirely to the municipal jurisdiction; an abuse which Alexander III. forbade as early as the year 1180, but to no purpose. As an authority for this abnormal custom was wanted, and none could be found, the Donation of Constantine—that large and inexhaustible treasury from which political and municipal privileges could be drawn just as they were wanted—must here also be brought into use.[1]

In the ideas of the people and laity generally, the Donation of Constantine had meanwhile acquired another and more comprehensive significance. In the whole of the later Middle Ages we see two diametrically opposite currents prevailing. On the one side was the effort to furnish the Church with

by the bishop, or archdeacon, or their substitute (Sendrichter) to try ecclesiastical offences, especially profanation of the Lord's day, and other violations of the decalogue.]

[1] The cardinals D'Ailly and Zaberella, on behalf of the bishops and their officials, lodged complaints respecting these fiscal gains of the ecclesiastical courts before the council of Constance, and requested that provision might be made against them (See Von Der Hardt, *Concil. Const.*, i, p 8, p. 421, and p 9, p. 524). But the mischief continued in Germany, and contributed not a little to the general bitterness against the hierarchy and the clergy, as one sees from the *Gravamina Nationis Germanicæ*, c. 64, of the year 1522, not to mention other indications of the same fact.

considerable donations, to create for her a broad foundation of extensive landed property, and to raise the number and condition of clergy living on ecclesiastical endowments; but side by side with this was the view which had been making way ever since the twelfth century, that the great possessions and large revenues of the Church were a grievous evil, the sources of nearly all existing abuses, and the causes of a moral deterioration of the clergy.[1] This view

---

[1] [We find this expressed in very strong language in some of the political and satirical songs of the thirteenth and following centuries. Such songs took a new tone in England just about that age. The civil commotions of the reign of John, and the weak government of Henry III., afforded every party abundance of material for satire, and plenty of opportunity for giving it free utterance. The clerk with his Latin, the courtier with his Anglo-Norman, and the people with their vigorous old English, all had their word to say. It may be worth while to give a few examples from Mr. Wright's collection of *The Political Songs of England.*

"Roma mundi caput est, sed nil capit mundum;
Quod pendet a capite totum est immundum;
Transit enim vitium primum in secundum,
Et de fundo redolet quod est juxta fundum.
"Roma capit singulos et res singulorum;
Romanorum curia non est nisi forum.
Ibi sunt venalia jura senatorum,
Et solvit contraria copia nummorum."
"Solam avaritiam Roma novit parca,
Parcit danti munera, parco non est parca:
Nummus est pro numine, et pro Marco marca,
Et est minus celebris ara quam sit arca," &c., &c.

From the *Invectio contra avaritiam* about the time of the interdict.

THE DONATION OF CONSTANTINE.

gradually assumed a form of serious and threatening import to the clerical body, as the notion was developed out of it that originally the clergy had been poor, had lived solely upon freewill offerings, and had remained poor upon principle, until Constantine by his Donation put an end to the former

> "Jacet ordo clericalis
> In respectu laicalis,
> Sponsa Christi fit venalis,
> Generosa generalis;
> Veniunt altaria,
> Venit eucharistia,
> Cum sit nugatoria
> Gratia venalis."
>
> From a *Song against the Bishops*, about 1250.

> "Les contre-estanz abatent li fiz de felonie;
> Lors perit seinte eglise, quant orgoil la mestrie.
> Ceo sustenent li prelaz ki s'i ne peinent mie,
> Pur dreiture sustenir nolent perdre vie."
>
> From a *Song of the Times*, about 1274.

See also *Piers the Ploughman's Crede* (about 1394) passim, and the pelican's charges against the clergy in the *Complaint of the Ploughman*.]

[Walther von der Vogelweide sings thus on the subject:—

> "Solt ich den pfaffen râten an den trinwen mîn;
> sô spræche ir haut den armen zuo 'sô daz ist dîn,'
> ir zunge sunge unde lieze manegem man daz sin;
> Gedæhten ouch daz si durch Got ê wâren almnosnære:
> dô gap in êrste geltes teil der künec Constantîn.
> Het er gewest daz dâ von übel künftec wære,
> sô het er wol underkomen des riches swære;
> wan daz si dô waren kische und übermüete lære."
>
> No. 111, p. 113, Simrock's edition, Bonn, 1870.

His poems abound in anti-papal sentiments.]

state of poverty, especially in Rome, and pope Sylvester by his acceptance of it gave an example eagerly followed by the clerical body generally, and ineradicably implanted in them the passion for acquiring wealth. The view that the wealth of the Church was the great obstacle in the way of all clerical reform gained ground more and more. Sectarianism, which from the middle of the twelfth century onwards assumed numerous and various shapes in Italy, France, and Germany, made common cause with this view, or fostered it and spread it assiduously. It ended in becoming part and parcel of public opinion.

It was precisely this which won for the fabulous Donation of Constantine such universal acceptance, that the fiction so exactly corresponded with the feelings and needs of the people at that time. The Middle Ages, with their natural propensity to imagine definite actors, and an act producing effects once for all, in the case of circumstances which really had been gradually and slowly developed, could not account for the fact that the formerly poor Church had gradually become rich, otherwise than by representing this change as having been instantaneous. The Church, which till yesterday had been utterly without property, became suddenly possessed of a

superabundance of earthly goods, through the **acts of
the two Heads, the imperial giver, and the accepting
pope. And** therewith, said numberless persons, the
hitherto closed Pandora-box had been opened for the
Church; all the **evils from which she was** suffering
were to be **attributed** to this source of mischief. [1]
Even **men who stood on the heights in their own**
age, saw **the matter thus,** and **their grief at the in-**
firmities **of the Church, the** degeneracy **of the clergy,**
and the ceaseless conflict between the spiritual **and**
temporal power, clothed itself in lamentations **over**
Constantine's well-meant, but ill-advised munificence.
Thus two contemporaries, whose sentiments agree in
many points, Dante [2] and Ottokar of Horneck. The

---

[1] With what naïveté even ecclesiastics **and** historians **up** to tho close of the Middle Ages placed themselves **quite at the** stand-point of the popular view, **is shown from the following** passage of **the** monk Bernhard White (about A.D. 1510) in his *Historia Westphaliæ,* Monast., 1775, p. 61: "Silvestro pontificante . . . **ecclesiarum** "Prælati, qui hactenus in paupertate vixerunt, imo nihil habentes **et** "omnia possidentes, possessiones habere inceperunt."

[2] Inf., XIX., 115-17:

["Ahi Constantin, di quanto mal **fu matre,**
Non la tua conversion, ma **quella dote,**
Che da te prese il primo ricco patre!"

"Ah, Constantine! of how much ill was mother,
Not **thy conversion,** but that marriage dower,
Which the first wealthy **Father** took from thee!"
                                     Longfellow's Translation.

Dante deplores the supposed Donation no less heartily in the *De*

former especially bewails avarice and simony, as the unhallowed fruit of that Donation; but the latter says Constantine added a sword, which they did not know

Monarchiâ: "O felicem populum! O Ausoniam te gloriosam! si vel "numquam infirmator imperii tui extitisset; vel numquam sua pia "intentio ipsum fefellisset." **Lib.** II., sub finem.

Ariosto places the Donation in the moon, among the things which **have been lost or** abused on earth:

> "Di varj fiori ad un gran monte passa,
> Ch' ebber già buono odore, or puzzan **forte,**
> Questo era il dono (se però dir lece)
> **Che Constantino al buon** Silvestro fece."
>
> *Orl. Fur.*, c. XXXIV., st. 80.

> "Then passed he to a flowery mountain green,
> Which once smelt sweet, now stinks as odiously;
> This was that gift, if you the truth will have,
> That Constantine to good Sylvester gave."
>
> **Milton's** Translation. *Prose Works*, i., p. 11, ed. 1753.

From Cary's note on Dante, Inf., xix., 118.

But perhaps the strongest passage in Dante against the Donation is Par. **xx.,** 55, where Constantine is found in Paradise, *in spite of* the Donation.

> "Lo altio, che segue, con le leggi e meco
> Sotto buona intenzion, che fe mal frutto,
> Per cedere al pastor si fece **Greco:**
> Ora conosce, come il mal dedutto
> Dal suo bene operar non li è nocivo,
> Avvegna che sia il mondo indi distrutto."

> "The next who follows (Constantine), with the laws and me,
> Under the good intent that bore bad fruit
> Became a Greek by ceding to the pastor;
> **Now knoweth** he how all the ill deduced
> From his good action is not harmful to him,
> Although the world **thereby may be destroyed."**
>
> **Longfellow's Translation.]**

how to wield, to the stole of the priests, and thus broke the strength of the empire.[1]

This view, that the Donation had brought ruin into the Church, assumed in that legend-producing age the form of an actual occurrence. An angel was said to have cried from heaven, "Woe! woe! This "day hath poison been infused into the Church." The legend is to be found as early as the commencement of the thirteenth[2] century, in Walther von der Vogelweide. "The angel hath told us true," says this poet, but he is thinking chiefly of the weakening of the empire, which appears to him to be the evil fruit of the Donation :

> "alle vürsten lebent nû mit êren,
> wan der höhste ist geswachet,
> daz hat der pfaffen wal gemachet."[3]

So, also, the Strasburg chronicler, Königshofen. "Then was a voice heard over all Rome, which said, "'This day hath gall and venom flowed into holy

---

[1] Cap. 448, in Pez., iii., 446.

[2] [Simrock assigns this poem to A.D. 1198. The one in which the poet talks of having sung for forty years, "von minnen und als "iemen sol," is assigned to the year 1228. This would place his birth about 1168. He took part in the sixth crusade, and probably died soon after his return.]

[3] [That is, "all the princes now live with honours, since the highest (the emperor) is weakened. The election of the clergy has brought about this." No. 5, p. 36, Simrock's edition.]

"'Christendom,' and know ye that this also is source and ground of all war between popes[1] and emperors."

Contemplation of the mischief which the hatred between Lewis the Bavarian and the French popes had created, moved the Minorite John of Winterthur also to complain, that "at this time one sees plainly enough how truly the angel spoke, in saying that through that well-meant, but in its consequences most unhappy, rich dotation and fat present, which Constantine conferred, poison had flowed into the Church."[2]

Even theologians were not ashamed to appeal to the saying of the angel. John of Paris concludes from it that the Donation had displeased[3] God. A hundred years after him Dietrich Vrie, an Augustinian at Osnabruck, says that poison certainly at that time had been administered to the Church, but yet only through the *abuse* of the Donation; for wealth in itself

---

[1] In the Vienna manuscript, *Hist. Eccles.*, 29, fol. 64 (in thirteenth century), the reason given for the voice of the angel is, "quia (ecclesia) major est dignitate, minor religione." The story about the angel is found also in the *Chron. Mona.t. Mellicensis*, in Pez, *Scr. Austr*, i, 182, in the chronicle of Theodore Engelhusen, in Leibnitz, *Scr. Brunsvic.*, ii., 1034.

[2] In Eccard, i., 1889.

[3] In Schard, *Sylloge*, p. 210.

THE DONATION OF CONSTANTINE. 173

was by no means a calamity for the Church.[1]. At last this saying of the angel passed into a proverb, common even in the mouth of the lower orders.[2]

At first, however, this angel, who proclaimed the poisoning of the Church, seems to have been a fallen one. For the first who narrates the miracle, Giraldus Cambrensis (about the year 1180), (and, as bishop Pecock of Chichester (1450) assures us, the other chroniclers merely copy Giraldus,) makes the "old enemy" speak the words.[3] At any rate, this "evil one" shortly afterwards transformed himself into an angel of light.

The sects of the twelfth and thirteenth centuries, especially the Catharists and Waldenses, proceeded on the principle, that every possession of the Church was in itself objectionable, and that it was damnable for the Church to devote anything more than the mere freewill offerings of the moment, towards supplying

---

1 *Hist. Concil. Const.*, in Von der Hardt, i., 111.

4 Ab omnibus recitatur, tempore quo Constantinus M. incoepit dotare ecclesiam, audita est vox in aere: "Hodie effusum venenum "in ecclesia." Jo. Major, *de Pot. Papæ.* In Gerson's Works, ii., 1159.

1 "The oold enemy made thilk voice in the eir." Pecock's *Repressor*, ed. by Churchill Babington, London, 1860, p 351. According to Pecock's statement, the passage is to be found in the *Cosmographia Hiberniæ* of Giraldus. It is not in the printed *Topographia Hiberniæ*; but it is possibly in the still unprinted *Descriptio Mundi* of Giraldus.

means of life to the clergy. The [1] endowment, therefore, of the Church by Constantine was considered by them as a decisive turning-point, involving the ruin of the Church, nay, its utter destruction. Until Sylvester, they said, the Church existed; in him it fell, and became extinct by receiving from the hand of Constantine riches and worldly power, until it was once more revived by the "Poor men of Lyons."[2] With the end of its poverty ended the very existence of the Church: property was the poison of which it died. Sylvester is, therefore, that mighty, bold, and crafty king prophesied of in Daniel[3] viii. 24, who

[1] [This was the doctrine so widely spread by the Abbot Joachim of Fiore, Dolcino of Novara, and the Fraticelli. The primitive Church had held that poverty was better than riches. That period had come to an end with Sylvester. Since his time all popes had been prevaricators and deceivers, except Celestine V. He alone had understood and practised the blessed state of poverty. The Cathari argued that, as Constantine's empire was one of wrong and violence, and he had ceded it to Sylvester, the popes since Sylvester were successors to an unrighteous kingdom, not to an apostolic Church. This view had its effect also on the various *prophecies* which were circulated in the fourteenth century under the name of Joachim, and others. See a most interesting essay by Dr. Döllinger in Raumer's *Historisch s Taschenbuch*, Leipzig, 1871, on *Der Weissogungsglaube und das Prophetenthum in d r christlichen Zeit*, pp. 264 265, 282, 283.] [This essay is translated in the present volume.]

[2] Rainer. Sacchoni, in Martene Thesaur. v., 1775. Moneta, *Advers. Cathar. et Vald.*, p. 412.

[3] ['And in the latter time of their kingdom, when the trans-"gressors are come to the full, a king of fierce countenance, and "understanding dark sentences, shall stand up. And his power

destroys "the people of the holy ones"—[das Volk der Heiligen ;—so the Hebrew, and the *margin* of the English version]. He is also Antichrist, the Man of Sin, and Son of Perdition, of whom St. Paul[1] speaks [2 Thess. ii. 3]. Valdez, on the other hand, the founder of the "Poor men of Lyons," is the Elias, who, according to the words of Christ (Matt. xvii. 11), shall come and restore all things. Later, however, the Waldenses discovered that a Church which for eight hundred years, from Sylvester to Valdez, had entirely vanished, and then had been called into existence again out of nothing, was a nonentity. They maintained, therefore, that their sect or church had not had its first beginning with Valdez, but had already been in existence in the time [2] of Sylvester, and that since that pope all the clergy, and those who

---

"shall be mighty, but not by his own power; and he shall destroy "wonderfully, and shall prosper, and practise, and shall destroy the "mighty and the holy people. And through his policy also he shall "cause craft to prosper in his hand; and he shall magnify himself "in his heart, and by peace shall destroy many; he shall also stand "up against the Prince of princes, but he shall be broken without "hand." (Daniel viii. 23–25.) Only by considering Sylvester as having become, through the Donation, potentially a Gregory VII., an Innocent III., a Boniface VIII., can we understand how this prophecy could ever have been quoted as referring to him.]

1 Moneta, iv., 263.

2 Petrus de Pilichdorf; *Contra Waldenses*, in Bibl. Patr. Lugd, xxv., 278.

followed them, were damned.[1] The name Leonenses (i.e. of Lyons) then gave occasion to the invention of a Leo as the supposed founder of the sect. A pious man of this name in the time of Constantine, "disciple "and fellow of pope Sylvester," is said to have separated from the now wealthy pope, in order to show his abhorrence of the latter's avarice, and serve the Lord in voluntary[2] poverty.

This notion, that utter poverty of the clergy, and rejection of all property, were among the conditions of the Church's existence, and that, consequently, Constantine and Sylvester were the authors of the Church's ruin, was at that time so prevalent, and so much in harmony with the characteristics of the age, that it was always reappearing. The Dulcinists[3] or Apostolic Brethren at the beginning of the fourteenth century, who aspired to realise the primitive Church in its purity, as they conceived it, said that it was Sylvester who had reopened the doors of human society and of the Church to Satan.[4] Dolcino

---

[1] *De Hæresi Paup. de Lugd*, in Martene, Thes. v., 1779.
[2] So Conrad Justinger in Bern, about A.D. 1420, in his chronicle of Bern.
[3] [The followers of Dolcino of Novara. Clement V. condemned him and others to death. His flesh was torn away from his body with hot pinchers, and his limbs then wrenched off, A D. 1304.]
[4] "Quando paupertas fuit mutata ab ecclesia per S. Silvestrum "tunc sanctitas vitæ fuit subtracta ecclesiæ et diabolus intravit in "hunc mundum." So the Dulcinist Peter of Lucca, in Limborch *Hist. inquis.*, p. 360.

himself, in his first letter to Christendom, declared Sylvester to be the angel of Pergamus, who "dwells "where Satan's seat is." (Rev. ii. 13.)

The English precursor of Protestantism, Wyclif, shared this view. Constantine, he says, foolishly injured himself and the clergy, in burdening the Church so heavily with temporal goods.[1] In the *Trialogus* he represents Antichrist as produced by the Donation of Constantine, and thence deduces the downfall of the Roman empire.[2]

The days of the Donation of Constantine were, however, numbered. Already, in the year 1443, Æneas Sylvius Piccolomini, afterwards pope Pius II., then secretary to Frederick III., had recommended that emperor to summon a fresh council, at which, among other things, the question of the Donation of Constantine, "which caused perplexity to many souls," should on Frederick's proposal be finally decided. He himself was well known to be convinced of its unauthenticity, and he notices that neither in the ancient historians nor in *Damasus*, that is, in the Pontifical book, was anything about it to be found. Its unauthenticity, therefore, was to be proclaimed by

[1] Thomas Waldensis, *Doctrin. Fidei*, ed. Blanciotti, ii., 708, quotes his words from his book *De Papa*.
[2] *Tracts and Treatises*, ed. Vaughan, 1845, p. 174.

the council, and Æneas joined with this the *arrière pensée*, that Frederick should again take possession of at least a part of the territory included in the Donation, as belonging to the empire, and thus gain a firm basis in the peninsular for the imperial power, which otherwise would vanish into air.[1]

Three men appeared almost simultaneously in the middle of the fifteenth century, to prove on historical grounds, that the *fact* of the Donation no less than the document was an invention;—Reginald Pecock, bishop of Chichester, cardinal Cusa, and Lorenzo Valla. In contrast to the uncertain vacillation[2] of Cusa, Pecock's exactness of historical investigation, an exactness proportionate to his knowledge of authorities, is very remarkable.[3] In Paris, where scholasticism still held the sceptre, criticism had not

---

[1] *Pentalogus*, in Pez. Thes. Anecd iv., p 3, 679.

[2] The passage out of his *Concordantia Catholica* is printed in Brown, Fasciculus, i., 157.

[3] *Repressor*, p. 361-67. [Pecock gives eight reasons for maintaining that the Donation is a fiction, most of them tolerably conclusive; e. g. the silence of Damasus, who mentions other small gifts of Constantine; the silence of credible historians; the fact that Constantine bequeathed the very territory in question to his sons, and that Boniface IV. asked the emperor Phocas to give him the Pantheon as a church, A. U. 608, &c., &c. By "Damasus" Pecock no doubt means the *Liber Pontificalis* or *Anastasius* (falsely so called), which was usually quoted as a work of pope Damasus in the Middle Ages.]

advanced so far as this fifty years later, as Almain shows. Valla certainly went much farther than Pecock and Cusa; he undertook to prove that the pope had no right to the possession of Rome, and the States of the Church in particular, that he was "tantum "Vicarius Christi et non etiam Cæsaris." His treatise was rather an artistic, rhetorical production, an eloquent declamation, than a calm historical investigation.[1] He himself considered it as the *chef d'œuvre* of his eloquence. And yet after his treatise had been circulated everywhere, and had caused the greatest excitement, Valla was invited to Rome by Nicolas V., taken into the service of the pope, and received both from Nicholas V. and from Calixtus III., various marks of favour, without any retractation whatever being required of him.

The jurists meanwhile did not allow themselves to be put out of countenance, and held fast to the fiction for about a hundred years longer.[2] Antonius, archbishop of Florence, calls attention to the fact that the passage in Gratian's decretals does not exist in the

[1] Poggiali, *Memorie di Lorenzo Valla*, Piacenza, 1790, p. 119. [A full account of this treatise of Valla is given in the *Presbyterian Quarterly Review*, Jan. 1861, pp. 381–411, by Rev. E. H. Gillett, D.D.]

[2] "Apud Canonistas nulla ambiguitas est, quin perpetua firmitate "subnixa sit," says Peter of Andlo, *De imperio Romano*, p. 42, in the *Tractatus varii de R. G. Imp. Regimine*, Norimb., 1657.

more ancient manuscripts of the collection, but at the same time, remarks that the legists (professors of civil law) disputed the legal validity of the Donation, while the canonists and theologians upheld it. He himself adopts the idea [1] of a universal dominion of the pope, resting on a divine dispensation, and accordingly sees in the Donation nothing more than a restitution. Meanwhile, defenders of its legal authenticity were not wanting even among the professors of civil law. [2] Above all others Bartolo must be mentioned here (about 1350), to whom formerly, as Tiraboschi says, almost divine honour was paid. But as he calls attention to the territory in which he and his hearers happen to be, he lets one divine his true meaning. [3] On the other hand, Nicolas Tudeschi, who was considered by his contemporaries as the greatest of all canonists, declares that he who denies the Donation lies under the suspicion[4] of heresy. Cardinal P. P.

---

[1] The passage out of his *Pars Historialis* is found in Brown, Fascic., i., 159.

[2] The jurists had discovered a passage in proof of the Donation even in the Corpus juris civilis. That is to say, Cod. 5, 27, in a law of the emperor Zeno, they read, " Divi Constantini, qui ... Roma-" num *minuit* imperium," instead of " *munivit*."

[3] " Videte, *quia nos* sumus in terris Ecclesiæ, idcirco dico quod illa " donatio valeat." In prœm., ff. n. 14.

[4] *Concil.* 84, n. 2, in cap. per venerabilem, and elsewhere. Compare Francisci Bursati *Consilia*, Venet., 1572, i, 359.

Parisius, and the Spanish-bishop, Arnold Albertinus, declare the same. Whosoever pronounces the Donation to be null and void, says the latter, comes very near to heresy; but whosoever maintains that it never took place at all is in a still worse case.[1] Antonius [2] Rosellus, and Ludwig Gomez[3] are of the same opinion; and cardinal Hieronymus Albano declares thus much at least, that there exist shameless persons who refuse to submit to the " unanimis consensus tot ac tantorum " Patrum," respecting the Donation; or, according to the expression of Petrus Igneus, to the "tota acade- " mia Canonistarum et Legistarum," with the whole host of theologians to boot.[4] But after cardinal Baronius had once for all confessed the unauthenticity of the Donation, all these voices, which had shortly before been so numerous and so loud, became dumb.

Only one remark more need be added in conclusion. In consequence of its naturalization among the Greeks, the Donation in its full extent found admittance even into Russia, for it exists in the *Kormczaia Kniga*, the Corpus juris canonici of the Græco-Slavonic Church, which was translated from the Greek

---

[1] *De Agnoxendis Assert. Cath. et Hær., quæst.*, 17, n. 14.
[2] *Tr*:ct. *de Potest. Papæ*, Lugd. s. a., p. 320.
[3] In Bursatus, l. c. 360ᵇ.
[4] Bursatus, l. c., quoted all these, and many others.

by a Servian or Bulgarian, in the thirteenth or fourteenth century.[1]

[One [2] further argument may be noticed, not as being needed, but as being in itself almost conclusive. Among the innumerable monuments of Roman art, from the fourth century onwards, some of which have direct reference to Constantine, no reference whatever is made to the Donation. Would it not have been a favourite subject, had it ever been a fact? There appears to be only one representation in mediæval art of the Donation of Constantine. It is a mosaic from the "zophoros," or frieze of the Lateran basilica. Some of the details of the costumes show it to be *not earlier than the twelfth century.* On one side, " Rex " baptizatur et lepræ sorde lavatur ; " on the other, " Rex in scriptura Silvestro dat sua jura."]

---

[1] Wiener *Jahrbücher der Literatur*, Bd. xxiii., 265.

[2] *The Testimony of the Catacombs and other Monuments of Christian Art*, etc., by Wharton B. Marriott, London, 1870, p. 99.

VI. LIBERIUS AND FELIX.

It will be necessary first to give the true history of these two men, the sources of which happily flow with all the clearness that could be wished. In this way the origin and tendency of the fable will become more plainly apparent.

The emperor Constantius, under the influence of his eunuchs and certain Arian bishops, wished to force Arianism on the Church and bishops of the West, in that weakened and half ashamed form which the Eusebians had given to it. He, as well as his satellites, made use of all means of seduction, intimidation, and brutal violence, in order to accomplish this object. The Roman bishop, Liberius, first at Rome, and then at Milan, whither he had been summoned to the imperial court, steadfastly resisted the efforts of Constantius and his eunuch, Eusebius; he was accordingly banished to Berœa, in Thrace, in the year 354. In his place Constantius caused the Roman deacon, Felix, to be consecrated by three Arian bishops (one of whom was the Anomœan Acacius of Cæsarea), in the presence of three eunuchs. Felix had not formally rejected the Nicene Creed, but he held ecclesiastical communion with Arians, which was all that the leaders of that party needed then ; for the remainder, viz., the predominance of their doctrine, would gradually follow of itself. In Rome, where Liberius was personally much beloved, the people re-refused to enter the churches in which Felix showed himself. The whole clergy publicly promised, with an oath, before the congregation, that as long as Liberius lived they would recognise no other. It ended at last in an insurrection, in which some persons were killed.[1] When Constantius came to Rome two years later, he found the Roman populace still true to Liberius. The Roman ladies besought him earnestly to give them back their bishop, and he granted their request to this extent, that he decreed that Liberius and Felix (to the latter of whom the greatest number of the clergy had meanwhile joined themselves) should for the future rule the Roman Church in common. But the people assembled in the circus cried out, " One God, one Christ, one bishop." Liberius was, however, not recalled ; until in the following year, 357, broken by the sufferings and privations of his exile, pressed with threats, and deprived even of the man who hitherto had been left to him as servant and companion,

---

[1] Athanas. *Hist. ad monachos*, p. 389. Faustini and Marcellini *Libell.* præf. Socrat., 2, 37 ; Rufin., 1, 22 ; Hieron. *Vir. Illustr.*, c. 109 ; *Chron.* ad. a. 354.

the deacon Urbicus, he determined to sign a creed which was laid before him, to refuse to hold communion with Athanasius, and in consequence with all decided Nicæans, and thus to enter the Arian court party. He signed the first formula of Sirmio, which was inoffensive in other respects, and left nothing to be desired but the Homoüsion. He went further; he declared himself unable to hold communion with Athanasius, and accordingly entered into communion with the most decided Arians, such as Ursacius, Valens, and Germinius. He courted the favour of the influential protégés of the emperor, the Arian bishops, Epictetus and Auxentius. Later on (in the year 358), he was summoned from Berœa to the imperial court at Sirmio, and, at Constantius' bidding, signed a fresh and still worse formula, which the Arian and Semiarian bishops, just then assembled at a synod in Sirmio, had drawn up. In this formula, with a view to obtaining an express rejection of the Homoüsion, the decisions of the synod at Antioch [1] against Paul

---

[1] Not merely of the synod held at Antioch in 341, as Hefele states (*Concilien-Geschichte*, i., 662); for this did not occupy itself either with the case of Paul of Samosata, or with that of Photinus; but also of the synod of 269, which rejected the Homoüsion in the false sense given to it by Paul of Samosata. The object now in view was no longer a mere abstaining from the use of the hated word, but a formal condemnation of it; because, as was represented, under the pretext of the Homoüsion, certain persons (Athanasius

of Samosata, and the later ones against Photinus and Marcellus of Ancyra, together with one of the formularies of the synod at Antioch, in A.D. 341, were incorporated. Liberius was thus reduced to accepting precisely the position of the Semiarians, now so influential with Constantius. He gave his adhesion to their expression, "substantial likeness," sacrificed the Nicene doctrine, and apprised the eastern Arians of his entry into their communion, and of his separation from Athanasius. It was chiefly on account of this weakness exhibited at Sirmio, under the double influence of the emperor and the bishops, and not on account of what had taken place before at Berœa, that Liberius drew upon himself the reproach of his contemporaries, of being heretical, and an ally of heretics. And, indeed, no other judgment was then possible. He had granted communion to the very worst Arians, such as Epictetus of Centuncellæ and Auxentius of Milan.[1] It was Fortunatianus, bishop

and all who held firmly to the Nicene doctrine) wished to set up a sect of their own. Sozomen, 4, 15. Philostorgius (4, 3), moreover, does not say, as Hefele represents, that Liberius signed the *second* Sirmian formula. Of the one signed at Berœa he says nothing whatever; but he does mention the one accepted by Liberius afterwards at Sirmio, that is the *third;* and of this he says quite correctly, and in agreement with Sozomen, that Liberius thereby condemned the Homoüsion and Athanasius.

[1] Hilar. *de syn.*, Opp., ii., 464; Frag., 6, ii., 680; Sozom., 4, 15. The letters of Liberius in Coustant, *Epistolæ Pontiff.*, 442 sqq.

of Aquileia, who, according to Jerome, persuaded Liberius to such apostasy.

This was the price at which Liberius purchased his return to Rome, where the people joyfully welcomed the bishop, whom they personally loved in spite of his fall. The whole community was, and remained, Catholic. The people of the West had as yet occupied itself but little with the controversies about the consubstantiality of the Son with the Father; they scarcely understood the question at issue or its import. Liberius was therefore able quietly to resume his office without retracting. It had been determined at Sirmio, that Liberius and Felix should preside over the Church of Rome together; for Felix, in consequence of his holding communion with the Arian bishops, was still high in favour at court. At Rome, however, disturbances with wide reaching consequences took place. The clergy were divided, for the majority had broken the oath of fidelity which they had taken to Liberius before his banishment, and had recognised Felix. But the latter was obliged to withdraw from the city, because the people would not tolerate him; and long afterwards when he attempted to get possession of a church on the other side of the Tiber, he was again driven out. He lived eight years from that time without being able to set foot in Rome;

but after his death (November 22nd, 365) Liberius pardoned the clergy of his party, and allowed them to resume their position.[1]

Nothing is told us of Liberius own position. He appears not to have retracted what he did at Berœa and Sirmio, and not to have ceased to hold communion with the Arians; otherwise Constantius would not have allowed him to remain long in Rome. The synod of Rimini however, towards the end of the year 359, and in the year 360, gave him an opportunity of proving his orthodoxy. He rejected the synod, and ordered that those who had taken part in it should be admitted to communion only on condition of retracting; and it was he who, in the year 366, demanded of the Semiarians an adhesion to the Homoüsion, which he had formerly rejected himself, as a *sine quâ non* of their being recognised by the Church. He might have been led astray at Sirmio, in that the misuse which Paul of Samosata, and Marcellus of Ancyra, and Photinus had made of the Homoüsion was represented to him as a just ground for refraining from using so double-edged a weapon as this word had proved, and for forbidding the employment of it; moreover, they had held up to

---

[1] Marcellini et Faustin. ad *libell. prec.* præf. Both these Roman priests were eye-witnesses, and Jerome confirms their statement.

him the authority of the synod of 269. When he assented to the *substantial likeness* of the Son to the Father, he might (like other otherwise good catholics of that time) have been convinced, that in the Godhead substantial equality and substantial likeness are necessarily equivalent. Thus much may, perhaps, be said in extenuation of his error; but it certainly gives no excuse for his rejection of Athanasius, or for his entering into communion with the leaders of the Arian party. He must however have made good this grievous error even before the synod of Rimini was held (359). Without doubt events since 358 had taught him that that dogmatic word was indeed quite indispensable for the Church; that it, as he says in his epistle to the bishops of the East, in the year 366, was "the sure and impregnable bulwark, against "which all attacks and stratagems of Arianism shat- "tered." [1]

Liberius, therefore, at no time in his life was actually heretical; but his eagerness to see himself freed from the sufferings of a lonely exile and restored to the bosom of his people, who loved and honoured him, blinded him. He sacrificed the Church to the Arians, he perplexed the consciences of his people in regard to Church matters, and one knows, of course,

---

[1] In Coustant, *Epp. Rom. Pontiff*, p. 460.

that Hilary anathematized him. But he remained throughout the rightful bishop of Rome; and his opponent, Felix, was and remained an illegitimate intruder, in respect to the Arian trouble still more culpable than Liberius. For Felix received violent handling from no one, and obtained and kept his position only by getting himself ordained by Arians, and by ensuring them communion; especially the court bishops, and those who hung about the emperor. Whereas Liberius did not succumb to the ill usage to which he was subjected until after several years of steadfast endurance.

At the death of Liberius, in the year 366, the split which the intrusion of Felix and the secession of many of the clergy to him had called into existence, broke out afresh, this time with bloodshed. A numerous faction of the people, urged on by some of the clergy, wished to decree that none of those who, in violation of their oath, had recognised Felix ten years before, should succeed to the office of bishop. On this ground, Ursinus was set up in opposition to Damasus, who had been elected by a majority of the clergy. A regular civil war was the consequence. They fought in the streets and in the churches with such animosity, that on one occasion,[1] one hundred and thirty-seven dead bodies, mostly from the faction

---

[1] Ammian. Marcell., 1, 27, 3, 12.

of Ursinus, were found in the Sicinian basilica. Damasus himself could not restrain his own party; and only by the banishment of Ursinus and seven others of this faction, and by the strong measures of the prefect Juvencus, was some sort of order at length restored in the city. The supporters of Urşinus, however, continued their schism and their meetings in the cemeteries of the martyrs, which led to fresh bloodshed and fresh banishment of clergy belonging to this faction. Thus passed several years in perpetual disquietude; and thus from that violent act on the part of Constantius there grew so long afterwards the bitter fruit of a disturbance in the Church, which was not completely healed until a whole generation had died out.

It is very remarkable that the later myth or intentional fiction, which dates from the sixth or seventh century, has metamorphosed this history entirely to the disadvantage of Liberius, and in favour of Felix, who was dubbed an ecclesiastical hero and martyr. And it came to this; that this perjured antipope, consecrated by fanatical Arians, and intruded on the Romans only by the temporal power, was honoured as a saint, and reckoned in the list of the popes as pope Felix II.; while Liberius, even in Rome itself, was represented as a blood-stained tyrant, a heretic, and persecutor of the faithful.

One cannot fail to see that all this was invented with a view to placing the cause of that numerous portion of the Roman clergy who broke their oath and adhered to Felix, in a favourable light, and to represent them as the rightful party, who had withstood heresy and the heretical pope, and had been persecuted on that account. Nevertheless, these fictions must be assigned to a late period, the sixth or seventh century, as it would appear, when only hazy recollections of the events of the fourth century still survived in Rome, and when the story of the Roman baptism of Constantine, with its train of myths, had already disturbed all historic consciousness there, and had thrown into confusion the historical continuity and order of events. There are three documents in which the fictitious history was incorporated, and from which all later ones have been made: the biographies of Liberius and of Felix in the *Liber Pontificalis*, the *Acts of Felix*, first edited by Mombritius, and the *Acts of Eusebius*.[1]

These *Acts* have manifestly been invented with

---

[1] They are to be found in the Baluze-Mansi Collection, i., 33, and throughout the whole of the Middle Ages were constantly used and copied.

a view to branding the memory of Liberius, and representing him in the most glaring way as an heretical apostate and persecutor of the Catholic confessors, so that the party of Felix might appear as the oppressed orthodox. Hence the narrator makes pope Damasus condemn Liberius in a synod of twenty-eight bishops and twenty-five priests, immediately after Liberius' death. At the same time, also, this opportunity was seized, in order to give a fresh security against the contradicting testimony of antiquity to the story of the Roman baptism of Constantine,—the pet story of those by whom and for whom the invention was made. Hence the biography of Felix begins with a statement, made with affected precision, to the effect that he had declared the emperor Constantius, son of Constantine, a heretic, who had got himself baptized a second time by Eusebius, bishop of Nicomedia,[1] in the villa Aquila (Achyro), near to Nicomedia.

Here, then, what the father did is transferred to the son, and the intention in Constantine's case to put Rome in the place of Nicomedia, and Sylvester in the place of Eusebius, is unmistakeable.

The following narrative was substituted in place of

[1] In Vignoli, i., 119.

the true one in the two first-mentioned documents, which really hang together.

When Constantius banished Liberius on account of his defence of the Catholic faith, the Roman clergy elected and consecrated the presbyter [1] Felix as bishop,[2] under the advice and with the consent of Liberius. Felix forthwith holds a council of forty-eight bishops, and finds here that two presbyters,[3] Ursacius and Valens, agree with Constantius, and condemns them. The two persuade Constantius, and with his consent go to Liberius and offer him return from banishment on these terms :—that there should be communion between Arians and orthodox, but that the latter should not be required to be

---

[1] Felix was only a deacon. Rufinus, 2, 22; Marcellin. *Libell. Prec.* præf.

[2] This would only have been possible if Liberius had abdicated at the same time, which he did not do. That one bishop should appoint another co-ordinately with himself, or cause himself to be represented by another during his absence, was contrary to ecclesiastical law, especially to one of the Nicene canons. When after all Valerius, bishop of Hippo, did so, Augustine himself, whom he caused to be consecrated with the permission of the primate of Carthage, found that is was "contra morem ecclesiæ," and accordingly gave orders that at every ordination the canons should be read beforehand, in order that such a transgression might not occur again.—Possid. *Vit. Aug.*, c. 8.

[3] Both were bishops, Ursacius of Singidon in Mysia, Valens of Mursa in Pannonia, and had no relations whatever to the Roman Church. The main supporter of Arianism in the Roman territory was Epictetus, bishop of Circumcellæ.

re-baptized.[1] Liberius consents, comes back, and takes up his abode in the cemetery of St. Agnes with the emperor's sister, Constantia.[2] She is urged to gain admittance for him into Rome by intercession with her brother, but declines as a true catholic. Constantius, however, summons Liberius **to Rome** without the intervention of his sister by the advice of the Arians, gets together a council of heretics, and with its help deposes the catholic Felix **from his** episcopal[3] office. The very same day **a bloody** persecution commences, conducted by Constantius and Liberius in concert. The presbyter Eusebius (who distinguishes himself by his courage and catholic zeal, and gathers the people together in his house) reproaches the emperor and Liberius with their crime, declares to the latter that he is no longer in any way the rightful follower of Julius because he had fallen from the faith, and to both, that, in satanic blindness, they have driven out the catholic blameless Felix. Whereupon Constantius, by the advice **of** Liberius, has him shut up in a deep hole only four

---

[1] There was no discussion about re-baptism at that time, or for a long time afterwards. The Arians **before** Eunomius considered catholic baptism to **be** valid.

[2] A confusion with the sister of Constantine the Great.

[3] **All this time, and so** long as Liberius was in office there, Constantius was **not in** Rome. The narrative, however, gives one to understand that he lived there regularly.

feet broad, in which he is found dead at the end of seven months. The presbyters, Gregory and Orosius, relations of Eusebius, bury him; upon which the emperor gives orders to **shut** up Gregory **alive** in the same vault in which they had placed the corpse of Eusebius. Orosius drags him out from the vault by night half dead; he dies, however, in his arms, whereupon the other, Orosius, records the whole history. **Felix, who had reproached** the emperor with **his re-baptism, is** beheaded by the emperor's **command.** The persecution rages in Rome until the **death of Liberius.** Constantius publishes an edict **that every one who** does not join Liberius shall **be executed** without trial. Clergy and laity are now murdered in the streets and in the churches. At last Liberius dies, and **Damasus** brands his memory with infamy in a synod.

The description in the *Acts of Eusebius* is considerably more highly coloured than the representation in the *Liber Pontificalis*, where the circumstances are toned down somewhat; but the object in view, viz., to quash Liberius and make him appear as Constantius' companion in guilt, shines through it all from beginning to end. That the acts of Eusebius were composed in the interest of the antipope Felix, has been already remarked by

Cavalcanti.[1] It appears to me that there was another object joined with this, viz., to place the bloody scenes, which occurred in consequence of the divided election of Ursinus and Damasus, and which may have left behind them a misty recollection even two centuries later in Rome, in a light more favourable to the clergy of the time; and, by this means, the events were ante-dated by two years, and represented as persecutions of the staunch catholic clergy by the two Arians, the pope and the emperor. And they even went so far in their rejection of Liberius and efforts to put Felix in his place, that in the chronological notices of the Liberian basilica, built by that very pope, they passed Liberius over altogether, and placed Felix alone between Julius and Damasus.

Thus, then, Felix was gradually thrust into the lists of the popes, the liturgies, and martyrologies, as rightful pope and a holy martyr; not, however, until a late date, and, as regards the martyrologies, only slowly. Optatus and Augustinus had passed him over in their lists of the bishops of Rome. The twenty-ninth of July was the day which had been dedicated to his memory. But here, when the calendars and martyrologies were examined and compared, the deception became palpably manifest,

[1] *Vindiciæ Rom. Pontiff.*

and showed that the **Felix** there celebrated was quite a different one; and that not until the eighth century, after the false legends about Felix and Eusebius had been forged, did it occur to people to declare that this Felix was the rival of Liberius. The oldest document as yet known is the **Roman** calendar, which Martene has published in the fifth volume of his *Thesaurus*. He assigns it to the beginning of the fifth century; and rightly, for, with a single exception (Sylvester), it contains festivals of martyrs only, and Sylvester is the latest of the saints mentioned in it. Hence Damasus, though canonised at an early date, is wanting. Here, then, the twenty-eighth of July was marked as [1] **natalis s. Felicis, Simplicii,** Faustini, et Beatricis. In all other cases the designation "papa" is added to the names of the popes in this calendar. Several martyrologies, which bear the name of St. Jerome, and, [2] judging from their chief contents, belong to the fifth century (the period before Cassiodorus), agree with this. That of Bede likewise, without mentioning Rome. Then the *Martyrologium Ottobonianum* of the tenth, and the *Kalendarium Laureshamense* [3]

---

[1] So also the *Sacramentarium Gregorianum*. Elsewhere it is always the twenty-ninth.

[2] In Martene, *Thes.* iii., 1558.

[3] Both in Giorgi's edition of Ado, p. 683, 692.

of the end of the ninth century. On the other hand, that of St. Jerome in D'Achery separates Felix from the three others which manifestly belong to Rome, and transfers [1] him to Africa. The Vatican calendar itself, of the beginning of the eleventh century, [2] agrees also with this. But how Felix got transferred from Africa to Rome is explained by a martyrology of Auxerre, which falls well into the end of the ninth century (the latest of the numerous popes mentioned in it is Zacharias), (741-752) and is especially rich in Roman material, and accurate in local notices; so that there can be no doubt as to its Roman origin. This is what it says at the twenty-ninth of July :—" Romæ via Aurelia translatio "corporis beati Felicis episcopi et martyris qui iv. "idus Novembris martyrio coronatus est. Eodem "die ss. mm. Simplicii, Faustinii et s. Beatricis m. "sororis eorum." [3] It appears, therefore, that the bones of the African martyr, Felix, were brought to Rome, and that only on account of this translation, which took place on the twenty-ninth of July, Felix was joined with the Roman martyrs Simplicius, Faustinus, and Beatrix, to whom this day was

---

1 *Spicileg.*, ii., 15, nov. ed.
2 In Giorgi, p. 699.
3 In Martene, *Coll. Ampl.*, vi., 712.

already dedicated. Thus there are other martyrologies and missals, in which Felix is not found, but only the three others. In the so-called *Sacramentarium* of Gelasius he is wanting also, although Simplicius, Faustinus, and Viatrix (or Beatrix) are celebrated.[1] In the later Gregorian *Sacramentarium*, on the other hand, the day is given as the birthday of the four saints, but in such a way that in the Oratio Felix alone is celebrated, and that as "martyr et "pontifex." In the martyrology of the year 826,[2] found at Corbie, as well as in the *Martyrologium Morbacense*, and in the *Calendarium Anglicanum*, only Simplicius, Faustinus, and Beatrix are mentioned.[3] Most of them simply mention Felix without further designation, along with the other three; or, like the Neapolitan of the ninth century, say[4] "Felicis "et Simplicii;" or, "in Africa Felicis," &c., as the calendar of Stablo.

With the eighth century, however, begins, on the other hand, the line of calendars and martyrologies which make Felix a pope, and of course mean one to

[1] In Muratori, *Liturgia Romana Vetus*, i., 659; ii., 106.
[2] D'Achery, *Spicil.*, ii., 66.
[3] The *Calendarium Anglicanum* (of the year 1000) in Martene Coll. ampl, vi., 655. The *Martyrologium Morbacense* in Martene, *Thesaur.*, iii., 1570.
[2] In Mai. *Coll.*, v., 63.

understand the antipope of A.D. 356. The first is the Roman calendar of the middle of the eighth century, edited by Fronto.[1] **Next to** this comes the martyrology which Rosweyde was **the first to print**; which, however, is not a Roman one, as the editor and the Bollandists have stated.[2] **It already** contains the fable of Felix's martyrdom under Constantius. It is from this source, or **from the** legends, or from **the** book **of the** popes, that Ado has drawn; and the subsequent martyrologists for the most **part have** copied **him.** Usuard, Notker, Rabanus, Wandelbert, follow in the same track.

St. Eusebius, celebrated on the fourteenth of August, is found in almost all calendars and martyrologies, with the exception of the oldest, which belongs to the fifth century. This one, however, mentions the church of St. Eusebius as already existing in Rome, because here was a "statio" on the Friday in the fourth week of Lent. In the martyrologies of St. Jerome, and in that of Bede, one reads at the fourteenth of August, "Eusebii tituli conditoris." From which it appears that his festival in the first instance was celebrated only in the church which he had built,

---

[1] *Epistolæ et Dissert. Eccles.*, ed. Veron, 1733, p. 185. Exaratum intra tempora Gregorii II. and III., according to Borgia, *De Cruce Vaticana*.

[2] See on this point argument of Fronto, l. c., p. 137.

thence passed into the Roman calendars, and from them into those of other countries. Nearer notices of him do not exist, and even from the sixth century and further were not to be found. Hence it was all the more easy for the intentional fiction, which aimed at distorting the history of Liberius and Felix, to make use of his name, and transform him into the hero of a tragedy, which should set forth the Arianism and cruelty of Liberius in strong colours.

Here, then, as in other cases, it was the *Liber Pontificalis* that created the new tradition, which has influenced chroniclers and the papal biographers. The glaring contradictions of the *Liber Pontificalis*, which resulted from the unthinking interpolations of later hands, were at that time not observed. In the biography of Liberius, which was correctly composed before any one thought of giving Felix a special biographical article, Felix dies peacefully (requievit in pace) on his own estate, on the first of August. On the other hand, in the article respecting him, a few lines farther on, he is beheaded with many clergy and laity, on the eleventh of November. The author of this article, in order that nothing should be wanting for Felix's papal dignity, wished to represent him also as the builder of a church, and so represents him as again building the very " Basilica in via Aurelia," which in the article on Felix the First (A.D. 269-275) had already been mentioned as Felix's work. All the following writers of papal history have therefore naturally followed this account:—Pseudo-Luitprand, Abbo of Fleury, the anonymous chronographer in Pez,[1] Martinus Polonus, Leo of Orvieto, Bernard Guidonis, Amalricus Augerii. Felix is set forth as the thirty-ninth rightful pope. The revelation of the secret, that Constantius had caused himself to be re-baptized by Eusebius of Nicomedia, costs him his life, and Liberius reigned for five years, as an Arian, and by his Arianism caused the martyrdom of many clergy and laity. Nevertheless, all that he did and ordered was declared null and void after his death by Damasus. Bernard Guidonis makes the addition of a martyrdom, which Eusebius is made to endure because he proclaimed Liberius to be a heretic.[2]

From that time onwards the theologians accommodated themselves to the prevailing view, especially in Rome itself. Who does not know, says the Roman presbyter Auxilius, the defender of Formosus, that Liberius gave his assent to the Arian heresy, and that at his instigation the most horrible abominations were practised?[3] And towards the middle of the twelfth

---

[1] *Thes. Anecd.*, i., p. 343. [2] In Mai, *Spicileg.*, vi., 60.
[3] *De Ordin.*, i., 25.

century Anselm, bishop of Havelberg, reproaches the Greeks, because Constantius had caused Felix to be put to death for revealing the fact of his second baptism. But he makes excuses for Liberius, who no doubt had allowed much that was heretical, but had nevertheless steadfastly refused to allow himself to be re-baptized.[1]

The Abbot Hugo of Flavigny (1090–1102) goes a step farther in his chronicle; he makes Liberius also receive baptism a second time as a thorough[2] Arian. Eccard, in his most influential chronicle,[3] Romuald of Salerno, the papal historian Tolomeo of Lucca, the *Eulogium* of the monk of Malmesburg, all follow the usual fabulous tradition, that Liberius remained till the day of his death—six, or (according to Tolomeo[4]) eight years—persistently heretical, while Felix is the catholic martyr. Nevertheless, with Marianus Scotus, Gottfried of Viterbo, and Robert Abolant, the authority of Jerome is still so powerful, that they narrate how Felix was violently thrust into office by the Arians.

When at last the era of historical criticism and theological investigation came in with the sixteenth

---

2 *Dialog.*, iii., 21, in D'Achery, *Spicil.*, i., 207.
3 In Pertz, x., 301.
4 Pertz, viii., 113.
5 "Vixit in hoc errore annis octo."—Muratori, *SS. It.*, xi., p. 833.

century, no small amount of helplessness was exhibited. Hitherto Felix had been regarded as rightful pope, and the time of his pontificate was reckoned at a year and somewhat more. According to this view, Liberius would be deprived of his office by sentence of the church, on account of his lapse into Arianism, and then Felix came in as rightful pope, until at the end of a year he suffered martyrdom. Liberius, however, is said to have survived him by several years, and to have remained an Arian till his death. He could not therefore again become lawful pope after the death of Felix. Nor was the hypothesis of a vacancy of the see for several years either admissible or attempted. On the contrary, an interregnum of thirty-eight days is all that the *Liber Pontificalis* records after the death of Felix. This created a difficulty for the theologians, of which they did not know how to dispose, if Felix was to be retained in his position as pope and saint; and the historians could not deny the irreconcileable contradiction to all contemporary information. Cardinal Baronius had already composed a treatise to show that Felix was neither a saint nor a pope. Gregory XIII. had appointed a special congregation to decide the question. And then (1582) during some excavations under an altar dedicated to SS. Cosmo and Damian, a body was found with an inscription on stone—"Corpus S. Felicis Papæ et Martyris qui condemnavit Constantium." The stone with the inscription vanished again soon afterwards, and Schelstrate[1] laments that search was made for it in vain. The wording of the inscription in itself would have been quite sufficient to prove it at once to be the clumsy invention of a later age. But Baronius and the congregation thought otherwise; and so Felix kept his place as pope and martyr in the corrected Roman martyrology. Nevertheless, the place was[2] expunged from the subsequent editions of the older Roman breviaries, in which the martyrdom of Eusebius, for merely rebuking the Arianism of Liberius, was related in the words of Ado. Moreover in the Oratio of the breviary the designation of Felix as "pope" was removed. But even such a man as Bossuet could allow himself, on the strength of documents so palpably forged, to represent Liberius as an obstinate heretic and bloody persecutor of true[3] catholics. Still he contends against Baronius, who had accepted the wholesale persecution and butchery of the catholics in Rome under Liberius as a literal fact.

1 *Antiquit. Illustr.*, i.
2 See Launoi, *Epist.* 5, p. 41.
3 *Defens. Decl. Gall.*, p. 3, 1. 9, c. 33.

To complete it all, in the year 1790, a Roman ecclesiastic, Paul Anton Paoli,[1] undertook in a lengthy work to prove the legitimacy of Felix, and the authenticity of his sufferings and acts. He has succeeded, he says, in accomplishing the feat, hitherto considered an impossibility, of making *both* the rivals, Liberius and Felix, appear as innocent and guiltless, both of them together, as legitimate popes. All, according to him, rests upon misunderstandings and untrue reports. Athanasius, Hilary, Jerome, all their contemporaries, have been found to be in unintentional and unavoidable error. In Rome men were obliged to believe that the papal chair became vacant through Liberius' guilt, which, however, in reality was not the case, and hence Felix was elected. The Acts of Eusebius are genuine and contemporary. All the awkward statements which they contain are set aside by the convenient and never-failing resource of supposing them to be later interpolations. Moreover, the author has fortunately discovered that Felix lived concealed in the neighbourhood of Rome for thirty-four years after he was driven out of the city; although contemporaneous evidence makes him already dead in the year 365, and, although there was

---

[1] *Di San Felice Secondo Papa e Martire Dissertazzioni,* Roma, 1790. With a supplement of over 400 pages quarto.

no conceivable reason for his concealment, after the death of Constantius.

The whole is a structure of ill-conceived hypotheses and conjectures, which crumbles to dust at the first breath of sober historical investigation.

That Felix was never rightful bishop of Rome, but a mere tool of the Arians, foisted upon the people, and successfully rejected by them, has been admitted by all the better ecclesiastical historians, Panvinius, Lupus, Hermant, Tillemont, Natalis Alexander, Fleury, Baillet, Coutant, Ceillier. In Rome itself cardinal Orsi [1] has let his own view, which agrees with theirs, shine through, partly by a meaning silence, partly by the appellation "antipope," which he gives to Felix, though he only mentions him once in passing. Saccarelli [2] has shown, quite decisively and with correct judgment, that it is historically necessary to strike out Felix from the list of Roman bishops. Saccarelli's contemporary, the Augustinian monk Berti, in one of his treatises on ecclesiastical history, has stated the reasons usually given for and against Felix having a place in the list of the popes in such a way, that he makes one sensible of the weakness of the *former;* and then [3] adds, as if by way of a joke,

[1] *Istori. Eccles.*, vi , 201, ed. in 12mo.
[2] *Hist. Eccles.*, v., 334. Rome, 1777.
[3] " Hæret, ut aiunt, in aqua: neque enim tarditate ingenioli mei

that he does not venture to decide. Later on, three other Roman authors, Novaes, Sangallo, and Palma, the two first in their biographies of the popes, the last in his ecclesiastical history, have given up the case[1] of Felix as untenable.[2]

"percipere possum, quomodo, sedente Liberio, Felix verus Pontifex "sit habendus," etc.—*Historia Eccles. s. Dissert. hist.*, iii., 466, Aug. 1761. This reluctance to speak his meaning openly is easily explained by the fact, that cardinal Lambertini (afterwards pope Benedict XIV.) in his work *De Canoniz. Sanctorum*, 1, 4, p. 2. c. 27, 14, had just maintained, to the no small astonishment of all who were acquainted with ecclesiastical antiquity, "De S. Felicis II. "sanctitate et martyrio nullam amplius superesse dubitationem, sed "disputari ab eruditis duntaxat de qualitate rationeque martyrii." When therefore cardinal Borgia, in his *Apologia del Pontificato Benedetto X.*, says, "passa quasi per dimostrata a legittimità del ponti- "ficato di St. Felice per quelli che suppongono la caduta di Liberio," he is stating what is manifestly incorrect.

1 Novaes, *Elementi della Storia de' Sommi Pontefici*, Roma, 1821, 1, 128; Sangallo, *Gest. de' Pontef.*, iii., 496; Palma, *Prælectiones Hist. Eccles.* ii., 129.

2 [In the busts of the popes in the cathedral at Sienna the bust of Pope Joan has been transformed into pope Zacharias. (See p. 30.) Felix, however, retains his place there to this day.]

VII. ANASTASIUS II.

DANTE sees in hell, in the circle of false teachers and their followers, the cover of a large tomb, with an inscription stating that this tomb contains pope [1] Anastasius,

> "Whom out of the right way Photinus drew."

Now, it must always be a matter for astonishment that the great poet, when it occurred to him to represent a pope as suffering the fate of a heretic, should have chosen precisely this one, one of the least known in the Roman list. One would have thought

---

[1] *Inf.* xi., 9.

> [E quivi per l' orribile soperchio
> Del puzzo, che 'l profondo abisso gitta
> Ci raccostammo dietro ad un coperchio
> D'un grand' avello, ov' io vidi una scritta,
> Che diceva : "Anastagio Papa guardo,
> Lo qual trasse Fotino della via dritta"—xi., 4-9.
>
> And there by reason of the horrible
> Excess of stench the deep abyss throws out,
> We drew ourselves aside behind the cover
> Of a great tomb, whereon I saw a writing,
> Which said : "Pope Anastasius I hold,
> Whom out of the right way Photinus drew."
>
> Longfellow's Translation.

"The commentators are not agreed concerning the person who is "here mentioned as a follower of the heretical Photinus. By some "he is supposed to have been Anastasius II.; by others, IV.; while a

ANASTASIUS II.

that Liberius or Honorius would have been much more ready to his hand for this purpose, the first especially, who, **according to** the account which prevailed everywhere in the Middle Ages, ruled at Rome for several years before his death as a notorious Arian, so that, as was supposed, ardent catholics died as martyrs because of him.

It was Gratian's *Decretum* which, directly **or** indirectly, determined the Florentine poet **in his** choice. That is to say, Gratian, according **to the** precedent of the Ivonian decretal, inserted a passage from the Pontifical[1] book, in which it is said that

> "third set, jealous of the integrity of the papal faith, contend that
> "our poet has confounded him **with** Anastasius I., emperor of the
> "**East.** Fazio degli Uberti, like **our** author, makes him a pope:—
>> "Anastasio papa in quel tempo era
>> "Di Fotin vago a mal grado de sui,—*Dittamondo*, ii., 14."
>
> Cary's note **in loco.**
>
> Those who **would save the** pope at the expense of the emperor say that Photinus died before the time of pope Anastasius **II. Both** pope and emperor were called heretical **out** of respect **to the** memory of Acacius. But the emperor need not be considered **here.** Dante probably knew what he meant, **and** when he says **pope,** means pope, and not emperor.]

1 *Decret.*, i., dist. 19, 9. [Gratian's *Decretum* appeared at Bologna, the first school of law in Europe, **about** 1150. It combined the Isidorian forgeries with those of Deusdedit, Anselm, Gregory of Pavia, and Gratian **himself.** It displaced all the older collections of canon law, and became the usual manual **for canonists and theolo-** gians. No book has ever had such influence in the Church, although **it** teems with errors, both intentional and unintentional. For further particulars, **see** Janus, *Der Papst und das Concil*, iii., p. 154-162.]

many persons in Rome separated themselves from the company of Pope Anastasius, because he had entered into church communion with the deacon Photinus of Thessalonica, and intended secretly to bring Acacius again into honour in the Church. For which reason God had punished him with sudden death. Throughout the Middle Ages Gratian's *Decretum*[1] was accounted a decisive authority; it did not readily occur to any one to doubt the facts and doctrines stated in it; and hence it comes to pass that the memory of pope Anastasius II. has come down to posterity as that of a man prone to heresy, from whose communion in the Church it was right to withdraw oneself, pope though he was; and only by his sudden death was still greater mischief warded off from the Church. Now what was there to justify this view?

The Byzantine emperors were perpetually finding themselves impelled by the political condition of the empire to endeavour to reconcile the powerful party of the Monophysites to the Church, and thus heal, not merely an ecclesiastical, but also a political disorder, and ward off the grave danger which was

---

1 [It became *comparatively* obsolete after Gregory IX. caused the five books of Decretals to be published by Raimond de Pennafort in 1234. It was, in fact, insufficient for the increasing usurpations of the popes.]

threatening the State. **With** this object, the emperor Zeno, advised by Acacius, patriarch of Constantinople, had published the *Henoticon* (482), **which** declared the binding authority **and dogmatic decisions of** the **council** of Chalcedon, so hateful **to all** Monophysites, **to be** an open question. This ended in **pope Felix II. calling a** synod, **and** declaring **Acacius anathema.** Acacius **himself certainly** remained **all the while** catholic in his doctrine, **but he sacrificed the council** of Chalcedon for the **sake of peace**, and **entered into** church communion with all Monophysites who had accepted the *Henoticon*. Acacius had almost the whole East on his side, and as Rome broke off from **every one who remained in communion** with Acacius, a schism in the Church between East and West for thirty-five years was the consequence.

The successors **of** Acacius were **bidden to strike** his name off the **diptychs as** one who **had died under** excommunication; **and the popes Felix** and **Gelasius** demanded this as a condition of communion. **This, however, the** patriarchs dared **not do,** for **fear of a popular commotion; and** Rome **would not give** way, **although** Gelasius himself confessed **that** the **expectation, that the** Orientals would **prefer communion with the See of Rome to** every **other consideration, had proved**[1] **a delusion.**

[1] *Concilia*, ed. Labbé, iv., 1173.

The separation had lasted already eleven years, when pope Anastasius ascended the papal throne. He had peace with the Eastern Church more at heart than his two predecessors had had. He did, therefore, what Gelasius had refused to do, even at the request of the patriarch Euphemius; he sent two bishops as his legates to Constantinople, still, however, contending that the name of Acacius must no more be mentioned at the altar. In a contemporaneous Roman fragment mention is made of the letter which the pope sent at the time to the emperor. The reader will thence see on what worthless grounds the still continuing schism between the East and the West [1] rested. At this point Photinus arrived in Rome, a man who seems to have been active in ecclesiastical negotiations, and who probably had received a commission from the Orientals to win the pope over to the cause of union. Anastasius admitted him to communion, although from the Roman point of view he belonged to the schismatical party, that is to say, remained in alliance with those who honoured the memory of Acacius. And the pope showed himself [2] ready to give way in

---

[1] In Blanchini, *Notæ Varior. ad Anastas.* iii., 209.
[2] The expression of the biographer in the Pontifical book, "occulte "voluit revocare Acacium," is to be understood of the re-insertion of his name in the diptychs. "Id nonnisi de illius nomine sacris "diptychis restituendo intelligi potest," says Vignoli (*Liber. Pontif.*,

the question of mentioning Acacius name at the altar, and thus renounce the haughty bearing which, as exemplified in the conduct of his predecessors,

1, 171) quite rightly. Cardinal Mai, following in the track of many others (Baronius, Bellarmine, Sommier, &c.), says in his note to Bernard Guidonis (*Spicil.*, vi., 98), that the statement in the Pontifical book cannot be true; Anastasius cannot have cherished the intention of securing for the name of Acacius mention in the liturgy, because he, like his predecessors, in the letter which he sent to the emperor immediately after his promotion to the papacy, had demanded that this name should be suppressed. But, in matters of history, it can scarcely be thought possible to build on such weak arguments. Certainly Anastasius *did* do this in the first few weeks of his pontificate, on entering upon the heritage of his predecessors. But what can be more natural than that a peace-loving pope, having become convinced of the impracticability of his own hard requisition, one which shocked the feelings of millions [nearly the whole East remained true to Acacius], should have shown a disposition to renounce a demand, with the surrender of which not a single essential principle of church discipline was surrendered. If it was possible in the case of a man, who for a hundred and thirty years after his death had remained in the enjoyment of church communion and intercession (Theodore of Mopsuestia), at last to expel him, when men became convinced of the fundamental heterodoxy of his writings, it surely was possible, in the case of a bishop, who had always acknowledged catholic dogma, and had only erred in a formal way, and under very extenuating circumstances, to release him after his death from the anathema which had been pronounced on him, when on this act of clemency depended the well-being and peace of the whole Church.

[The anathema against Acacius was pronounced by Felix in an unusually strong form. It was declared to be irreversible by any power, even by Felix himself: "Nunquamque anathematis vinculis "eruendus."—*Epist. Felic. ad Acacium.* In a subsequent letter to Zeno, Felix maintains this inexorable position : " Unde divino judicio " nullatenus potuit, *etiam quum id mallemus,* absolvi."—*Epist.* xi. Writing to Fravitta, who succeeded Acacius in a brief patriarchate of four months, Felix intimates that Acacius is doubtless with Judas in hell. But the anathema was almost a *brutum fulmen* in the East. Acacius maintained his patriarchate till his death, and the other three patriarchs of Antioch, Alexandria, and Jerusalem remained in communion with him.—Milman's *Latin Christianity,* bk. iii., c. i.]

had given such offence to the East. But in Rome, where it was considered a duty and point of honour not to depart from the path of Felix and Gelasius, this excited great displeasure; and it came to a formal separation from Anastasius, for being willing to sacrifice the righteous cause of the Roman See, the authority of his predecessors, and the validity of the Chalcedonian decrees for the sake of an insecure peace. The premature and unexpected death of the pope at this position of affairs was regarded by those who had separated from him as a providential deliverance of the Church from very great danger.

The later commentators on Dante—Poggiali, Lombardi, and Tommaseo—think that Dante, misled by Martinus Polonus, has confused pope Anastasius with the emperor, his contemporary and namesake. This, as one sees, is not the case.[1] Philalethes also thinks that, as Acacius had already been dead some time, the whole story rests on an error; that is to say, he supposes that the author of the Pontifical book means one to understand the still-living Acacius, because he makes use of the expression (explained in the note) "to recall" [revocare Acacium]. There is, however, no necessity for this adoption of a glaring anachronism. It is

---

1 *Dante's Divine Comedy*, Dresden, 1839, 1., 69. [by the King of Saxony.]

certainly a disfiguring blot in Dante's sublime creation that he has placed an innocent and doctrinally blameless pope, whose desire for peace would have been accounted as a high merit in another age, in hell with the eternally lost heretics. But the error, into which the greatest of Christian poets thus fell, lay not in the historical fact, but in the judgment respecting the fact; and this erroneous judgment Dante shared with his contemporaries, and with the Middle Ages generally.

In the Pontifical book it is stated, that Anastasius was not able to accomplish his intention with regard to Acacius,[1] because death overtook him as a judgment from heaven. This statement is not sufficient for the chroniclers of the thirteenth and fourteenth centuries. The catastrophe must be more distinctly

---

[1] Cardinal Mai also, following in the steps of Bellarmine, Baronius, and Novaes, maintains that the author of the *Liber Pontificalis* would lead one to suppose that the pope was struck by lightning, and that this was a confusion with the emperor Anastasius, who had met with this kind of death. Entirely without foundation. The Pontifical book does not say one word about lightning. Nothing more than this is conveyed in what it says: that the pope, owing to his opportune, and, as it were, divinely-sent death, was prevented from carrying out his ruinous intention. And that the emperor of like name was killed by a flash of lightning is a late fable, unknown to his contemporaries or to the next generation, and at the time when the biography of pope Anastasius was written, was not invented.—Conf. Tillemont, *Hist. des Empereurs*, vi., 585.

marked, and the fate which overtook the heretical pope must be such as to excite horror and disgust. They transferred, therefore, the story of the sudden death of Arius to Anastasius. He had gone aside to satisfy a call of nature, and was found afterwards with his intestines out. So Martinus Polonus, Amalrich Augerii, Bernard Guidonis.[1] Dante's commentators in the fourteenth century have followed them. According to them Acacius is the associate (compagno) of Photinus, and canon of Thessalonica; but Photinus seduced the pope into denying the divinity of Christ. A great disputation between the pope and the cardinals, bishops, and prelates, who rebuked him for his false doctrine,[2] precedes the catastrophe. The gloss to the *Decretum* makes the pope struck with leprosy.

[1] The papal biographer, Du Peyrat, on the contrary, contents himself with saying, "Anastasius damnatus est et reprobatus,"—*Notices et extraits*, vi. [Anastasius, the Librarian (*Patrol.* cxxviii., 439), says that the pope, in punishment for his error, "nutu divino "percussus est."—Robertson, *Hist. of the Christian Church*, i., p. 527.]

[2] So the "false Boccaccio," or the *Chiose sopra Dante*, composed in 1375, Florence, 1846, p. 87, and the Latin commentary published by Nannucci under the name of Petrus Allegherius, Florent., 1845, p. 137; and then the *Ottimo Commento*, p. 199, which confuses Photinus with the heterodox bishop of the fourth century. So also Francesco da Buti, *Commento*, i., 301. Where Graul (*Dante's Hölle*, p. 116) found the story that Anastasius denied the divine nature of Christ, I do not know.

It was Gratian therefore, mainly, who fixed the judgment of the Middle Ages respecting Anastasius. This pope,[1] he says, is rejected by the Church of Rome. So says also the anonymous writer of Zwetl in his History of the Popes. "The Church [2] rejects "him and God smote him." The gloss adds that two popes, Gelasius and Hormisdas, excommunicated him. The fact that Gelasius was Anastasius' *predecessor* was overlooked.[3] But it was now hereby established, as a certain fact, that Anastasius was an heretical pope; and so he was henceforth usually quoted along with Liberius as a second instance of papal heresy. Since Gratian's time theologians were accustomed to appeal to the chapter "Anastasius" in the *Decretum* and to the gloss on it, when they discussed the question of heretical error in a pope, and of the conduct of the Church in such circumstances. The schoolman, Alger [4] of Liege (about A.D. 1150), must certainly have had other sources than Gratian before him when he asserted that pope Anastasius was condemned along with his Decree, because in it he

---

1 "Ideo ab Ecclesia Romana repudiatur."—*Distinc.*, 19, c. 8.
2 Ap. Pez, *Thesaur. Anecd.*, i., p. 3, 351.
3 [Felix II.,   A.D. 483   Symmachus, A D. 498
   Gelasius I.   "   492   Hormisdas   " 514.]
   Anastasius II.   "   496.
4 *Liber de Misericordia et Justitia*, c. 59. In Martene, *Thes. Anecd.*, v., 1127.

had declared that the baptisms and ordinations performed by Acacius after the sentence which had passed on him at Rome were valid. In this [1] he contradicted the decisions of his predecessors. Alger here agrees in the main with his contemporary Gratian. Gratian has quoted the declaration of Anastasius,—according to which the efficacy of sacraments is not dependent on the character of the dispenser, and, consequently, even the sacraments administered by a bishop who has lapsed into heresy are valid, and under proper conditions efficacious,—as an instance of a false decision in matters of faith given by a pope, respecting which the Roman correctors have since contradicted him. [2]

On the other hand, William of Saint-Amour (about

---

[2] Alger himself does not mean, as he afterwards explains, that the sacraments administered by Acacius were forthwith null and void. He distinguishes thus: "Quod vera, quamvis non rata pos-"sint esse sacramenta cujuslibet mali sacerdotis, vel hæretici, vel "damnati."—c. 83. But he fancies that Anastasius erroneously declared that the sacraments administered by Acacius were "rata." That is to say, he starts from the principle which certain short-sighted defenders of papal supremacy had already put forth, that a pope who became heretical, immediately, and before even he had in any way made known his heretical opinions, ceased to be pope, and hence all that he subsequently did was null and void. In which case the Church, which nevertheless, could not possibly do otherwise than recognize him all the while, would find itself in unavoidable error.

[1] *Decret. distinc.*, 19, c. 7, 8.

A.D. 1245) confuses Anastasius with Liberius. He knows nothing more than that in the time of Hilary, a pope lapsed into heresy, of whom it is recorded "nutu divino fuit percussus;" and he conjectures[1] that this may have been Anastasius II., mentioned by Gratian.

Alvaro Pelayo, who, next to Augustine of Ancona, furthered the aggrandisement of the papal power, with the greatest zeal, beyond all previous bounds, and almost beyond all limits whatever, in his great work on the condition of the Church, makes mention of the judgment[2] which came upon Anastasius, in order to prove his dictum, that a heretical pope must receive a far heavier sentence than any other. Occam,[3] also, makes use of the "heretical" Anastasius as an instance to prove, what was his main point, that the Church erred by his recognition. The council of Basle in like manner, with a view to establishing the necessary supremacy of an œcumenical council over the pope, did not fail to appeal to the fact, that popes who did not obey the Church were treated by her as heathens and publicans, as one reads of Liberius and Anastasius.[1]

---

2 *Opera.* ed. Cordes, Constantiæ (Parisiis), 1632, p. 96.
3 "Divino judicio percussus fuit, nam dum assellaret intestina emisit."—*De Planctu Ecclesiæ*, 2, 10, Venetiis, 1560, ii., 38.
4 *Opus Nonaginta Dierum.*, Lugd., 1495, f. 124.
1 In Harduin, viii., 1327.

"The pope," says Domenicus dei Domenici, bishop of Torcello, somewhat later, in a letter addressed to pope Calixtus III. (1455–1458), "the pope by himself "alone is not an infallible rule of faith, for some popes "have erred in faith, as, for example, Liberius and "Anastasius II., and the latter was in consequence "punished by God."[1] After him the Belgian John le Maire, also, says (about 1515), Liberius and Anastasius are the two popes of ancient times, who, subsequent to the Donation of Constantine, obtained an infamous reputation in the Church as heretics.[2]

[1] *De Cardinalium Legit. Creat. Tract.*, in M. A. de Dominis, *De Republ. Eccl*, Londini, 1617, i., 767 ss.
[2] "In hæresin prolapsus est, et reputatur pro secundo Papa infami "post donationem Constantini."—*De Schismatum et Concil. Differ.* Argentor, 1609, p. 594.

VIII. THE CASE OF HONORIUS.[1]

WHILST Anastasius, most undeservedly, was counted as a heretic, the memory of Honorius, on the other hand, was held in honour; and the fact that a general council had pronounced an anathema on this pope for holding heterodox opinions and countenancing heresy, was in the Middle Ages usually ignored. The circumstances were as follows: The Monothelite heresy was a dangerous and unhappy attempt to reunite the Monophysites with the Church by means of a very comprehensive concession, devised and introduced into the Church, by certain Oriental prelates, who herein had probably an understanding with the emperor Heraclius, and were acting in accordance with his wishes. The point of difference was this: the council of Chalcedon had declared that the two natures in Christ are united without any confusion or changing of one into the other; there must, therefore, be also a duality of wills, and a human and a divine will be distinguished in Christ. The Monophysites,

[1] [On this case see a translation of Bishop von Hefele's essay on Honorius, with notes, by H. B. Smith, in the *Presbyterian Quarterly and Princeton Review*, New York, April, 1872.]

on their side consistent, made the human will vanish in the presence of the divine, allowing to the Logos alone in Christ the full exercise of the power of volition. The Monothelites, who had formed themselves into a middle party, having for its object the reconciliation of the Monophysites with the Church, on this point agreed with the latter; and thus Cyrus, in Alexandria, brought about a union between the followers of Severus there and the Catholics. Sergius, patriarch of Constantinople, who had an understanding with Cyrus, sought and obtained the assent of pope Honorius against the opposition raised by Sophronius. The manner in which the pope and the two patriarchs of Constantinople and Alexandria held essentially the same view, was this: Honorius had declared, quite in the sense of the other two, that the two decisive texts, in which the human and created will is most clearly distinguished from and opposed to the divine will of the Logos, are merely an "economy" in Christ's mode of speaking, that is to say, an accommodation to be taken only in a figurative sense, by means of which Christ merely intended to exhort us to submit our own wills to the divine will. He was compelled therefore, equally with the Orientals, to recognize only a single will in Christ, the divine or theandric, that is, a will having its source in the Logos, and, as it were, merely *flowing through* the human nature—a will in which merely the Logos is the willing power and active principle, while the human nature is purely passive; so that its power of volition is either non-existent, or, at any rate, quiescent. And this he said in so many words: "We recognise," he says, conceding the point to Sergius, but expressing himself with more decision than Sergius, "we recognise "one will in Christ." And thereupon Honorius, like the Monothelites of the East, troubled himself with the notion, that a human will, as belonging to man's sinful nature, must always strive against the Divine; whereas the idea was not far to seek, that the human will, having its root in the sinless nature of Christ, conformed to the divine will, so that a moral unity co-existed with an actual duality of will.

On the other hand, Honorius, taking the word "energy" (i. e. mode of operation), which had been used by the Greeks, in a sense altogether different from theirs, gave as his decision, that one ought not to speak either of one or of two energies; for that Christ, by virtue of His one theandric will, showed many modes of operation and activity. Therefore there is unity of will, says Honorius, for it is the Person that wills, and not the natures, and there is multiplicity (not unity, nor duality) of energies or modes of operation. In this way, then, Honorius would have the controversy put down; viz., that it was preposterous to contest about one or two energies in Christ, because neither the one nor the other expression could be used in a rational sense. At the same time, however, it was set forth that all men should be united in the acceptance of a single power of volition. The emperor Constantine stated subsequently in his edict, that Honorius had not only taught a false doctrine, but also contradicted himself, merely because he, being used to the oriental terminology, did not understand the sense in which Honorius used the word "energy." Honorius meant by it, *manifestations of activity in the Person*, which are many and various. But the emperor understood by it, *modes of operation in the natures*, of which there must be two, or (according to the Monothelites) on account of the unity of will, only one.

This doctrine of Honorius, so welcome to Sergius and the remaining favourers and supporters of Monothelitism, led to the two imperial edicts, the *Ecthesis* and *Typus*. It led to them to this extent, that Heraclius was thereby justified in concluding that the Roman See would not oppose such a doctrinal decree as the *Ecthesis*; and the *Typus* of Constans was nothing more than a weaker echo of the *Ecthesis*. The result, however, was different from what had been hoped at Constantinople. The whole East rose up in arms against the new doctrine, and it forthwith became evident that Honorius, with his mode of understanding the question, stood alone in Rome and in the West. For some time efforts were made to excuse Honorius. Pope John IV. (A.D. 640-642) stated in his[1] apology that his predecessor had merely rejected the fond notion of two *mutually opposing* wills; as if, that is to say, Christ had a will tainted with sin. No doubt the fear, that in admitting the double will one would be irresistibly driven on to accept two mutually opposing wills, was a very considerable element in the declaration of Honorius; only it remains a riddle how a man, who certainly had no Monophysite tendencies, could allow himself to be influenced by so unfounded an apprehension. The excuse which Maximus, appealing to the statement of the papal secretary, brings forward for Honorius is still more forced and untenable. Honorius, he says, only

---

[1] Mansi, x., 683. [Severinus, the immediate successor of Honorius, had a brief pontificate of only three months; and appears to have rejected the Ecthesis. John IV. did so in solemn council. Heraclius thereupon wrote to the pope to disown the document, saying that he had only published it at the urgent request of Sergius.—Robertson, *Church History*, ii., 45.]

wished to guard against the supposition of two *human* and mutually[1] opposed wills. Manifestly the pope had never thought of any such absurdity. Rather his decision and the cause of his error may be briefly expressed thus: One Willer, therefore one will; for the will is the attribute of the Person, not of the natures.

Honorius had written again to Sergius to the same effect, as well as to Cyrus and Sophronius, and hence it was quite natural that he should come to be regarded as one of the supporters of Monothelitism. The patriarch Pyrrhus, successor of Sergius at Constantinople, had accordingly appealed to him and, at the Lateran synod in the year 649, the writings of the Monothelites, which claimed for themselves the authority of Honorius, were publicly read. No one there spoke a word in defence of Honorius. Complete silence was observed respecting him, although the five prelates who were accounted the originators and main supporters of the false doctrine—Theodore of Pharan, Cyrus of Alexandria, Sergius, Pyrrhus and Paul, patriarchs of Constantinople—were condemned by pope Martin and the synod.

At last came the decisive council of A.D. 680. And here took place what preceding events would lead

---

[1] Mansi, x., 687, 691, 739.

one to expect. Honorius, as partaker in the Monothelite heresy, was treated in the same way as the other prelates who had already been condemned at Rome, along with them was placed under anathema, and the council insisted upon cursing "the heretic Honorius" by name. He joined himself, it is stated in the decree, in all particulars to Sergius; he spread the heresy of the one will abroad among the people; he deserved to be placed under the same anathema as Sergius, for his dogmatic writings were completely opposed to the doctrine of the apostles and decisions of councils, tending towards the same godlessness as the writings of the most pronounced Monothelites. The emperor Constantine [IV., Pogonatus] in particular, who had taken a [1] very active part at the council, expressed himself to this effect in the letter which he wrote to the pope. And in the edict which was affixed to the great church of the capital, it was said of Honorius that in all points he was[2] to be treated like Sergius and Theodore, as "the companion and associate of

---

[1] [There were eighteen sessions, lasting from Nov. 7th, 680, to Sept. 16th, 681. The emperor presided in person at the first eleven sessions, and at the eighteenth. In his absence the president's chair was left empty. The number of bishops increased gradually to nearly two hundred.]

[2] Mansi, xi. 697-712. ["Qui fuit cum eis in omnibus cohæreticus " et concurrens et confirmator hæresis."—Harduin, iii, 1638.]

"heretics and the sanctioner of heresy." The council[1] itself, after subjecting the writings of Sergius and Honorius to a careful investigation, declared respecting the two men, "whose godless doctrine we "abominate," that "we deem it necessary to cast their "names out of the Church."

That it was the intention of the council to condemn Honorius for actual heresy, and not merely for weakness or negligence or imprudence in his mode of contending against heresy, there cannot be any doubt. And yet it is certain that he[2] was not heretical in the

---

1 ["Duas igitur in eo naturales voluntates (φυσικὰ θελήματα), et "duas naturales operationes (φυσικὰς ἐνεργείας), communiter atque "indivise procedentes prædicamus; superfluas autem vocum novi- "tates, et harum adinventores procul ab ecclesiasticis septis abjici- "mus, et anathemati merito subjicimus; id est, Theodorum Pharani- "tanum, Sergium et Paulum, Pyrrhum simul et Petrum, qui Con- "stantinopoleos præsulatum tenuerunt, insuper et Cyrum, qui "Alexandrinorum sacerdotium gessit, et cum eis Honorium, qui "fuit Romæ præsul, utpote qui eos in his secutus est."—Labbe, *Concil.*, vi., 1053; Harduin, *Concil*, iii., 1422.]

2 [See on this point the essay of Bishop of von Hefele, referred to above. He shows that Honorius taught heretical doctrine. He says, that "Honorius confounded the *energy*, or mode of working in itself, with its single manifestations.

"His words, bearing on this, read literally : 'It is not right to give the authority of ecclesiastical dogmas to opinions which do not seem to have been submitted to the examination of Synods, nor to have the authority of ecclesiastical canons ; as is the case with those who presume to predicate *one* energy or *two* energies of Christ, etc.' (*Mansi*, Collect. Concil. T. xi. p. 542.)

"And afterwards he says: 'For we have not learned from the

strict sense of the term; though assuredly it is equally clear that Cyrus, Sergius, Pyrrhus, and Paul were neither more heretical than Honorius, nor less so. The question at issue was one which had not been raised or discussed before, it then for the first time occupied men's minds; a question in which the danger of falling into one of two opposite errors— Nestorianism or Monophysitism—was very imminent. In such cases a certain amount of time and of controversy is always needed, in order that the consciousness of the Church may find its bearings and

Holy Scriptures that Jesus Christ and his Holy Spirit have one mode of operation, or two, although we have learned that He worked in manifold ways.' (*Mansi, ubi suprâ.*)

"And at the close: 'This, my brother, you will also preach as we do . . . and we exhort you, that, avoiding the new mode of operation, you proclaim with us one Lord Jesus Christ.' (*Mansi*, p. 543.)

"Honorius here not only rejects the *orthodox* technical term of *two energies*, but at the same time prescribes a *heretical* phrase as a rule of faith when he says: 'On this account we too confess *one will* (ἐν θέλημα) of our Lord Jesus Christ, since our nature but not our guilt was manifestly assumed by the divinity; and this nature, too, as it was created before sin and not as it was vitiated by the fall. That is, the corrupted nature was not assumed by the Saviour, for this would be repugnant to the law of the Spirit.' (*Mansi*, p. 539.)

"The result is that Honorius (*a.*) rejected the technical orthodox term of *two energies* (δύο ἐνέργειαι); (*b.*) and declared the specific heretical term, *one will* (ἐν θέλημα) to be correct; and (*c.*) prescribed this two-fold error as an article of faith, in this instance to the Church of Constantinople." *Presb. Quarterly*, April, 1872, p. 284, H. B. S.]

define itself. In the primitive Church the erroneous enunciations of individual bishops on questions which had not yet been decided and formulated by the Church were treated with gentleness and forbearance, especially if such men had died in communion and peace with the Church. But after the fifth great council at Constantinople (A.D. 553) had set the example in anathematising Theodore of Mopsuestia, —not merely his writings, but himself,—and the popes after some opposition had accepted this, and at last carried into effect through the whole West, the case was altogether altered. In the synod of 649 (First Lateran), five prelates had been condemned in Rome as Monothelites, among them three who were already dead. One of these was the patriarch of Constantinople, Paul II., who had written to pope Theodore to say that he followed the doctrine of Honorius, and who had thereupon accepted the *Typus* of the emperor Constans. The *Typus*, however, did not go so far as the letter of Honorius; for while this declared expressly for the doctrine of one will, the *Typus* merely commanded silence about the whole question. It was only natural and human that the Orientals assembled at the sixth council would not allow the reproach and disgrace of heresy to fall exclusively on the heads of their own patriarchs, but seized the opportunity, not altogether unwillingly, of making the patriarch of Old Rome, as he was then called, appear for once among the guilty. And the papal legates, who had just before made a protest respecting a charge of false teaching brought against pope Vigilius, could make neither formal nor material objection to the perfectly regular course taken in the case of Honorius; they were therefore obliged to join in voting for his condemnation. For even the inflexible Monothelites at the council, Macarius, patriarch of Antioch, the monk Stephen, and the two bishops of Nicomedia and Klaneus, had just before declared that they had promulgated no innovation, but merely the doctrine which they had learnt from Honorius and the patriarchs. The assembled Fathers had no alternative, but either to excuse all the six deceased originators and favourers of Monothelitism, or to condemn them all. The Lateran council had rendered the first course impossible; and the Roman legates would probably have protested against a decision which would have compelled the Western Church to make a sentence pronounced by itself in a large synod, of no effect. Hence the second course was all that remained.

The reception which the decree would meet with in old Rome might well be watched with anxiety in the new imperial city. A new and hitherto unheard of event had taken place. A pope had been condemned as heretical by an œcumenical council, and the Romans were required to strike out his name, which no one hitherto had thought of aspersing, from the intercessions of the Church. Pope Agatho had made an attempt to avert the threatening blow. Without mentioning his predecessor, he had in his letter given utterance to the general assurance, that the Roman See had never swerved from the path of apostolic tradition, never allowed itself to be tainted with heretical innovations. The council answered this with the counter-statement, that they had passed judgment upon the condemned theologians, Honorius included, in accordance with the sentence originally pronounced by Agatho. It was, however, precisely Honorius who had been passed over by Agatho in his letter.

Agatho meanwhile had died at Rome;[1] and the task of speaking out respecting the condemnation of Honorius fell on his successor, Leo II., who had translated the acts of the council from the Greek. Leo saw that both prudence and justice required him to recognise the judgment of the council, that an attempt still to draw a distinction between Honorius

[1] [January, 662, while his legates were still at Constantinople.]

and the Oriental bishops had no longer any prospect of success. He therefore sent an acknowledgment to the emperor, containing an express condemnation of Honorius, because,[1] "instead of enlightening the "Roman Church with apostolic doctrine, he had "surrendered its primitive spotlessness to be defiled "by an impious betrayal of the faith (profana per-"fidia)." This was going almost beyond what was warranted by historical fact. Honorius, as it happened, was the only person in Rome who cherished the doctrine laid down in his letter; nothing is known of any other convert which the Monothelite doctrine had made in Rome. However, in his letter to the Spanish bishops and king Erwig, Leo noticed the transgression of his predecessor in less strong expressions. According to this,[2] Honorius had merely allowed the pure doctrine to be falsified or tainted with error. He had merely been wanting in watch-

---

[1] ["Necnon Honorium, qui hanc apostolicam ecclesiam non apos-"tolicæ traditionis doctrina lustravit, sed profana proditione imma-"culatam fidem subvertere conatus est."—Harduin, *Concil.*, iii., 1475.]

[2] ["Cum Honorio, qui flammam hæretici dogmatis non, ut decuit "apostolicam auctoritatem, incipientem extinxit, sed negligendo "confovit."—*Epistola ad Episcopos Hispaniæ*. "Et una cum eis "Honorius Romanus, qui **immaculatam** apostolicæ traditionis re-"gulam quam a prædecessoribus suis suscepit, maculari consentit." —*Epistola ad* **Erviyium** *Regem Hispaniæ*, Ap. Harduin, *Concil.*, iii., 1730, 1735.]

fulness and foresight. In this, however, he altogether contradicted the declaration of Agatho, that all popes had done their duty with regard to false doctrine.

It was natural that the circumstance should be looked upon in Rome as a mortifying humiliation in their relation to the Byzantines. Nevertheless, after the decision of the council, no further attempt was made to withdraw the fact from notice, even in the West. On the contrary, as if it was desired to give it the greatest possible publicity, it was inserted in the confession of faith which every newly-elected pope had to sign. Thus it is found in the *Liber Diurnus*,[1] the official book of formulas of the Roman Church at that time, intended for the use of the papal curia. The sixth œcumenical council, at which pope Agatho presided in the person of his legates, is here noticed with explicitness of detail. Then follows, after an exposition of the doctrine of two wills, the condemnation of those who opposed the doctrine. Sergius, Pyrrhus, Paul, and Peter, the four patriarchs of Constantinople, together with Honorius, who assented to and promoted (fomentum impendit) their false doctrine, are anathematised together with Theodore and Cyrus.

All the more astonishing is it that the other official

[1] Ed. Garnerii, Paris, 1680, p. 41.

work of the **Roman** Church at that time, the Pontifical book, maintains an unmistakeable silence with anxious **care respecting all that concerns** the part taken by Honorius in the Monothelite **controversy** and his condemnation. And yet in other respects it contains **good** and contemporary **accounts of this period.** First under **the popes** Theodore **and Martin, the** appearance **of Pyrrhus in Rome, the dispute with Paul** about the *Typus*, the Lateran council of A.D. 649, and the tragical end of pope Martin, are all noticed. The biographer of Agatho in this collection evidently had the diary before him, which **was** kept by the papal legates sent to the council of A.D. 680. These legates, among whom [1] were three bishops, relate that **it** was they themselves who had challenged the Monothelites at **the** council **to** produce the **authority of** the Apostolic See, **to** which they appealed. [2] **Thereupon** the delighted Monothelites laid before the council **the** letter of pope Vigilius to Mennas. Investigation, however, showed that the passage **in** point had been interpolated. There is not a word about the fact that the Monothelites had above all appealed to Honorius, that the two letters of Honorius, both in Latin and

---

[1] [Abundantius, bishop of Paterneum, John, bishop **of** Portus, John, bishop of Rhegium, together with the sub-deacon Constantine, the presbyters Theodore and Gregory, and the deacon John.]

[2] *Liber Pontificalis*, i., 279, ed. Vignoli.

Greek, had been laid before the council, examined, and rejected as heretical. Either the legates suppressed all this, because they had received very different instructions from Agatho, which they found it impossible to follow at the council, or the compiler of this portion of the Pontifical book, in copying their diary, has omitted all that relates to Honorius. Seeing that the legates produced the acts of the council, and the canons which they themselves had signed, including the condemnation of Honorius, one would rather suppose that the latter alternative was the fact; the more so inasmuch as the compilation, or at any rate the last revision of this part of the Pontifical book, was probably conducted by Anastasius the librarian, who two hundred years after the event, in his letter to the Roman deacon John, took great pains to try and excuse Honorius. The contents of Honorius' letter he did not venture to justify, as later apologists [1] of this pope have done; but, he adds, we cannot be certain that the secretary did not possibly misunderstand the pope's dictation, or arbitrarily alter the words out of malevolence or caprice. He bethinks himself, however, that this

---

[1] [For example, the archbishops of Westminster and Baltimore in their recent pastoral letters. The archbishop of Malines also in his controversy with Père Gratry. See Appendix F.]

secretary was a very holy man, the abbot John; and now he directs his indignation against the sixth council itself, which, contrary to the command of scripture, had condemned a man who was voiceless and defenceless in his grave;—quite forgetting that the Roman synod of A.D. 649 had done precisely the same in the case of five prelates. The dogmatic decisions of the council were no doubt binding as a rule of faith; but just as the Roman See had rejected the twenty-eighth canon of the council of Chalcedon without detriment to the dogmatic authority of that assembly, so, he thinks, it is possible to reject also the sentence pronounced on Honorius. Did Anastasius not know what Leo II. had done, what stood written in the pope's confession of faith? The only thing in point which he produces is the remark, that no doubt the council condemned Honorius as a heretic, but that, properly speaking, no one could be called a heretic who did not add to his error contentious obstinacy (contentiosa pertinacia).

The silence in the biography of Agatho has nevertheless not prevented the biographer of Leo II., in the very same Pontifical book, from citing the name of Honorius under the head of those who were condemned by the sixth council as Monothelites; and as the lessons for St. Leo's day were taken word for word from this biography, the condemnation of Honorius has been transferred to the older versions of the Roman breviary, no doubt without the following point being observed.

In the East it was natural frequently to recur to the condemnation of Honorius, without, however, exactly calling attention to it as anything extraordinary and astonishing. The patriarchs Tarasius of Constantinople, and Theodore of Jerusalem, mentioned him at the time of the seventh council [1] (A.D. 787) under the head of those who were condemned for Monothelitism; so also the deacon Epiphanius. [2] It occurred to no one to make a difference between him and the other Monothelite leaders* who were condemned for heresy. Pope Hadrian II. specially remarked in the letter of his which appended to the acts of the eighth council, that Honorius was accused and condemned on account of heresy; and moreover, that his condemnation had taken place only in consequence of the Roman See having given its assent. [3]

It is Hincmar of Rheims who mentions the affair of Honorius for the last time in the West, adding the

[1] [Of Nicæa, which anathematised the Iconoclasts, and restored image-worship.]
[2] *Concilia*, ed. Labbe, vii., 166, 182, 422
[3] See Garnier's note to the *Liber Diurnus*, p. 41.

remark, that he must have deserved anathema in his life, otherwise those who sat in judgment upon him would have harmed themselves rather than [1] him. After him the recollection of the circumstance perished in the western churches. Of course, in the notices of the sixth council, as they existed in this or that chronicle, and in the Roman breviary, the name of Honorius, without further explanation, was still read along with the rest who had been condemned by this council. But seeing that all these others were Orientals, that the Monothelite controversy had left no traces behind it in the West, and that none of the historical works in general use in the Middle Ages contained any particulars of the Monothelite question, it no longer occurred to any one that the Honorius thus expelled from communion with the Church was the pope. Beyond everything else the silence of the Pontifical book decided the point in this direction. Hence it came to pass that not one of the numerous compilers of histories and lists of popes gave even the slightest hint of so remarkable a circumstance, one quite unique in its kind. The pseudo-Luitprand, Abbo, Martinus Polonus, Leo of Orvieto, Bernard Guidonis, Gervasius Riccobald of Ferrara, Amalrich

---

[1] In the treatise *De una et non trina Deitate*, cf. Chmel *Vindiciæ Concil*, vi., Prague, 1777, p. 137.

Augerii—all these writers of histories of the popes are silent. They sometimes relate about him some unimportant things, such as small liturgical directions; they mention that Leo II., understanding Greek, translated the Acts of the sixth council into Latin. But an event, which in Rome itself appeared so important that it had been expressly included in the pope's confession of faith, they one and all leave unmentioned, not perhaps of set purpose—only of the compiler of the Pontifical book can it be said that he purposely suppressed the proceeding—but openly, because they knew nothing whatever about it, although three œcumenical councils, the sixth, the seventh, and the eighth, had pronounced or confirmed the sentence of anathema on Honorius.

And this was universally the case with the Latin writers from the tenth to the fifteenth century. True that the chronicle of Eccard,[1] that Ado and Marianus Scotus mention Honorius among those who were condemned by the sixth council, but this name without any further description was, for those times, mere empty sound, conveying no ideas to any one. When, therefore, Cardinal Humbert, in his writing against the Greek Nicetas,[2] inserts a notice of the sixth

---

[1] In Pertz, viii., 155.
[2] In Baron., Append. ad tom. xi.; *Annal.*, p. 1005, ed. Colon.

council, and in this mentions Honorius also as one of those condemned, we may be certain that he had no suspicion of the rank of the person mentioned; otherwise the Byzantines would have been precisely the people in whose minds he would have avoided awakening such a recollection. The oblivion into which the fate of Honorius had fallen is specially astonishing in the letter of Pope Leo IX. to Michael Cerularius, patriarch of Constantinople, and to Leo [1] of Achrida, in which all the scandals and heretical errors of their Church and its bishops are set before these prelates. The pope confidently contrasts the

---

[1] Harduin, iii., 921. [Michael Cerularius and Leo, archbishop of Achrida and metropolitan of Bulgaria, provoked the correspondence in 1053, by a letter to the bishop of Trani, in Apulia, warning him against the errors of the Latins. The pope replied from his virtual captivity at Benevento. After quoting the text, "Ego autem rogavi " pro te, ut non deficiat fides tua; et tu aliquando conversus confirma "fratres tuos," the pope proceeds: "Erit ergo quisquam tantæ " dementiæ, qui orationem illius, cujus velle est posse, audeat in " aliquo vacuum putare? Nonne a sede principis Apostolorum, " Romana videlicet ecclesia, tam per eumdem Petrum quam succes-" sores suos, reprobata et convicta, atque expugnata sunt omnium " hæreticorum commenta; et fratrum corda in fide Petri, quæ " hactenus nec defecit, nec usque in finem deficiet confirmata?

"Præterimus nominatim replicare nonaginta et eo amplius hæreses "ab Orientis partibus, vel ab ipsis Græcis, diverso tempore ex diverso "errore ad corrumpendam virginitatem catholicæ ecclesiæ matris "emergentes. Dicendum videtur ex parte, quantas Constantino-"politana ecclesia per præsules suos suscitaverit pestes; quas " viriliter expugnavit, protrivit, et suffocavit Romana et Apostolica "sedes."]

steadfast orthodoxy of the bishops of Rome with the numerous cases of heresy which had occurred in Constantinople, and calls attention to the way in which the popes, especially in the Monothelite controversies, had continually exercised their judicial office over the patriarchs of Constantinople, and had condemned them; evidently not having the slightest suspicion that Michael and Leo, by quoting the condemnation of Honorius, pronounced at Constantinople and accepted at Rome, could have demolished his whole argument. On the contrary, deceived by the Roman apocryphal documents, he represents to his opponents that Sylvester had decided that the First See (that is the Roman) can be judged by none, and that Constantine, together with the whole council of Nicæa, had approved this.[1]

Again, Anselm of Lucca would not have maintained with such confidence that at the eight œcumenical councils which had been held up to that time, it had been proved that the patriarch of Rome was the only one whose faith had never wavered, if he had known that it was precisely at the last three of these

---

[1] ["Illi nempe facitis præjudicium, de qua nec vobis, nec cuilibet "mortalium licet facere judicium; beatissimo et Apostolico Ponti- "fice Silvestro divinitus decernente, spiritualique ejus filio Constan- "tino religiosissimo Augusto cum universa synodo Nicæna approbante "ac subscribente, ut *summa sedes a nemine judicetur.*"]

eight synods that Honorius had been condemned for heresy.[1] In like manner, Rupert of Deutz would not, as he has done, have contrasted the steadfast orthodoxy of the popes with the heretical aberrations of the patriarchs of Constantinople, if he had not shared the general ignorance respecting the sixth council.[2]

Accordingly, in the West, as often as cases had to be quoted in which popes had erred or become heretical, people appealed to those of Liberius and Anastasius, sometimes also to that of Marcellinus; never to Honorius. This ignorance appears in a very astonishing way under Clement V. At that time there was on the part of the French a pressing desire for a formal anathema on Boniface VIII. The defenders of this pope contended that as being a dead man who could no longer answer for himself, he was exempt from all human judgment, and therefore even from that of the Roman See. The instance of Honorius would have been very welcome to the agents of the French court; for by means of it they could have proved in the most emphatic way that the Church had certainly sat in judgment on a defunct pope, and had condemned him. The fact, however, had long since vanished from the memories of jurists no less

---

1 *Contra Guibertum Antipapam*, **Bibl. Patrum Lugd.**, xviii., 609.
2 *De Divinis Offic.*, 2, 22.

than of theologians; and hence in the long controversy and legal discussion the name of Honorius was never mentioned.

Hence it has come to pass that Platina has even made Honorius a decided *opponent* of Monothelitism, and he represents Heraclius as banishing Pyrrhus and Cyrus at the suggestion of Honorius. But that towards the close of the sixteenth century the learned Panvinio, whom Cianoni then copied in turn, should allow this to pass unchallenged, is scarcely conceivable.

The fact that Honorius was condemned by the sixth general council was first brought back to the memory of the Western Church by a Greek living in Constantinople, Manuel Kalekas, who in the year 1390 wrote a work against the Byzantines for being separated from the West. The papal nuncio Anton Massanus, a Minorite, brought the book from Constantinople to the papal court in 1421; whereupon Martin V. had it translated by the celebrated Camaldulensian abbot, Ambrose Traversari. From it cardinal Torquemada,[1] who wrote his *Summa* about the year 1450, first learnt the condemnation of Honorius, which disturbed him greatly; for by no

---

[1] Quetif et Echard, *Scriptores O. P.*, I., 718.

sort of means would it work into his system.[1] Kalekas had made light of the affair in his controversy with the Greeks. He had contented himself with referring to the excuse which Maximus makes for Honorius, without troubling himself with the consideration that the judgment of an œcumenical council must have **an** authority **very** different from the evasive answer **of a theologian, who knew of no other way** of helping his case than to make **the** secretary answerable for the errors contained in **the** pope's[2] letter. Now Torquemada was acquainted with the declaration of Hadrian II. from the Acts of the eighth council, to the effect that Honorius had been anathematised for heresy. Nevertheless, he says that we must suppose that the Orientals were misinformed about Honorius, and so had condemned him under[3] a mistake. His sole **ground** for saying this is, that pope Agatho, **in** enumerating **the** Monothelite leaders, has not mentioned Honorius among them.

This attempt to load an œcumenical council with

---

[1] *Summa de Ecclesia*, 2, § 3, ed. **Venet.**, 1560, f., 228. This is the most important work of the Middle **Ages** on the question of the extent of the papal power.

[2] *Contra Græcorum errores*, Ingolst., 1608, p. 381.

[3] "Creditur quod hoc fecerint Orientales ex **mala et falsa sinistra** "informatione de præfato Honorio decepti."

the charge of a gross error, merely to rescue the honour of one pope, remained, however, on the whole, unobserved, and stood alone at that time. For then, as through the whole of the Middle Ages, the view still prevailed that a pope could certainly apostatise from the faith and become heretical, and in such a case both could and ought to be deposed.

Not until after the middle of the sixteenth century did any one occupy himself seriously with the question of Honorius. The fact of the condemnation was irreconcileable with the system then developed by Baronius, Bellarmine, and others. Attempts were accordingly made to set it aside. It was pretended, that is to say, that the Acts of the sixth council had been falsified by the Greeks of a later age, and all therein that concerned Honorius had been interpolated by them, in order that the disgrace of so many Oriental patriarchs being condemned for heresy might be lessened by the shame of a pope being found in the same predicament. Then it became necessary to declare that the letter of Leo II. was also interpolated. And on this Baronius, Bellarmine, Hosius, Binius, Duval, and the Jesuits Tanner and Gretser determined. But when the *Liber Diurnus* came to light, the nullity of this attempt was disclosed. Another mode of getting out of the difficulty proved still more untenable; this was to deny the condemnation of Honorius at the sixth council, and transfer it to another purely Greek synod (the quinisext [1] council of A.D. 692 is apparently the one meant), the Acts of which were then inserted in those of the sixth council. This was the device resorted to by Sylvius Lupus, and the Roman oratorian Marchese, who has set forth this idea in a book of his own.[2]

That the letters of Honorius were forgeries, or that they had been interpolated, was somewhat more conceivable; at least the supposition demanded no such immense and elaborate apparatus of falsification as Baronius and Bellarmine pictured to themselves, or at any rate to their readers. This mode of escape therefore was chosen by Gravina and Coster; Stapleton also and Wiggers were inclined[3] towards it.

---

[1] [Called *quinisext*, as being supplementary to the fifth and sixth councils. It is also known as the *Trullan*, from the *Trullus* or vaulted hall, in which it was held. The date of it is doubtful; 636, 691, 692 have all been suggested. Harduin places it as late as 706. The two papal legates signed its 102 canons; but pope Sergius I., to the chagrin of the emperor Justinian II., declined to do so. The council was recognised by the East only, *where its Acts were quoted as those of the sixth council;* and this was the first grave step towards the schism between the East and the West.]

[2] *Clypeus fortium, sive Vindiciæ Honorii Papæ.* Romæ, 1680.

[3] Against endeavours such as these of Bellarmine, Baronius, and others after them,—to set aside well-attested historical facts by

Seeing, however, that the letters of Honorius were laid before the council, examined, and condemned *in the presence of the papal legates*, who at any rate must have known their contents, it was found necessary to abandon *this* method of getting out of the difficulty also. Several, therefore, preferred to maintain that Honorius himself had taught what was orthodox, and had only been condemned by the council because he had shown leniency to heresy from an ill-timed love of peace, and had favoured it by rejecting a dogmatic expression which had become indispensable. So De Marca, Natalis Alexander, Garnier, Du Hamel, Lupus, Tamagnini, Pagi and many others.

This method of defending Honorius became a very favourite one after the outbreak of the Jansenite troubles. It is chiefly owing to the Jansenists that the question of Honorius has become a *quæstio vexata*, in which every effort has been made to

throwing suspicion on the witnesses and documents, because they will not square with the system of a particular school or party,— cardinal Sfondrati has spoken out very strongly on this very question of Honorius. "Quid hoc aliud est, quam contra torrentem " navigare, omnemque historiam ecclesiasticam in dubium vocare? " Sublata vero historia et consequenter traditione usuque Ecclesiæ, " quæ tu arma contra hæreticos satis valida habebis? Male ergo, ut " nobis quidem videtur, Ecclesiæ illi consulunt, qui ut Honorii " causam tueantur, historiam Ecclesiamque exarmant. Ergo si " testibus agenda res est, Honorius Papa hæreticus fuit."—Eugenii Lombardi *Regale Sacerdotium*, p. 721, sq.

confuse and set aside the facts, and with which since
1650 almost every theologian of note has occupied
himself. So that within a period of about 130 years
one may say that more has been written on this one
question of ecclesiastical history than on any other in
1500 years. For the Jansenists it was all-important
to invalidate the judgment which the Church had
pronounced on the work of Jansen. Accordingly they
put forth the theory that the Church both **could err**
and had erred; not, indeed, in the setting forth of
doctrine, but in "dogmatic questions of fact," that is
to say, in its judgment on a book, or its interpretation
of a dogmatic text. They set themselves therefore
on the side of Honorius against the council, and
readily pursued the course which had already been
opened by cardinals **Torquemada, Baronius,** Bellarmine, De Laurea, and Aguirre,[1] maintaining that

[1] For these writers, foreseeing that the theory of a falsification of
the Acts would not hold water, **had** already taken up the other
alternative, that the council had **made a** mistake in its judgment on
the decretals of Honorius—Bennettis (*Privil. Pontif. Vindiciæ*,
Rom., 1759, P. ii., T. V., p. 389) **admits,** "Turrecrematæ, Baronio,
"Bellarmino ac Spondano locutiones excidisse minus accuratas ac
"paulo asperiores." They **have simply** sacrificed the authority of
an œcumenical **council, and of a decision accepted by the** Papal See
itself, to the interests of their own theory. [So also Père Gratry:
"On m'accuse de manquer à l'Église, notre mère, parce que je
"dénonce le pernicieux mensonge des décrétales dans les leçons du
"Bréviaire romain. Le bréviaire est-il donc l'Église, et les légendes

grievous wrong had been done to Honorius and his letters by the judgment of the council. The council, in spite of the care which it bestowed, and although the matter in question was at that time current with every one, had been mistaken in their decision! The opponents of the Jansenists, who would not allow that the Church had condemned a pope as heretical and expelled him from communion, preferred rather to do violence to the clear words of the council, in order to say that Honorius had become subject to the anathema of the council, not on account of positive, but only of "negative" heresy; that is to say, merely because he had countenanced other heretics and favoured their false [1] doctrine. But Fénélon had already pointed out that, with all the artifices and

"sont-elles donc le bréviaire? Mais, quoi! si l'on manque à l'Église
" pour vouloir effacer des erreurs dans les leçons du Bréviaire
" romain, que dire de ceux qui veulent effacer des décrets de foi
" dans les conciles œcuméniques? . . . Oui, je demande ce qu'il
" faut dire de ceux qui traitent ainsi les décrets des conciles; qui,
" voyant Honorius condamné par trois conciles œcuméniques, sans
" compter vingt papes, répondent tous simplement que ces con-
" ciles se sont trompés!"—*Troisième lettre à Monseigneur l'Archevêque de Malines.* Paris, 1870, i., p. 5.]

[1] It is specially the Jesuit Garnier, who, in his notes to the *Liber Diurnus*, has expended great pains on this point. A whole host of theologians have followed him. At last Palma (*Prælectiones Hist. Eccles.*, ii , 127), whose efforts go beyond everything with this conclusion, asserts that the council certainly invoked an anathema on Honorius, but in the expression of it was not quite in earnest.

explanations by means of which the orthodoxy of Honorius was to be saved, nothing after all was to be gained. For the paramount question must always be this:—Has the Church, represented by a full œcumenical council, **declared the dogmatic** writings of a pope to be heretical, and *thus recognised the fallibility of popes?* If this question must be answered in the affirmative, then it matters very little for the interests of the Roman See whether the synod, in the application of the principle to a particular case (the meaning of the letter of Honorius), has made a mistake or not.[1]

Some Italians of the last century—for example, bishop Bartoli and the librarian Ughi—once more took refuge in the favourite and most convenient falsification theory, which makes very short work of every stubborn fact. According to Bartoli,[2] the letters of Honorius are forgeries. At the same time, however, Bartoli adopted the discovery which had already been made by the Augustinian Desirant, that besides this the Greeks had forged also the letters of Sergius; so that the doubly-deceived synod had regarded the letter of Honorius also, which agreed

---

[1] *Troisième instr. pastor. sur le Cas de Conscience.* Œuvres, éd. de Versailles, xi., 483.

[2] *Apologia pro Honorio I. Rom. Pontif.*, Ausugii, 1750.

with that of Sergius, as heretical. Ughi[1] admitted that the synod openly condemned Honorius for heresy; but thinks that it acted carelessly and without thought in so doing, because it allowed itself to be deceived by the letter which had been foisted upon Honorius. And, not to adopt any half measures, he declares that the letters of Leo II. are also spurious. The French theologian, Corgne, likewise has resorted to this lamentable expedient.[2]

Arsdekin and Cavalcanti thought of another loophole, through which it was possible to escape from the unwelcome conclusion, viz., that it was the Greeks alone who, at the sixth council, pronounced the unjust sentence upon Honorius; the Latins present had not taken part in this mistaken proceeding.

On the other hand, their contemporary, bishop Duplessis d'Argentré, maintained that the council had condemned Honorius *as a heretic*, and with justice, for God had allowed him to fall into these errors in his letter to Sergius, in order that popes

---

[1] "Quæ omnia," he remarks, after quoting the most decisive passages from the acts of the council, "nullo unquam temperamento "emollita . . . manifeste demonstrant, fuisse Honorium non solum- "modo tanquam desidem, sed—tanquam verum hæreticum a synodo "VI. proscriptum."—*De Honorio I. Pontif. Max. Liber*, Bononiæ, 1784, p. 94, cf p 98.

[2] *Dissertation critique et théologique sur le Monothélisme*, Paris, 1741, p. 56 sq

might learn by his example that freedom from error in the setting forth of doctrine was assured to them only on condition of their taking proper counsel, which he had neglected to do.[1] Cardinal Orsi also has fully recognised the untenableness of the efforts to save the orthodoxy of Honorius, and the openings for attack which were thus exposed by shortsighted theologians. He withdraws, therefore, back to the point of view, that Honorius spoke only as a private teacher, neither as pope, nor in the name of the Roman Church giving a solemn decision after the necessary taking of counsel (*ex cathedrâ*). Cardinal Luzerne has subjected these tenets to a sharp[2] criticism. One cannot say, he justly remarks, that Honorius gave his opinion on the Monothelite question not as pope, but only as a private teacher. The question was put to him as pope, and he answered as pope, in the same tone and style in which his predecessors, Celestine and Leo, had answered on dogmatic questions. Orsi, however, is quite right on his side, when he argues that Honorius gave his decision without a council and on his own

---

[1] *Collectio Judiciorum de Novis Erroribus.* Paris, 1724, T. I., præf., p. 4. And in his *Variæ Disputationes theol. ad Opera.* M. Grandin, Paris, 1712, ii., 220.

[2] *Sur la Déclaration du Clergé. Œuvres*, Paris, 1855, ii., 42, and 190 sq. [On decisions " *ex cathedrâ*," see Appendix E.]

responsibility; without troubling himself about the doctrine held by the Churches of the West, which from the first had always believed in a duality of wills; without even giving the Roman Church itself the opportunity of making known its creed as regards this question. If the idea of a decision *ex cathedrâ* be duly expanded, and only those dogmatic announcements be reckoned as *ex cathedrâ* which a pope issues, not in his own name and for himself, but in the name of the Church, *with full consciousness of the doctrine prevailing in the Church, and therefore after previous inquiry or discussion by a council*— then, and only then, can one say that judgment about Honorius was not given [1] *ex cathedrâ*. Neither the Roman Church, nor the Western, nor the greater part of the Eastern Church, has ever been Monothelite. Nevertheless, Honorius sent letters to the Eastern Church, about the Monothelite meaning of which assuredly not a doubt would ever have been raised, but for the fact that the author was a pope. Accordingly, the old Roman breviary designates him simply as a Monothelite.[2]

1 [With this interpretation one would readily admit that not only the pope, but every bishop is infallible, when he speaks *ex cathedrâ*.]
2 Hefele, in his *Conciliengeschichte*, and in the discussion in the *Tübingen Quartalschrift*, year, 1857, has treated the question of Honorius with philosophic impartiality, accuracy, and thoroughness. [See also four letters to Monseigneur Deschamps, archbishop of Malines, by A. Gratry, priest of the Oratory. Paris, 1870.]

IX. POPE GREGORY II. AND THE EMPEROR LEO THE ISAURIAN.

According to later historians, who have been eagerly followed by many theologians, Gregory II. deprived the iconoclast emperor Leo of the kingdom of Italy, and induced the Italians to throw off their allegiance to him, because he attempted to carry his edict against the use of images into effect in Italy as well as in the East. Baronius, Bellarmine, and others have made this supposed fact a main support of their system with regard to the authority of popes over the temporal power.

Of the biographers of popes in the Middle Ages, Martinus Polonus is the only one who, while he makes a confusion by transferring the matter to Gregory III., asserts that the pope, recognising in the emperor Leo an incorrigible iconoclast, induced Rome, Italy, Spain, and the "whole of the West" to throw off their allegiance to the emperor, and forbade all payment of taxes to him. We have here another proof of the incredible ignorance of Martinus Polonus, in representing Spain—Gothic and even Saracen Spain—as throwing off their allegiance. And besides that, what we are to understand by the "whole of the West," he himself would have had some difficulty in showing. The other papal biographers, Amalrich, Guidonis, Leo of Orvieto, and others, know nothing of the secession of Italy from the empire. But before Martinus Polonus, Sigebert of Gemblours, Otto of Freysingen, Gottfried of Viterbo, Albert of Stade, and the so-called Landulf, the late compiler of the *Historia Miscella*, had already accepted the statement that pope Gregory induced the Italians to revolt from Leo. All of these, as well as the Byzantines Zonaras,[1] Cedrenus, and Glykas, received the statement from one and the same single source. This source is the chronicler Theophanes, who wrote the history of this period eighty years after it (he died not earlier than A.D. 819); and his work, in the abbreviated Latin translation of Anastasius Bibliothecarius, was used by the above-mentioned Latin chroniclers either directly or indirectly.

It is altogether futile, therefore, to pile up names of witnesses to this supposed fact (after the manner of Bianchi[2]), and add to these Nauclerus, and Platina also. All these witnesses resolve themselves into one; and the investigator has merely to show (1) that

---

[1] [Zonaras and Michael Glykas bring their chronicles down to the death of the emperor Alexis I., Comnenus, 1118; Cedrenus, to 1057.]

[2] *Della Potestà e della Polizia della Chiesa.* Rom., 1745, i., 382.

Theophanes [1] is a late authority, very little acquainted with Italian affairs ; (2) that the two contemporary Italian witnesses, Paulus Diaconus, and the anonymous biographer of Gregory in the Pontifical book, state just the opposite of what **Theophanes says** ; and (3) that Zonaras, in the twelfth century, and **certainly** Cedrenus (both of whom merely copied **Theophanes**) are here utterly unworthy of consideration. The special object of Zonaras, **moreover, is to** throw the blame of the loss of its Italian possessions by the Greek empire on the papacy. Accordingly he decorates the erroneous statement of Theophanes with the further statement that Gregory made an alliance with the Franks, who hereupon got possession of Rome, a statement which he thrice repeats. That is, he transfers events, which first took place under Pepin and Charles the Great, to the time of Gregory II. and Charles Martel.

The truth of the matter is, then, that, according to the accounts of the two Italian contemporaries and

[1] [Theophanes was born about A.D. 750. He was a most zealous advocate of the use of images at the second council of Nicæa in 787. Leo the Armenian made him an object of persecution for his support to the cause of **image-worship**, imprisoned him for two years, and finally banished him to Samothrace, where he died almost immediately, March, 818. His chronicle is a continuation of that of his friend Syncellus, commencing with the accession of Diocletian in 284, and going down to 813.]

Gregory's own statements in his letter to Leo, this pope, far from wishing or effecting the overthrow of the Byzantine dominion in Italy, was rather the only, or at any rate the principal, cause of its maintenance. It is true that, when Leo ordered the destruction of pictures and dismantling of churches, the Romans and inhabitants of Eastern [1] Italy, from Venice to Osimo, flung off the Greek yoke, and even wished to elect an emperor of their own. But Gregory strained every nerve to prevent this, and exhorted them unceasingly to maintain their allegiance to the Roman empire of the East.[2] The biographer in the Pontifical book, who, from the fullness, insight, and liveliness exhibited in his narrative, is easily seen to be a contemporary and eye-witness, gives only one circumstance which seems to go beyond the line of loyal obedience otherwise observed with great strictness by Gregory, and has given Theophanes an opening for his misrepresentation. The patrician Paul, he says, on becoming exarch, made an attempt on the life of the pope, because he attempted to hinder [3] the imposition

---

[1] [The Greek dominions in Italy at this time were:—(1) the exarchate of Ravenna, (2) the duchy of Rome and Naples, (3) the cities on the coast of Liguria, and (4) the provinces in the extreme south of Italy.]

[2] Paul Diac., *de Gestis Longob.*, 6, 49; *Liber Pontif.*, ed. Vignoli, ii., 27–30.

[3] "Eo quod censum in provinciâ possit præpediebat," l. c., p. 28.

of a tax in the province, and would not consent to the plundering of the churches—that is, the carrying off of pictures and of vessels ornamented with figures of saints. Here the point at issue was hindering the levying of a new impost, in which the pope did no more than set a precedent, which was then followed by others, of refusing to pay a new impost out of the great and numerous patrimonies of the church. But Theophanes and the Greeks [1] after him represent this as an injunction issued to the Italians not to pay any more taxes whatever.

Hefele, following Bossuet and Muratori, has set the events which took place in Italy at that time in their true light, and has shown how devoid of foundation the Greek statement [2] is. It would have been sufficient merely to call attention to this, had not

---

[1] [In this they are followed by Gibbon. "The most effectual and "pleasing measure of rebellion was the withholding the tribute of "Italy, and depriving him of a power which he had recently abused "by the imposition of a new capitation." In a note he adds, "A "*census*, or capitation, says Anastasius (p. 156): a most cruel tax, "unknown to the Saracens themselves, exclaims the zealous Maim- "bourg (*Hist. des Iconoclastes*, l. 1.), and Theophanes (p. 334 [tom, "i., p. 361, ed Bonn,]) who talks of Pharaoh's numbering the male "children of Israel. This mode of taxation was familiar to the "Saracens; and, most unluckily for the historian, it was imposed a "few years afterwards in France by his patron Louis XIV."—*Decline and Fall of the Roman Empire*, chap. XLIX., note 38.]

[2] *Conciliengeschichte*, iii., 355 ff.

Gregorovius lately revived once more the old view of Bellarmine, and represented the pope as in open revolt against the emperor. "Gregory," he states, "now "decided upon open resistance .... he armed him-"self, as the Pontifical book says, against the emperor "as against a foe .... The act of open rebellion, at "the head of which the pope boldly placed himself, "was perhaps even definitely declared by refusal of "the tribute from the duchy of Rome,"[1] &c. But in manifest contradiction to this view, he states further on, "Gregory could not withdraw himself from the "tradition of the Roman empire, the seat of which "was Byzantium; with prudent moderation he "restrained the rebellious Italians, and appealed to the "legitimate rights of the emperor, whom he had no "longer much need to fear" (page 257).

Is it conceivable that so prudent a man as (on Gregorovius' own showing) this pope was, should first have set himself at the head of an open rebellion, and then directly afterwards, without any external compulsion, should again have quashed the rebellion, and come forward as champion of the emperor's rights? For the view that the pope originated and directed the revolt of the Italians, Gregorovius has given no other evidence than his quotation of the words of the

[1] *Geschichte der Stadt Rom.*, ii., 255.

Pontifical book, "he armed himself against the "emperor as against a foe;"[1] but the words which immediately follow, and which explain the meaning of this "arming" he omits, namely, the words, "in "that he rejected the emperor's heresy, and sent "letters everywhere, bidding Christians to be on their "guard against the new form of impiety that had "appeared." Gregory, therefore, kept himself rigorously within the sphere of ecclesiastical matters, declared himself the opponent of the imperial decree against the use of images, and charged the faithful not to destroy their images. But at the same time he exhorted them to show civil obedience to the imperial power, so much so that he used all his influence to preserve Ravenna for the empire, when the Lombards were threatening to seize it; and he placed [2] forces at

---

[1] [Gibbon quotes the whole passage, but draws the same conclusion as Gregorovius. "Without depending on prayers and miracles, "he boldly armed against the public enemy, and his pastoral letters "admonished the Italians of their danger and their duty." To which he subjoins in the note: "I shall transcribe the important "passage of the *Liber Pontificalis*." "Respiciens ergo pius vir "profanam principis jussionem, jam contra Imperatorem quasi "contra *hostem* se armavit, renuens hæresim ejus, scribens ubique "se cavere Christianos, eo quod orta fuisset impietas talis. *Igitur* "permoti omnes Pentapolenses, atque Venetiarum exercitus contra "Imperatoris jussionem restiterunt: dicentes se nunquam in ejusdem "pontificis condescendere necem, sed pro ejus magis defensione "viriliter decertare" (p. 156), l. c., note 37.]

[2] [This was partly the result of the interference of the Lombard

the disposal of the imperial governor Eutychius, by means of which Eutychius was able to put down the revolt of Tiberius Petavius in Tuscany.

A glance at the position of affairs shows that Gregory,[1] straitened as were the limits within which the difficulties of his surroundings allowed him to act, nevertheless well understood how to maintain the true **bearing which prudence and duty** alike dictated.

king himself (see next note). It is the more remarkable, **inasmuch as** Eutychius, the last exarch of **Ravenna**, had come on **an iconoclastic mission from Constantinople**; and it was commonly believed of him, as of other imperial emissaries before him, that he meditated **the assassination of the pope. It was thanks to** Gregory that Eutychius was not assassinated himself.]

1 [Gregory was under the influence of two violent and conflicting feelings, horror of an iconoclastic emperor (an iconoclast in the eyes of an Italian was scarcely a Christian), and horror of a Lombard supremacy. When Ravenna was taken by the Lombards, he organised a league between Venice, the exarch Scholasticus, and Rome; and the forces thus raised recaptured Ravenna while Luitprand was away at Pavia, A.D. 727. Two years later, however, we find Liutprand acting the part of mediator between Gregory and the exarch Eutychius. As regards the question of iconoclasm, it was one fanatic against another. Leo was at least as fanatical in his attack on the use of images, as Gregory in his support of it. And when it is urged in proof of the pope's rebellion that he excommunicated the emperor, we must remember that at that time excommunication of a prince did not necessarily carry with it a release of his subjects from their allegiance; it did not even cut off the prince himself from all spiritual privileges. It merely declared in solemn terms that the pope declined to communicate with him. But "si "quis .... imaginum sacrarum .... destructor .... extiterit "sit extorris a corpore D. N. Jesu Christi vel totius ecclesiæ "unitate," is strong language.]

The gravest peril, the most pressing and disastrous fate in the eyes of the Romans at that time, and especially of the popes, was to be swallowed up by the Lombards. Gregory shared the general feeling, and he, too, speaks of the "gens nefanda Longobardorum."[1] And this fate, to become the prey of the detested foreigner, was inevitable for Rome and the rest of Byzantine Italy, as soon as the power of Constantinople in the West was broken. That these provinces, if left alone, could not maintain themselves against the overwhelming power of the Lombards, Gregory was well aware.[2] Above all would protection be needed for the Roman See; and at that time the Frankish kingdom alone, under its prince, Charles Martel, could have given this protection. Charles Martel, however, was fully occupied with perpetual wars against the Saxons, Frisians, Saracens, and people of Aquitaine; and, moreover, was on friendly

---

[1] [Gregory commences his letter to Ursus, doge of Venice, on the subject of united resistance against the Lombards, in these words: "Quia, peccato faciente, Ravennatum civitas, quæ caput extat "omnium, a nec dicendâ gente Longobardorum capta est."—Labbe, *Concil.*, vi., 1447. The Lombards, on their side, had a similar style of abuse. If they wished to express the bitterest contempt for a foe, they called him a Roman.]

[2] [Yet, as Dr. Döllinger remarks in Essay V., "Gregory II. made "an attempt to form a confederation of states, which was to maintain "itself independently of both Greeks and Lombards, the head of it "to be the Roman See," p. 121.]

terms with the Lombard king. Thus he was both unable and unwilling to take serious part in Italian affairs. Hence it came to pass that lower Italy, in which the richest possessions of the Roman Chair lay, remained then, and for some time longer, faithful to the Roman emperor in the East. Not a single attempt was made there to revolt from him; and if the influence of the pope had been exerted to bring such a result about, it would certainly have failed. Had Gregory then, as Gregorovius represents, placed himself at the head of a rebellion, he would have entered upon a hopeless undertaking, involving the most ruinous losses to the Roman See.

X. SYLVESTER II.

A POPE, who was held in great honour by his contemporaries, who was renowned as the most learned scholar and the most enlightened spirit of his time, whose memory remained unsullied for a century after his death, becomes gradually an object of suspicion; the calumnies about him assume larger and larger dimensions, until the papal biographers of the later Middle Ages represent his whole life and pontificate as a series of the most monstrous crimes. According to them, Sylvester II. entered into a league with the devil, and exercised his pontifical office in the devil's service and in obedience to his will.

At first writers were content with the timid criticism that Gerbert had devoted himself with far too much zeal to profane sciences, and on that account stood so high in the favour of an emperor with such a thirst for knowledge as Otho III. This is the line taken by the chroniclers Hermann of Reichenau (died A.D. 1054) and Bernold. Hugo of Fleury (A.D. 1109) as yet knows nothing to the discredit of Gerbert; according to him Gerbert attained to such eminence merely by means of his knowledge. But his contemporary Hugo of Flavigny, whose chronicle ends with the year 1102, goes so far as to state that it was by certain sinister arts (quibusdam præstigiis) that Gerbert contrived to get himself elected archbishop of Ravenna.[1] The chronicler does not appear by this to have intended the interposition of demoniacal agencies; in which case he would certainly have used stronger language. He probably meant court intrigues, by means of which the Frenchman won the favour of the empress Adelaide, who at that time held Ravenna, and of the emperor Otho; so that the latter, evading an open election, simply nominated Gerbert.

Some years later we have Siegebert of Gemblours (died A.D. 1113) stating that some did not reckon Gerbert among the popes at all, but put in his place a (fictitious) pope Agapetus, because Gerbert had been addicted to the practice of the black art, and had been[2] struck dead by the devil.

Siegebert may have had before him the work of Cardinal Benno. The main features of the fable appear first in the writings of this calumnious enemy of Gregory VII. Benno, whose work must have been written about the year 1099, asserts that to a certain extent, during the whole of the eleventh century, a

---

[1] Pertz, x., 367.   [2] Bouquet, x., 217.

school of black magic existed in Rome, with a succession of adepts in this art, and he enumerates them in order. The most important personage among them is archbishop Laurentius of Amalfi, who at times gave utterance to prophecies, and could also interpret [1] the notes of birds. Theophylact (Benedict IX.) and the archpriest John Gratian (Gregory VI.) learnt the unholy art from Laurentius, and Hildebrand from John Gratian. But Laurentius himself was the pupil of Gerbert, who was the first to bring the art to Rome. And then Benno relates the story which has since been so often repeated, and which became so popular, that Satan promised his disciple Gerbert that he should not die until he had said mass in Jerusalem. Gerbert accordingly believed himself to be quite safe; for he thought only of the city of Jerusalem, without remembering the Jerusalem church in Rome. The message of death came to him as he was saying mass in this church, and he thereupon caused his tongue and hand to be cut off, by way of expiation.

Benno certainly did not invent this fable; he found it already existing in Rome. Before him there is no mention of it anywhere,[2] and it evidently sprang up

---

[1] *Vita et Gesta Hildebrandi*, in Brown, *Fascicul.*, i., 83.
[2] Though Dav. Koeler (*Gerbertus—injuriis tam veterum quam*

nowhere else but in Rome, just like the fable about Pope Joan. A foreigner, with his, at that time, unheard of and incomprehensible learning, who had acquired very questionable knowledge among those enemies of the faith, the Mohammedans in Spain, may well have inspired the Romans with something of awe and horror. At a time in which scientific studies had all but died out in Rome, in which the Roman Chair was under the control of aristocratic factions, and a pope without powerful relations was scarcely able to maintain himself, the populace could not understand how a man like Gerbert, of the very humblest extraction, by mere pre-eminence of intellectual culture, should have raised himself to the highest dignity in Christendom. That could not have come to pass by purely natural means.

Here also, as in the fable of Pope Joan, a verse plays an important part. It is the well-known line—

"Scandit ab R Gerbertus in R, fit postea Papa vigens R."

For it is well known that Gerbert was first archbishop of Rheims, then of Ravenna, and finally

recentiorem scriptorum—liberatur. Altorf., 1720, p. 33) supposes this, and Hock (*Gerbert und sein Jahrhundert*, s. 161) considers it as most probable.

The Benedictines in the Bouquet Collection, x. 244, certainly say "Antesignanos Benno habuit." I have not been able, however, to discover these predecessors.

became pope of Rome. Originally Gerbert himself was said to have composed the verse, in calm satisfaction after the attainment of the highest dignity.[1] Next the verse was ascribed to him as a prophecy respecting his future destiny, which was eventually fulfilled. And thus the way was prepared for the next step, which was to make the verse into a prediction or promise of the devil. By this means Gerbert was placed in the power of Satan; and his wonderful and, at that time, unexampled success must have been the work of the devil, the result of a compact entered into with him. For after the story of Theophilus, which arose in the East in the ninth century, had spread in the West also, and the notion of compacts with the arch-enemy (originally quite foreign to the Christian world) became naturalised, there was nothing to hinder even a pope from being represented as having attained to his dignity by such a compact.

And thus it is stated in Ordericus Vitalis, who wrote his chronicle about the year 1151, that Gerbert is said to have studied as a scholar with a demon, and this demon gave utterance to the famous verse. Soon after, however, in William Godell, who wrote some twenty years later, Gerbert has already done

---

[1] So Helgald, in Bouquet, x., 99.

formal homage to Satan, in order to attain the fulfilment of his wishes through his power. William of Malmesbury tells the story in its fully developed form. And now the Dominicans appropriate it; Vincent of Beauvais, Martinus Polonus, Leo of Orvieto, Bernard Guidonis; also Amalrich Augerii. Petrarch adheres to them faithfully. In their hands Sylvester II. becomes a successor of St. Peter, who early in life sold himself to the devil, and by his assistance ascends the papal throne. As pope he has daily and familiar intercourse with Satan, making him his counsellor. But when the entry of a troop of demons into the church warns him of the approach of his end, he publicly confesses his sins before the people, and thereupon has one limb after another hacked off, in order to show penitence for his enormities by means of such an agonising death. Since then the rattling of his bones in the grave is wont to give notice of the approaching death of a pope. On the other hand, Dietrich von Niem (about A.D. 1390) was not far from the truth when he said that the Romans had detested this pope on account of his extraordinary learning, and therefore had accused him of having used magic [1] arts.

[1] *Privilegia et Jura Imperii*, in Schardii *Sylloge*, p. 832.

PART II.

THE PROPHETIC SPIRIT AND THE PROPHECIES OF THE CHRISTIAN ERA.

I. *Introduction.*

THE prophetic spirit of classical antiquity was national and patriotic, and hence was restricted to the interests of the state and the fortunes of war; it did not aim to unfold the vision of a far-distant future. The Roman Empire did indeed represent a great community, combining many nations,—the *Orbis Romanus;* but this Empire was content with the prophetic announcement that it was destined to endless duration; and, in fact, the imperial era did not produce any vaticinations excepting some few about the life and death of one or another emperor. With the introduction of Christianity there was a change. Man's sphere of vision was at once enlarged; there was a general sympathy in the fate of all those nations which now confessed the same faith and were knit together as members of the one great Church.

From this time onwards the destiny of the great nations that took the lead in culture and history, was inseparably intertwined with the progress and the fortunes of the universal Church. Every one of these nations led, so to say, a double life, the national, moving in its peculiar circle of ideas, and a second life, by virtue of which each of the leading Christian nations fulfilled the mission assigned to it in the great Christian commonwealth. And so it was that in the middle ages Germans, French and Italians had the consciousness that to each one of them some special function and gift (*charisma*) had been assigned; that each of them upheld one of the three great Christian institutions, the *Imperium*, the *Sacerdotium*, and the *Studium*.

Upon a closer view of the prophetic materials found in the Christian era, it is at once evident that we must distinguish between four kinds or types of prophecies. For besides the purely *religious* predictions, there are also the *dynastic*, then the *national*, and another kind yet, which I will call the *cosmo-political*. In the last I include those that relate to the Christian Church; because, ever since the founding of Christianity, ecclesiastical fortunes and changes have in general been closely connected with the great progressive development of the world's history. For it is a characteristic of these ecclesiastical prophecies, that they usually relate to approaching ruptures, or to the healing of divisions already existing, or to divine judgments on account of prevalent ecclesiastical corruptions, deeply lamented; and they announce the coming of some great and longed-for reformation of the Church, or a reunion of the divisions in the Christian world. Single monarchies or whole nations are designated as the chosen instruments of these ecclesiastical changes; or, again, such changes are regarded as the causes of social and political catastrophes and revolutions; and, accordingly, events are foretold, which belong partly to the political, and partly to the ecclesiastical sphere, sometimes equally to both. Thus it happens, that those prophecies which relate to the condition of the world, or to the destiny of the great civilized nations, always have a religious side; and, on the other hand, it is not possible to predict momentous and deeply penetrating events and revolutions in the religious sphere, without at the same time holding up to view a corresponding reshaping of political affairs, related to the former as the effect to the cause.

Accordingly, the vaticinations current in the Christian era betray a three-fold origin. Sometimes they are, as it were, self-originated products of a certain state or tendency of things, shaped without conscious intention, and without the definite authorship of any one person. But we frequently find such as have the appearance of a deliberate intention to subserve some special interest. In fine, there are also vaticinations which originate from the conjectures or genial insight of some individual, who, having a correct understanding of the present, forms conclusions about the phenomena of the future in accordance with the laws of causal connection, and boldly proclaims these as facts. The result stamps such instances with the character of prophetic announcements. Some examples will explain and confirm this general view and these distinctions.

As the historian is a prophet looking behind, so the prophet is often but a historian gazing backwards, and announcing events that have already occurred as future. This happens, for instance, when future facts are to be corroborated by the past; as is the case in the well-known Lehnin prophecy.[1] This also occurs

---

[1] [See Gieseler, die Lehninsche Weissagung gegen das Haus Hohenzollern, als ein Gedicht des Abtes von Huysburg Nicolaus von Zitzwitz aus dem Jahre 1692 nachgewiesen, erklärt und in Hinsicht auf Veranlassung und Zweck beleuchtet. Erfurt, 1849. It is directed against the House of Hohenzollern; but its authorship is contested. H. Schmidt (Berlin 1820) ascribes it to Provost Fromm of Berlin, who in 1667 went over to the Catholic Church. Giesebrecht and Gieseler, with more probability, assign it to Chr. Heinr. Delven. It was first published in 1723 in G. P. Schulz's Gelehrtes Preussen, Theil 2. II. B. S.]

INTRODUCTION. 277

in those cases where, under the protecting form of prophecy, monarchs, or governments, or ecclesiastical affairs are denounced, warnings are uttered, and a change in the course and destiny of a state is looked for. An example of this genus is the poem upon the government of Edward III. under the name of John of Bridlington (written about 1370), with a gloss in prose, in which the author clothes in the costume of prophecy what he did not dare to utter in open speech,—his denunciation of the infamous abuses and prostitutions which abounded. [1]

This, too, was well understood in ancient as well as modern times, that a prophecy can be an effectual political agency, and that an event, whose occurrence is desired, can be more easily brought about if it be foretold. When Queen Christina wished to become Queen of Poland, she gave the order that a prophecy with reference to it should be adroitly spread abroad by a monk. [2] When Cromwell designed to bring about certain events, he had them put beforehand into the Almanac, whose astrologer thus attained high consideration. When William of Orange and his

---

[1] See Th. Wright, Political Poems and Songs relative to English History. Vol. i. London, 1859.

[2] "Vous pourriez aussi écrire au Frère (N. N.) qu'il publie adroitement la prophétie." So it reads in her letter of the year 1669, found in Arkenholtz, *Mémoires concernant Christine*, iii, 380.

party in England had determined upon the overthrow of King James II. there appeared, in March 1688, a printed letter of a so-called Quaker, in which it was reported that the Spirit had revealed it to an illuminated member of his Society, that next October a great change would come over the kingdom, and that the month after William would come over the sea. The prophet was at fault only about a couple of weeks, everything else came to pass.[1] As far back as the thirteenth century such craft was applied with good success. When the popes had determined to uproot the Hohenstaufen imperial house, and allow none of its offspring to attain either the German or Sicilian crown, there appeared in the year 1256 a prophecy in Latin verses, under the name of Cardinal Albius,—probably the Cardinal-Bishop of Albano. In this, after a general description of a chaotic period and of the oppression of the Church, it was announced: "Suddenly and unexpectedly a deliverer, a new king, will appear, who for the sake of the honor of the mother (the Roman See) will restrain the South, crush the Sicilians and Frederick's race, and destroy all the works of the emperor Frederick and his sons and adherents. Besides this he will also make the perverse Romans bow under the yoke of the

---

[1] Bayle, *Œuvres*, iii, 249.

Pope." In short, he will bring about just what the papal court at that time wished and needed. The whole sounded like a programme, written with prophetic elevation, of the negotiations about the Sicilian throne, which Alexander IV. was then secretly carrying on with the English prince Edmund; and it was intended to prepare the way for the spoliation. To prevent the Italians from expecting, according to the custom, largesses of gold from the future king, the prophecy did not forget to add, that the deliverer sent from heaven, though rich in virtue, was poor in money.[1]

As an example of *dynastic prophecy*, I may mention the prophetic vision which the Thuringian Basina, mother of Clovis, showed on the bridal night to her spouse Childeric, king of the Franks. At her instance he went out from the sleeping chamber three times during the night. The first time he saw a lion, a unicorn and a leopard. The second time he was shown bears and wolves. The third time he saw dogs and smaller animals biting about. The lion, said Basina to him, represents our son Clovis: his sons will be strong like the leopard and unicorn,—that is Theoderic, Chlodomir, Childebert, and Clotair. From

---

[1] The prophecy is printed in Lami's additions to the Chronicon Pontificum Leonis Urbevetani, in his *Deliciæ Eruditorum*, 1737, p. 323.

them others will be born, strong and ravenous as bears and wolves,—Charibert and Childeric and the rest to Clotair II. At last follow the weak Merovingians in the anarchical times preceding the change of dynasty. This prophecy is found as early as a codex of Fredegar, reaching back to the first part of the eighth century; consequently, before the accession of the Carlovingians to the throne. The intention of preparing for this change shines out in the ironical declaration of Basina: "These dog-like kings will be "the pillars of this empire!"

A kind of dynastic prophecy, whose origin is easily detected, was current in England as a popular rhyme, passing from mouth to mouth in the time of Queen Elizabeth, and even under James I.:

"When Hempe is spun, England's done." [1]

The word "Hempe" means the five monarchs of the Tudor dynasty, Henry VIII. Edward VI. Mary with her husband Philip, and Elizabeth; because the five letters of this word are the first letters of these names. This prophetic saying undoubtedly originated in a popular way from the feeling that, as Eliza-

---

[1] Lord Bacon says in his Essays (Works, Lond. 1856, i, 291), it was generally believed that after the death of Elizabeth "England should come to utter confusion." A fulfilment of this prophecy was found in the Civil Wars, which, however, broke out more than forty years afterward.

beth had no children, at her death either a war of succession would break out, or a stranger, the Scottish king, more feared than desired, would ascend the throne.

Among these dynastic prophecies we may also reckon the prognostications as to the succession of the popes, two of which have attained special celebrity. In the earlier part of the fourteenth century there was spread abroad, under the name of Joachim, a description with allegorical figures, of the popes from Nicolas III. to Clement V., which designated each one of these popes by a few, short, pithy words, expressing in a symbolical way the chief events of his reign. Like the other spurious Joachimite writings this one, too, proceeded from the bosom of the Franciscan order, that section of them called the *Spirituals* or *Zealots*, who were here veiled under the name of the " Dove," given to their order. That a description like this, which painted most of the popes of that period in so black colors, charging them with serious transgressions,—Celestine V. alone is judged more mildly—and making them appear to be the despots of the Church, could find so great sympathy and attain such repute, is a remarkable sign of the revolution which was then going on in the sentiments of the Italians. As early as the beginning of the fourteenth century, in the chronicles of the Bolognese Dominican, Pipin, these assumed oracles and emblems are individually mentioned and described; afterwards less **skilful hands** continued them; **a part** still going under **the name** of Joachim, and a part under the fictitious name of a bishop, Anselm of Marsica. But while the **earlier** ones, from Nicolas III. to Clement V., pre-supposing the stand-point of the author, are appropriate, and easily conceivable, the later ones, those actually imagined **before the event,** rapidly degenerate **into** unintelligible phrases and commonplaces that mean nothing.[1]

This fiction long ago died out; but another one of later origin still has consideration and is reverenced by many persons. It is wholly different from the incisive criticism of the Joachimite vaticinations, for it does not delineate the moral character of the popes **or** their mode of administering ecclesiastical affairs, but it attempts to make each one of them known by one or two words, describing some circumstance in his life,

[1] [On Joachim's prophecies, **see further,** Frederick, in *Zeitschrift für wissenschaftliche Théologie*, Bde. iii, **iv, 1859**; **X. Rousselot,** *Histoire de l'Evangile éternel*, etc. Paris, 1861; Gieseler, *Church History* (New-York ed.), vol. ii, pp. 433-435; Renan, in the *Revue des Deux Mondes*, July, 1866; Hagenbach's History of Doctrines (New-York ed.), i, 423, 465; ii, 119. For the literature compare *Notes and Queries*, London, Sept. 1862, pp. 181-3; and Watts' *Bibl. Britann.* II. B. S.]

or alluding to some single event in his career. Malachias, an Irish bishop of the twelfth century, well known by St. Bernard's biography of him, was chosen as the sponsor for these vaticinations, which begin with Celestine II. in 1143. As far down as 1590 (Urban VII.), they are to the point, or admit an interpretation not altogether forced. The work was completed in 1590, to promote the election of Cardinal Simoncelli, of Orvieto. He was to be the successor of Urban; and is described by the words, *De antiquitate urbis* (*Orvieto, Urbs vetus*). The mottoes relating to the following popes are for the most part interpreted in an insipid and ridiculous manner. But since, from time to time, one or another of these prognostications seemed to be applicable, they were printed and used in numberless editions, and even now do not lack believers. Thus, in the case of Pius VI., the words *peregrinus apostolicus*, and in the case of Pius IX., the phrase *crux de cruce*, bear a convenient sense; while, on the other hand, the *aquila rapax*, for Pius VII., resists all exegesis.

One prophecy, which, at the time of the Reformation, exerted a powerful influence upon men's opinions, and so upon the course of events, was indeed fictitious; but still it originated in a very natural way and without design. Huss was reported to have said at the stake: "To day you burn a goose" (this is the Bohemian meaning of his name), "but from my ashes a swan will arise, whom you will not be able to burn."[1] Luther, who first refers to this and expressly applies it to himself, most certainly did not invent the narrative. The occasion of it was a passage in a letter of Huss to the citizens of Prague, written at Constance: "The goose, a tame animal that cannot fly high, has not rent its fetters; but other birds, which soar aloft in upward flight by means of the divine word and its life, will bring to naught all their malice."[2] And to this is to be added, that his friend and disciple, Jerome of Prague, actually challenged those that condemned him, to appear after a hundred years before the judgment seat of God.[3]

No less clear an invention is the famous vision and prophecy ascribed to Cazotte, about the horrors of the French Revolution, which La Harpe has described in so dramatic a way, and of which he was the undoubted author. But, on the other hand, it is true that, fourteen years before the breaking out of the Revolution, a famous preacher, Beauregard, declared in the pulpit of Notre-Dame: "The temples of God will be

[1] Opera, ed. Altenberg, v, 599; viii, 864; ix, 1562.
[2] Hist. et Monumenta Joh. Hus et Hieroyni (Nürnberg, 1715) i, 121.
[3] Narratio de Mag. Hieronymo, in the Monumenta, ii, 531.

plundered and devastated, His festivals abolished, His name blasphemed, His service despised. Yes: what do I hear? what do I see? Instead of hymns in praise of God, jovial and profane songs will here be sung; and Venus herself, the **goddess of the heathen**, will have the audacity here to take the place **of the living God, to sit at the** altar, and receive the homage **of her** true worshippers." All this actually occurred some years later, and in the very church in **which the prophetic** words were uttered. Whoever **knows the condition** of Paris at that time, and considers, for example, what Walpole said of it in his letters, can **very well** understand how a man like Beauregard, whose vision penetrated the depths **of the abyss of the** reigning corruption, might very well prognosticate these things, which afterwards came to light as **the manifestations** of a spirit that for a long time had **been at work,** although until then only in a noiseless way.

II. *Prophetic Anticipations in the Early Mediæval Times:* *Antichrist, and the End of the World.*

To estimate aright the prime characteristics of the religious and political prophecies of the middle ages, we must go back to the earlier times of the Church. The first christians succeeded to an inheritance transmitted to them by the Alexandrian Jews with their Hellenic culture; for the latter had already fashioned Sibylline prophecies, which held out the prospect of a final victory of Judaism over heathenism, and its elevation into a religion for the world. These Sibylline-Jewish books or fragments were current in the last century before Christ, and again in the first and second centuries after Christ. To them were soon added Christian vaticinations, some of which were held in reverence by the heathen and by a part of the Christians, who took them under their protection or made use of them as genuine, giving to them the name of Sibyllists, as, for example, they were called by the philosopher Celsus. To the Roman authorities, however, it did not seem a matter of indifference to spread abroad expectations of an approaching destruction of the Roman Empire and of the abolition of the religion of the state; and so they forbade, under penalty of death, the reading of these books or "leaves."

As long as the Roman Empire existed in the west, down to the period of the great migration of the nations, there was no real ground for independent prophecies. The christian representations with respect to the future were wholly controlled by their prophetic book, the Apocalypse. While the heathen Romans thought that their empire was sure of endless duration, and the eternity of Rome was, so to speak, an official dogma, the Christians, on the other hand, knew that Rome, drunken with the blood of christian martyrs, must fall, that the Roman secular power would come to an end. Hence the vaticinations which they framed had reference, first of all, to this expected destruction of the Roman Empire, and were connected with the interpretation of the prophetic Apocalypse without further details. The Christians of those early centuries had no well-defined idea that a new christian order of things, a circle of christian states, would spring up from the ruins of the empire. They were not in a condition to look beyond the Roman horizon, and to anticipate the still slumbering powers of barbaric nations, who appeared to them to be only the instruments and forces of devastation. And so they cherished the belief that the destruction of the Roman

Empire would also be the end of the present order of the world; or, to speak more exactly, that the beginning of the end had come. They thought, in fact, that Rome itself with its universal power was still spared, so that the catastrophe of the end of the world might be kept in abeyance. Lactantius says: " She, Rome, is the city which still holds and bears all." They were all the more confirmed in this representation by an incorrect interpretation of the passage in Paul's second epistle to the Thessalonians, ii, 7, (rendering κατέχων, *qui tenet*, he that holdeth on), understanding by it the Roman Empire, whose overthrow was to be followed by the manifestation of " the Man of sin," and soon after by the end of the world.

And so in the christian world, until the heart of the middle ages, there were no proper prophecies of general significance and weight. The prophetic inclination natural to man rested satisfied with conjectures about the great enemy of christianity, the Antichrist, who was expected by every one in east and west to be a Jew and the restorer of Jewish dominion. Much also was said about the approaching end of the world. The formula of the tenth century, " appropinquante mundi termino," is well known. But this was to be preceded by the manifestation of Antichrist, whose dominion was to endure three and a half years. With him men's imaginations were chiefly busy, yet still within the bounds traced by the old tradition. He was to be of Jewish stock; in the far east, in Mohammedan surroundings, he was to appear as a victorious general and a devastator, and fill the world with the terror of his name. So long then as no personage appeared, who could be described as a Jewish prophet and mighty tyrant, nothing could be said of an immediate coming of the end of the world. The expectation sometimes became so impatient, that he was represented as already living, though still in secrecy, just delaying his appearance. But farther than this they could not go; and thus the great Antichrist, the apostasy he was to effect, his victory and his bloody though short dominion,—all this remained a phenomenon constantly expected, constantly feared, but never occurring, though his course was minutely described, and his acts and destiny recounted and imaged forth. But in every century there were forerunners to prepare the way for the great terror; that is, every party regularly accused its opponents of being such preparatory messengers and servants, but the lord of these servants showed himself never and nowhere. It was indeed from time to time proclaimed: He is already born, or he is now nine or ten years old; as, for example, St. Martin, Bishop of

Tours, about the year 380, gave out that the Antichrist was then living, though still a boy. Towards the end of the eleventh century, about 1080, Bishop Ranieri of Florence was entirely sure that Antichrist was born; and some decennia later Archbishop Norbert of Magdeburg gave the same assurance to St. Bernard. The famous popular preacher, Vincens Ferrer, thought that he had the most exact information: the birth of the great foe of christianity took place in 1403. Vincens in 1312 wrote to Pope Benedict XIII. that the Antichrist was already nine years old, that this had been revealed at the same time to many persons, and that there was consequently an urgent necessity of proclaiming it to the world, "so that the faithful might be prepared for the fearful battle immediately impending."[1]

Baring-Gould, in his *Curious Myths of the Middle Ages* (London, 1869), speaks thus of the literature respecting the Antichrist:

" The literature connected with Antichrist is volu-

---

[1] In Malvenda, *De Antichristo*, i, 119. [On Antichrist, see the article in Smith's Dictionary of the Bible, American edition; Moses Stuart, Commentary on the Apocalypse; Elliott, on Apocal. Jowett, on " Man of Sin," in his Epistles of St. Paul; Schneckenburger, in Jahrb. f. deutsche Theologie, 1859; Maitland, Prophecies respecting Antichrist, Lond. 1830; Knight, Lectures on Antichrist, Lond. 1855. J. H. Newman, Patristic Idea of Antichrist, in his volume " Discourses and Arguments", London, 1872. H. B. S.]

minous. I need only specify some of the most curious works which have appeared on the subject. St. Hippolytus and Rabanus Maurus have been already alluded to. Commodianus wrote " Carmen Apologeticum adversus Gentes," which has been published by Dom Pitra in his " Spicilegium Solesmense," with an introduction containing Jewish and Christian traditions relating to Antichrist.[1] "De Turpissimâ Conceptione, Nativitate, et aliis Præsagiis Diabolicis illius Turpissimi Hominis Antichristi," is the title of a strange little volume, published by Lenoir in A. D. 1500, containing rude yet characteristic woodcuts representing the birth, life and death of the Man of Sin, each picture accompanied by French verses in explanation. An equally remarkable illustrated work on Antichrist, is the famous " Liber de Antichristo," a block book of an early date. It is in twenty-seven folios, and is excessively rare. Dibdin has reproduced three of the plates in his " Bibliotheca Spenseriana," and Falckenstein has given full details of the work in his " Geschichte der Buchdruckerkunst."

[There is an Easter miracle-play of the twelfth century, still extant, the subject of which is the " Life

---

[1] [The best edition of this recently discovered work of Commodianus is by H. Rönsch, in the *Zeitschrift f. Hist. Theologie*, 1872, s. 163-303, with a revised text. H. B. S.]

and Death of Antichrist." More curious still is the "Farce de l'Antéchrist et de trois Femmes," a composition of the sixteenth century, when that mysterious personage occupied all brains. The farce consists in a scene at a fishstall, with three good ladies quarrelling over some fish. Antichrist steps in—for no particular reason that one can see—upsets fish and fish-woman, sets them fighting, and skips off the stage. The best book on Antichrist, and that most full of learning and judgment, is Malvenda's great work in two folio volumes, " De Antichristo, libri XII." Lyons, 1647." H. B. S.]

III. *National Prophecies.*

MEANWHILE, from early times, prophecies of another type were fashioned on the basis of *Nationalities*. In general it may be maintained, that the prophetic impulse, so far as it is a natural outgrowth and not conditioned by religious prescriptions, is the product of widely diffused expectations, cherished by whole nations, embodying their desires or fears. When a large mass of people long for something which cannot at once be brought about by their own powers, or which appears to them to be the probable consequence of previous events and present circumstances, this naturally clothes itself among the imaginative races in the drapery of prophecy.

The consciousness of guilt also readily takes the prophetic form. A nation whose moral standard, and consequently whose self-knowledge, has not yet perished, in case it becomes conscious of deep degeneracy and wide-spread moral corruption, is not able to shut out the conviction that the punishment for this degradation must come sooner or later, but inevitably. When the anticipation of such a judgment assumes a concrete, so to say a plastic, form, as is customary at certain stages of culture, it at once takes the shape of prophecy, confidently proclaiming the special mode of chastisement, the impending national catastrophes, and also even the avenging instruments. What thus holds true of nations is also applicable to single orders, to corporations and institutions.

When a people is oppressed by foreign violence, or driven from its earlier possessions, the universal longing to be freed from this yoke takes the form of a prognostication. Such prophecies are frequently the product, not of an individual, but of many persons; at least they cannot be traced back to any one individual. But at the same time a prophecy must not be without a name,—unlike a popular song the author of which no one asks for. A people may not trouble itself about the poet, but it has a deep interest in being able to name the prophet. Where this is wanting it is always invented, and thus, wholly apart from conscious fiction, we find in the history of modern prophecies so many mythical personalities or names without an owner (τυφὰ πρόσωπα).

The very first one whom we have here to mention is just such a mythical personage. Merlin is really the British Orpheus: his name in the early part of the middle ages was celebrated above all others, and he was made the father of very many prophecies which went into fulfilment.

It is still a contested question whether there was ever a historical personage actually bearing this name. Nash, in his introduction to the English "Merlin," a romance of the middle of the fifteenth century, has lately endeavored to show, against Villemarqué, that Merlin or Ambrosius is a pure product of fancy, and that that British Merlin, whom the chronicles transfer to the end of the fifth or the beginning of the sixth century, never existed. At any rate, he became later the hero of a whole round of legends which grew up in the heart of the mediæval literature; and here he appears, not as a bard, which Stephens[1] says he was never called, but as a prophet, an enchanter and the son of a demon.

By the constant progress and pressure of the Anglo-Saxons, the native Britons or Cymri were pent up, from the sixth century, in the western parts of the island, where they maintained a certain independence in some small states. In the twelfth century it was noticed that they were very much absorbed in vaticinations: numerous prophetic declarations were passing from mouth to mouth. They were the feebler stock, ever imperilled by a strong and superior neighbour; the consciousness of this state of things and the hope

---

[1] History of Welsh Literature; German translation by San-Marte, 1864.

of a favorable change expressed itself in their vaticinations. Merlin became in fact the personified prophetic spirit of the people, and his name was attached to every utterance. In the most ancient witness, the British historian Nennius, in the ninth century, he already appears in a purely mythical form,—the wondrous boy, who was in truth the son of a Roman consul whom the mother had never known. In a deep and hidden ground he discovers the two serpents, the white (Saxon) and the red (British), now struggling with each other. As the North Britons, in Scotland, also had their national prophecies, and as a sponsor was needed for these nameless and wandering sayings, a second Merlin was invented, the Caledonian, a counterpart of the first. Of him it was reported, that becoming crazed by the sight of two serpents hovering in the air, he fled into a forest and there ended his life; and so it came to pass there, as in Wales, that many, like the Scottish chronicler Fordun, imagined that they saw in passing events the fulfilment of a Merlin prophecy.

After the beginning of the twelfth century, Merlin also became celebrated as a prophet in the whole of Southern Europe, and his name, like that of "the Sibyl," was ready for the prophecies ever springing up. Galfried of Monmouth, Bishop of St. Asaph about

1152, helped this on the most by his History of the Britons. This work chiefly contributed to spread abroad upon the continent the fame of Merlin the prophet. Along with Turpin's " Life of Charlemagne," Galfried's charmingly told story of the old British Kings had the greatest influence upon the legendary sphere of the middle ages. To magnify his people, he took the narratives of Gildas, Bede, and Nennius, woven in with British legends and adorned with further traditions, and thus made up an attractive, smoothly running history, which long prepossessed the following generations. His allegation, that he only translated a wholly unknown British original work, is doubtless a fiction. He created in fact a fascinating romance, which in its turn became the direct or indirect source of innumerable romances and poems; and from this in the subsequent centuries, especially in the legend about Arthur and the Round Table, there flowed a broad stream of fanciful legends.

The long prophecy of Merlin, incorporated by Galfried into his work and also published by itself, deeply aroused the fancy, not merely of the Britons, but also of other people, especially the French, in the middle ages. Galfried appears to have spun out the sayings and images of Merlin, preserved by oral tradition, and to have arranged them in a chronological order.

The German Dragon, before which the Red Dragon must recede, is to be revenged by a people (the Normans) out of Neustria, clad in wood and iron. Some incidents taken from English history in the early part of the twelfth century, together with the seizure of Ireland, are annexed; and soon afterwards he predicts definitely as to the time of the great national resurrection of the Welsh race. Then is to come the overthrow of the foreigners, the Anglo-Saxons and the Normans. The streams will run red with blood. Armorica will pour out its springs (that is the Britons will conquer with the help of their kindred from Britany), and they will be crowned with the crown of Brut, the first fabulous British King; the island will be named again with the name of Brut (Brittany), and England, the name given by the strangers, will be used no more.

Galfried did not invent these things, but gathered them from popular tradition. Nothing of all this occurred, rather the opposite; and we can understand how Englishmen, like the chronicler William of Newbridge (about 1198), would be impelled to protest against these *divinationes fallacissimæ* and their fanciful propagators. On the other hand, it is a striking fact, that the prophetic fame of Merlin constantly held its ground, not only among the Britons, but also among the French and Germans. It was said of King Arthur in the prophecy: "His departure will be doubtful"; that is, it will be uncertain whether he is dead or still alive. But the people believed that he was alive and would come back; and, according to the commentator Alanus, in Brittany any one would be stoned who maintained that Arthur died like any other man.[1]

Even the English historians favored the universal belief in Merlin and his prophecies. How often they say: "Tunc impletum est illud Merlini," or: "Ut impleretur Merlini prophetia." Galfried in important respects altered the legend about Merlin,—he makes, for example, a demon, James, to be his father; and he cannot be freed from the reproach of thus favoring a baleful superstition, which cost thousands of men their lives, when Thomas Aquinas shaped it into a theological dogma.

According to the belief of the Britons, Merlin foretold not only the fall of the British Kingdom, the invasion of the Saxons and then of the Normans, but also the return of the kings Arthur and Cadwallader; he predicted that the Red Dragon would at last conquer the White, that the old British Kingdom would be at last built up; and so, as the monk of Malmes-

[1] Alani ab Insulis Prophetia Anglicana. Fref. 1603, p. 19, 20.

bury reports, the credulous Welsh people were constantly breaking out in insurrections and revolts, until at last in the beginning of the fourteenth century the English completely and permanently subdued the land. And thus the Welsh restlessness and fondness for insurrection and war were ascribed to the Merlin predictions.[1] The need of a prophecy of an opposite character, to pour water upon the too fiery wine of the Cymrian hopes, was urgently felt. And so, under the name of an old Welsh bard, Teliesin, who lived in the sixth century, there sprung up this prediction: "You will keep your language and your songs, but nothing will remain to you of your old landed possessions, excepting your rough Welsh mountains."[2] To effect a thorough cure of the Welsh from their hallucination about Arthur, as still living and some time to return, as late as the time of King Henry II., there was a pretended discovery of his grave, and the actual corpse of Arthur was declared to have been exhumed, after he had lain there for six

[1] "Hos consuevit fallere et ad bella impingere Merlini vaticinium," says the monk Ranulph Higden, about 1310, in his Polycronicon, ed. Babington, Lond. 1865, i, 410.

[2] In the *Cambro-Briton*, London, 1821, ii, 185, the prophecy, somewhat modernised, reads thus:

"Still shall they chaunt their Maker's praise,
Still keep their language and their lays,
But nought of all their old domain
Save Wallia's rude and mountain reign."

hundred years; he was then said to have died in the year 542 on the island Avalon. But the popular belief could not for a long time be rooted out. Meanwhile Merlin's prophetic fame spread over land and sea, so that in the thirteenth century, even in Italy, a prophecy of Merlin was found to be connected with every remarkable and influential event.

Merlin's reputation was still greater in France, where the Celtic sympathy for their oppressed race upon the Island, and early hatred of the Anglo-Saxons, lent special weight to the Merlin prophecies about the Britons. In Guillaume le Breton's poetical history of King Philip Augustus, at the close, King Louis VIII. is formally summoned to fulfil the promise of the British seer, and to tear away the sceptre from the " English Boy " (the young King Henry III. of England), so that he, Louis, may reign alone in both kingdoms; " and thus", adds the poet, " according to the prediction of the Briton seer (Merlin), the poison of the White Serpent (the Anglo-Saxon) with his whole progeny will be thoroughly rooted out of our gardens." [1]

We might naturally expect to find in Ireland a prophetic spirit akin to that of Wales; yet Ireland produced no Merlin. Here the predictions are ascribed to the old saints of the land, Patrick, Columba,

---

[1] In the *Recueil des Historiens de France*, xvii, 286.

Adamnan. But these predictions have no religious character. They relate in part to events, and very insignificant ones, in the endless feuds of individual Irish chieftains; or to the irruption of the Danes in the ninth century; or in fine to the Anglo-Norman settlement and gradual ravage of the country. The Englishman, Giraldus Cambrensis, called his history of the conquest of Ireland, written in the thirteenth century, a "Prophetic History" (*Historia Vaticinalis*); for he intended to show that the old prophecies of St. Columba and other Irish fathers were fulfilled in the irruption and the bloody successes of the English adventurers, Strongbow and De Courcy.

The suspicion that such oracles were then invented in the interest of the English invaders is heightened by the statement of Giraldus, that DeCourcy himself always carried round with him a book of Irish predictions.[1] And when it was further proclaimed in native prophecies that the English would never more be expelled from the possession of the eastern part of the island, but that in the last times they would rule over all Ireland,—the intent of these inventions is certainly manifest. A learned Irishman, O'Curry,[2] has lately

---

[1] In Cambden's Collection: *Anglica, Normannica, Hibernica.* Frankfort, 1605, p. 794 sq., 803.

[2] *Lectures on the Manuscript Materials of Irish History.* Dublin, 1861, pp. 382, 434.

sifted the mass of prophecies found in Ireland, the most of which are only in manuscript, and convinced himself that they were partly made after the events, and partly invented for the sake of the result. Those prophecies which, in Ireland as elsewhere, flatter the impoverished posterity of families once rich and noble, with the prospect of a revolution and restoration, here seem to be preserved rather as family traditions. O'Curry testifies that they are still prevalent.[1] He says, that " he himself knows hundreds of persons, among them highly educated men and women, who neglect the usual means of obtaining a position in life, in the hope nurtured by these prophecies, that a great restoration is to be completed in Ireland,—although these predictions do not give a single date."

The Scots, too, as was to be expected, also have their national prophecies, a collection of which was published by the Bannatyne Club in 1833. Yet almost all of them have plainly the impress of inventions following after the events. Some few of them, genuine of their kind, originated at the time when the Scots were made subject to the English supremacy, as was especially the case after 1355, and again after 1513. These national predictions comforted the subjugated people with the hope that " Albania "

1. *Lectures*, p. 431.

(Scotland) would be again raised up, and, in union with the descendants of Brut (the Welsh), would lay prostrate their arrogant English neighbor and make the soil of England reek with blood.[1] In later times, after the treaties between Scotland and France, these prophetic hopes that were never fulfilled became connected with the powerful aid of the French lilies.

In the south-western part of Europe, in after times, the kingdom of Portugal by its tragic fate became a fruitful soil for prophecies. This small country, through an able dynasty, the second Burgundian, was, in the course of the fifteenth century, elevated to the height of worldly power (the first in these modern times), by means of its discoveries and colonies in Asia and Africa; its chief city became the principal market of the world. Under its king Immanuel, rightly called the Great [1495-1521], the way to the East-Indies by sea was discovered, and Brazil was subdued. After the death of John III. [1557], the boy Sebastian ascended the throne, and, misled by the Jesuits, undertook a war in Africa with wholly insufficient armaments, and Portugal lost, in 1578, in the unfortunate battle of Alcassar, its king and its army, while shortly afterwards the Burgundian dynasty wholly died

---

4. See the Latin prophecy, as given in Wright's *Reliquiæ Antiquæ* (London, 1846), ii, p 246.

out in both its male and female lines. The country was in consequence conquered, plundered and made subject for sixty years to the hated Spanish bondage; and since then, under the national dynasty of Braganza, it has never been elevated to its former power and prosperity. In this state of things we there find, what formerly occurred in Germany after the death of the emperor Frederick II., that a deep longing for the vanished king (of whose death in the battle there was no sure account) was awakened in the unhappy nation. The Portuguese clung tenaciously to the comfort and hope that their king was not dead, and that at the right moment he would again appear and break the Spanish yoke in pieces. One false Sebastian came forward after another, undeterred by the fate of his predecessor; and the belief could not be eradicated, that the "hidden Prince" (o prencipe encubierto), as he was called, was living on a far island; the whole arsenal of predictions, from the time of Joachim and St. Bridget, was searched through, and soon some were found which might be interpreted about Portugal and its glorious future, and confirm the delusion of the Sebastianists. Nor were there wanting new oracles fresh from the cloisters; national prophets arose, chief among them the tailor Bandara, whose comforting verses the Portuguese knew by heart. Far beyond the years of human life there was a confident expectation of the appearance of a national king; and even the succession of the house of Braganza to the throne was not able to dissipate it. Count von Schomberg, coming from Portugal, said to king Louis XIV., "Half of this nation is looking for king Sebastian, the other half for the Messiah."[1] Sebastian was the Portuguese symbol and pledge of their irrecoverable national greatness and glory; and the thought of their colonies plundered by English and Dutch, of their scattered wealth and their lost traffic, kept the hope ever alive, that he, by whose disappearance all was broken up, would restore all when he came again.[2]

Even after the middle of the seventeenth century, when the house of Braganza was already firmly seated upon the Portuguese throne, a man appeared in the character of a political and religious prophet, whose name stands very high in the literature of his country, the Jesuit Vieira, the most famous sacred orator of his nation. Like the Joachimites, he only attempted

---

[1] "Que voulez-vous que je dise à votre Majesté d'une nation dont la moitié attend le roi Sébastien, et l'autre le Messie?" See Boutaric, Correspondance Secrète Inédite de Louis XIV. (Paris, 1867), i, p. 191. By "the other half" Schomberg meant the numerous Jews (in secret), who were then still called Portuguese.

[2] See Miguel d'Antas, Les Faux Don Sébastien; Etude sur l'Histoire de Portugal (Paris, 1866), pp. 450, 456). It is here stated that as late at 1838, there were still Sebastianists in the heart of Brazil

to interpret and apply prophecies already at hand,— the most of them by Spanish and Portuguese monks, including those of Bandara.

After investigations continued through twenty years, he published a key to the prophets and a "History of the Future" (chiefly based on Bandara),[1] in order to proclaim to his expectant and longing countrymen (the still numerous Sebastianists) that, "God will again raise up your king, and elevate his Portugal to be the heart and centre of a new universal empire, the fifth, according to the prophet Daniel,—since the fourth, the Roman-German, is already falling in pieces, and will be wholly dissolved at the coming of Sebastian. In the time of this fifth empire all Jews and heathen will be converted; and thus the prophecy about one shepherd and one fold will be fulfilled." The Inquisition of Coimbra investigated this affair, the pope confirmed its judgment, and Vieira was obliged to recant and was imprisoned for many years.

It is remarkable that, in the East Roman empire, the heathen institutions of the Old Roman state for

---

[1] *Historia do Futuro;* besides this, an unprinted MS. entitled: Esperanças de Portugal; quinto Imperio do Mundo; and another work, first published in 1856: *Discorso em que se prova a vinda do Senhor Rey D. Sebastian.* See D'Antas, p. 453; and the *Deductio Chronologica et Analytica* of Seabra Silvius (Lissabon, 1771), vol. ii, p. 328.

determining destiny, sometimes by oracles, sometimes by the interpretation of signs, were perpetuated or sprung up anew. In the imperial library of Constantinople there has been found, since the eighth or ninth century, a book of figures with explanatory text, called the Sibylline prophecies. The text is no less uncertain and ambiguous than the figures of men and animals which it was meant to interpret. Bishop Luitprand, in his correspondence as ambassador, mentions a Book of Visions (ὁράσεις), which does not seem to be different from the above. He says that the Greeks named it after Daniel, but he would call it Sibylline; that it contained the number of years that each emperor should reign and the fortunes of the empire under him; which probably only means that these details were reckoned out from certain signs and images.

How this was done may be seen from the application made of it by occasion of the murder of the emperor Leo the Armenian, according to the report of Zonaras. The pictures showed a lion with the Greek letter X on its back; and a man is piercing the lion right through the X. It was now discovered that this prefigured the assassination of the emperor on Christmas, Christ's day,—whence the letter X.

There exists an interpretation or paraphrase of these

oracles, ascribed to the emperor Leo the Philosopher; but it sounds like an independent prophecy, promising in obscure and rough speech the advent of an imperial deliverer, an oriental Frederick, who was to save the kingdom and the people. Coming forth from the Ishmaelites (the Mohammedans), he is to rule over them, adorned with all the virtues, an archangel of God in the form of a venerable old man, poor as a beggar, yet needing nothing. Two angels in the form of eunuchs are to accompany him; a voice from heaven will cry out to the nations: "Will you choose him?" and all will receive him with worship.

There is no hint about the time when this prophecy [1] first originated. It is remarkable, however, in representing the deliverance as coming from that hereditary foe, the Moslem;—or is there here already the anticipation of a Moslem ruler, subjecting the empire of East Rome? And then, too, poverty is named as the chief virtue of this deliverer; while in Anatolian christendom poverty did not by any means have the worth and the religious significancy ascribed to it by the Western nations since the thirteenth century.

Besides, the Germany of the Occident is distinguished by the expectation that its coming emperor,

---

[1] It is found, together with other writings of Leo, in vol. cvii of Migne's *Patrologia Græca*, p. 1141. sq.

the longed-for Frederick, is to be a genuine king's son, the offspring of the ruling race, and not an upstart. Such an one could only be expected, where enduring dynasties and dynastic attachments were almost unknown, and the name *Porphyrogenitus* (born in the purple) was a rare distinction.

Yet this Byzantine expectation of a Deliverer, called from the deepest poverty to the imperial dignity, of a beggar (πτωχός) whom God was to raise up out of penury (ἀπὸ πενίας), for a long time kept its ground. We find it in the tenth century in Nicephorus, the biographer of Andreas Salo.[1] This long-expected One was to lead the Byzantine empire into a golden age, to humble the sons of Hagar (the Arabs) and burn them up with their children. From the twelfth year of his reign all taxes are to cease. Illyricum (Bulgaria) and Egypt will again become kingdoms, and at last he will also tame the blond-haired nations (the Germans and Franks), and bear the sceptre for three and thirty years. Thus are the wishes of the Greeks transformed into prophecies. But the prophecy, in a characteristic way, goes on to say, that a period of darkness, and governments loaded with crime, will follow right after this brilliant dominion. There is to be a sudden transition from a time

---

[1] Acta Sanctorum, maji. vi, Append. p. 96.

of shining virtue and moral purity to an era in which all manner of **shameless crimes** will abound,—a revolution, the only cause of which (in correspondence with the Byzantine absolutism) **is** to be the personality, the will and the example of the monarch. In the principal **city** of the empire they already believed, as a prophetic certainty, that Constantinople, the city dedicated to **the Virgin, and by** her shielded, would never be sacked by foes. It will, they say, **be beleaguered**, but the enemy will raise the siege in disgrace.[1] This delusion was indeed destroyed by the Latin conquest in the year 1204. There is also a later Sibylline prediction,[2] probably devised before the year 1453. Here it is said that the crimes of Byzantium, the blood there shed, and its sins against nature will rise up before God ; the enemy will hurl himself against the city, annihilate its splendor **and** glory, desecrate its sanctuaries and women, give up its buildings **to** the flames, and make its woes resound abroad. Then, in obscure words, there is an intimation of a future revolution.

In the last times of the dying empire, such prophecies produced **very** injurious effects ; **they** confused

---

[1] This **was** announced **by Andreas Salo, ubi supra, 96.**

[2] To be found in Wolf's **collection,** *Lectiones Memorabiles* (Lauingen, 1600), **vol. i, p. 71.**

and disheartened the people. In a cloister of Constantinople there was found a tablet, which, like the other Byzantine predictions, was ascribed to the emperor Leo the Philosopher (886-911). This showed in two columns the succession of the emperors and the patriarchs; every name had its own compartment, and it was found that there was only a single empty one left, so that the present emperor Constantine was to be the last. On the other hand there was another prophecy, intended to inspire the Byzantines with confidence, which likewise had pernicious effects. It ran thus: When the Turks have forced their way into the city as far as the column of Justinian, then an angel will suddenly appear and annihilate all of them. The actual result of their firm belief in this miraculous deliverance was, that the people abandoned all part in the defence, leaving it to the garrison alone, which was altogether too weak.[1] A remarkable example of the influence of these Byzantine prophecies even upon highly cultivated and acute minds, is found in the zealous Aristotelian, Georgius of Trapezium, one of the most learned of the Greeks, driven into Italy by the Turkish conquests. The old vaticination about an emperor and universal monarch, to be raised up

---

[1] Laonicus Chalcondylus, 8, 215, p. 406, ed. Bonn. Leonard. Chiens. ap. Bzovium, *Annal. Eccles.* ann. 1453.

among the Ishmaelites, led him in the year 1469 at Rome, where he was a public teacher, to the conviction that the present Sultan, Mohammed II., the conqueror of Constantinople, was this very Ishmaelite,— who would soon be converted to the Christian faith, and, as the emperor Immanuel and sole monarch of the world, would call all nations to the true faith; and this conversion of the world was to take place of itself, without any special effort on the part of Christians. In Rome this harmless hope was imputed to him as a mischievous transgression; for it was thought that he must also mean that his "righteous emperor," in accordance with the wide spread occidental expectations about the coming emperor, would set on foot a general slaughter of the clergy. But Georgius did not at all mean this; the Byzantine prophecies knew nothing about such a bloody destruction of the clergy; for in the Eastern Church the relation of the clergy to the laity was not so perverted and inimical as it then was in the West. The unhappy man was seized by the Roman authorities, despoiled of his property and put in prison, until at last king Alphonso of Naples took his part and supported him until his death in 1483.[1]

[1] See about him, Aretin's *Beiträge zur Geschichte und Literatur*, ix, 837.

IV. *The Prophecy about Rome.*

ONE city has furnished ampler materials than many a great empire to inspire the spirit of prophecy. The city of Rome for two thousand years has stood alone and unapproached, as one of the great factors in the world's history; and, though it has been the grave of nations, yet it still draws men to it by a magnetic power,—an enticing object which every one longs to see once in his life. In the most extraordinary manner, the views held about the duration of this city, and the high protection it enjoyed, have in the course of time been totally transformed. Under heathen rule Rome was believed to be eternal, and the name "Eternal City," ruler of the world, was applied to it as a matter of course in poetry, history, and even in public life.

Under the christian emperors also, until the end of the fifth century, Rome retained its name "Eternal City," at least among heathen writers. Ammianus Marcellinus said: "It shall live as long as there are men."[1] This name was offensive to the Christians; for they thought that the "name of blasphemy" (Rev.

---

[1] *Rerum Gestarum*, 1. 16, c. 10, 14.

xvii, 3), written upon the forehead of the great whore, clothed in purple, contained an allusion to this predicate of eternity.[1] This proud name died out with the dissolution of heathendom, and the fall of the Roman Empire of the West (about 476), although other names remained, as, for example, Ausonius greets Rome as " the house of the gods, the mistress or head of the world." Even after the fall of the empire, after the devastation by Alaric the Goth and the sacking under Genseric, Rome still remained in the eyes of men the first of cities, the head of the world, apart too from its ecclesiastical relations. When Totila, the Gothic king, boasted that he would raze Rome to the ground, Belisarius (547) warned him in reply, that if he outraged this city, chief of all the cities, he would commit high treason against the whole human race.[2]

In the eighth century there are still found echoes here and there of the ancient opinion that Rome is the ruler of the world, but these are already mixed up with the later ecclesiastical views; as when the abbess Cengitha in 733 expressed to Boniface her desire to visit the *former* mistress of the world, and there re-

---

[1] See Hieronymi *Opera*, ed. Villarsi, i, 852; and the author of the work *De Promiss. et Prædictionibus Dei*, in the collection of Prosper's works (Paris, 1711), Appendix, p. 194.

[2] Procopius, *Bell. Gothic.* c. 23, p. 548.

ceive forgiveness of sin.[1] But the existence of the Roman Empire was no longer bound up, as in the earlier representations, with the continuance of Rome. Before the revival of the western Roman Empire by Charlemagne (800), the Roman Empire was continued by name in the east; for the Byzantine Greeks always called themselves Romans, and claimed that they were the only genuine and legal heirs and successors of old Rome. And since 800 Rome has never been the chief city of the empire in the west, never the seat of the emperors. In the thousand years, from 500 to 1500, as in earlier times, the end of the Roman Empire was thought to be necessarily connected with the end of the world; but yet during this period it was no longer imagined that the city of Rome would likewise endure until the end of time. On the contrary, by a closer study of the Revelation of John, the result was gradually reached, that the prophecy in the eighteenth chapter of the Apocalypse, about the judicial destruction of Rome, was not yet fulfilled, but was still to come, and this, too, long before the close of the present æon. According to the Revelation of John, the judgment upon the City of the Seven Hills is to come suddenly, in a day, with death, mourning, hunger and burning, and the city is to be wholly

---

[1] Bonifacii *Opera*, ed. Giles, i, 76.

consumed. These predictions did not come to pass in the storms of the Gothic wars, for then there was only a gradual and partial destruction of the city.

St. Benedict of Nursia, about 542, had predicted that Rome was not to be destroyed by foreign nations, but to be visited by natural events, storms, whirlwinds and earthquakes, and to die out in and of itself.[1] Since then more than thirteen hundred years have passed, and none of these physical devastations have occurred. The plain meaning of this prophecy of the Apocalypse afterwards forced interpreters to assume that there was still to be a future destruction of Rome by fire. The time for this was conceived as being near or remote, according as the interpreters had in mind, either the mere moral condition of its inhabitants, or as they connected this overthrow of the city with the corruptions of the Church and the degeneracy and guilt of the papacy. In the latter case they viewed the judgments upon this seat and centre of the government of the Church as merely a part of the whole, a single stage in the great process of the purification of the Church.

Thus it was with the *Spirituales* (*zelotes*) of the Minorite order, who interpreted the Babylon of the Apocalypse of the Roman Church, then at Avignon,

[1] M. Gregorii *Dialogi*, 2, 15, ed. Benedict. ii, 240.

which had become corrupt and sensuous; and who also looked for the destruction of Rome by fire. Saint Brigitta, who lived many years at Rome, prophesied, in accordance with a vision imparted to her, that first the sword, then fire, would come upon Rome, after which her soil was to be overturned by the plow.[1] Saint Francisca Romana (in 1439) believed that the destruction of the city had been determined by divine decree, but supposed that the calamity had been subsequently averted through her intercession. Later, however, she had another vision, in which the fall of Rome was shown to her to be imminent.[2]

In a moral poem, by an English monk, Richard Rolle de Hampole,[3] a general separation from the Roman Church, which no one was henceforth to obey, was associated with the expected destruction of Rome. About the same time it was believed that the Roman Church would some time perpetrate so monstrous a crime, that many churches would separate from her, and then, in accordance with the prediction of Saint Paul (2 Thess. ii, 13), the Man of Sin would be revealed.[4] In Germany, the catastrophe which

[1] *Revelationes*, ed. Antwerp. (1611) p. 257.
[2] *Acta Sanctorum Bolland.* Martii ii, 147.
[3] *The Pricke of Conscience*: it was written in the fourteenth century in the Northumbrian dialect, and was published a few years since in London. See the passage p. 111.
[4] Anselmi Opera (Cologne, 1612). 2 Epist. Thessal. i, 2, ii, 42.

threatened Rome was transformed, so as to represent that a German or Roman emperor should be the executor of the judgment upon the guilty city. An emperor was first to destroy Rome, then Florence, the old metropolis of the Guelphs, so hostile to the Germans and their rulers. Such was the myth and the expectation in the fifteenth and even into the sixteenth century.

In the year 1519, when Charles V. was elected, a prophecy was brought from Venice to England,[1] to the effect that the new emperor would subjugate all states and peoples, would force the Mohammedans to accept Christianity, after having destroyed Rome and Florence by fire, and would at last visit Jerusalem, lay down his crown upon the Mount of Olives, and die. Now Charles V. burned neither Rome nor Florence, but, to please Pope Clement, he besieged the latter city and conquered it; and how his mercenaries in the year 1527 captured and plundered Rome is known the world over.

But now, Berthold, Bishop of Chiemsee, in his work "The Burden of the Church,"[2] composed in the year 1519, reproduces this identical prediction with the

---

[1] Sanuto has incorporated it into his great Diary. See Rawdon Brown's *Calendar of State Papers in Venice*, 1509-19, p. 566.

[2] *Onus Ecclesiæ*, 48, 8, ed. 1531.

remark, that it was said to have appeared in the year 1505, in Italy, but had not fallen into his hands until the year 1519. When Berthold wrote, Charles had not yet been chosen emperor. So thoroughly had the way been prepared in Germany, that when the message of May 6, 1527, was received, the only emperor who had possessed any real authority for over a hundred and eighty years, seemed to be seriously thinking of putting the prophecy into execution. It can be distinctly seen in the literature of the times, that so extraordinary and unheard of an event,—for such a fate as this had never befallen another great city—made but a slight impression on this side of the Alps. A much severer calamity had been expected.

But even in Rome this fatality was not quite unexpected. Bartolomeo Brandano, hermit of Siena, appeared in the streets of Rome, not long before May, 1517, crying: "Woe to the city devoted to destruction, which must fall a prey to the transalpine nations, on account of the grave sins of the pope and prelates." The pope had him arrested and imprisoned, and then drove him from the city with the threat that he should be thrown into the Tiber if he came back again. However, Brandano came back and proclaimed that the vengeance of God would now visit the clergy and the city. Clement VII., true to his word, had him thrown from the Ponte St. Angelo into the stream, but Brandano saved himself. Again **imprisoned**, he was released by the imperial army, and this fulfilled his prediction. He seems to have followed closely on the heels of Pope Clement, for as the latter journeyed towards Orvieto, Brandano again appeared, and pronounced him **a** false pope (**on** account of his illegitimate birth), and declared his **official** acts and indulgences invalid.[1]

Rome in a few years had recovered from the **fearful** stroke of the year 1527, and soon, in spite of the great rupture, became richer than she had been before. Meantime the belief that in future times she was destined **to an utter** desolation by fire had become prevalent. Rome is now spoken of as the Babylon of the Apocalypse, the harlot, who says **in her** heart, " I sit as queen ; " and the **word of the** Scriptures, yet unfulfilled, awaits its accomplishment. As early as the fourteenth and fifteenth centuries, we find the statement, that with the fall of the Roman empire would be conjoined a release of the nations from the papal

---

[1] Guicciardini, *Storia del Sacco di Roma*, in Bernini, *Storia delle Eresie*, iv.—Raynald, *Annales.* **a.** 1527, p. **648.** All the historians of the Augustine Order, **to which** Brandano belonged, speak of him. The most exact accounts are in Bardi's *Storia di Siena*, and Pecci's *Notizie Storico-critiche sulla Vita di Brt. da Petrojo chiamato Brandano*, Lucca, 1763, p. 20. Among the people he then **had** the repute of sanctity, and his prophetic mission was believed in.

chair;¹ and not this only, but the inhabitants of Rome itself were to rise up against the papacy, which would be forced to take its seat elsewhere, and then the judgment would be fulfilled upon the city which was equally apostate with the empire. Precisely those theologians who were the most unconditionally devoted to the temporal authority of the papacy defended this view. Rome, they said, has been an adulteress of old ; in the conflicts between the popes and the emperors, the Romans have always shown themselves rather imperialists than papists.² All these sins of Rome will, by and bye, be requited in that devastating conflagration.³ The entire order of the Jesuits was for a time in favor of this explanation of the 18th chapter of the Revelation,—Ribera, Viegas, Lessius, Bellarmine,⁴ Suarez, Henriquez, Cornelius van de Steen (a Lapide), and others.

From this, it was necessarily inferred that, before the

1 So, for example, abbot Engelbert, *De Ortu, Progressu et Fine Rom. Imperii*, in the *Bibl. Max. Patrum*, vol. xxiv.

2 This was certainly, as early as the 13th century, manifested in a variety of ways, and was one reason why the popes, after Innocent IV., generally kept away from Rome, and preferred to reside in the small provincial towns.

3 This is especially brought out by the Roman Oratorian, Thomas Bozio, *De Signis Ecclesiæ* l. 24, c. 6.

4. Bellarmine is really wavering between opposite interpretations. See on this Malvenda, *De Antichristo*, i, 367, who excuses him on account of the obscurity and difficulty of the question.

judgment upon the city, the papal chair must be translated to some other place, for the continuance of the papacy was not a matter of dispute. Then the conclusion was readily drawn, that it was not an indissoluble bond, which bound together the highest ecclesiastical dignity and power with Rome and the Roman episcopate. For with the destruction of Rome ended at least the Roman episcopate, and yet the Church was to continue, and ought to continue, much longer. Many consequently were of the opinion that, as Antioch, while Peter resided there, had been the seat of the primacy before Rome, and as there was no divine command for transferring it from thence to Rome, so, in these later times, the papal power might be transferred to another city and another Church.

V. *The Characteristics of the Prophets.*

LOOKING more closely at the characteristics of the prophets, we soon perceive that when men of theological culture, like *Joachim* and *Savonarola*, supposed themselves to be endowed with the prophetic gift, they nevertheless remained under the influence of the prevailing opinions in the theology of the schools, concerning the nature and conditions of this endowment. It was the universal teaching of these schools, that the gift of prophecy was, of itself, no sign of especial piety or sanctity of life; that even bad men might receive this gift from God (they appealed here to the Biblical statements concerning Caiaphas). Accordingly it seemed no presumption, nor to imply any assumption of the heroic christian virtues, for a man to lay claim to the gift of foreseeing future events.[1] Not even a special spiritual endowment, nor

---

[1] Thus the Dominican, Bernadin Paulini, in the address he made before Paul IV., who was about to condemn the writings of Savonarola, says: Ora dunque, se Fra Girolamo fu santo; o tristo, io non ne parlo; basta che non è impossibile, ch' egli fusse Profeta, essendo, come si sa, date e concesse le profezie anche ai tristi"; in Quetif, *Vita P. Hieron Savonarolæ*, ii, 572. The doctrine that bad men may sometimes be true prophets has gone over into the canon law: see in Gratian's *Decretum*, Can. Multæ autem, and Can. Prophetavit, 19, 1.

an unusual susceptibility to spiritual influences, said the theologians, was necessary for the prophetic functions. They contested the opinion of the Rabbis, who required of the prophet a natural gift and a high degree of insight and wisdom. A double consciousness, however, they said, must concur, in order to constitute a genuine prophet. He must, to wit, know with entire certainty that what is revealed to him is true, and he must be convinced with equal certainty that God is the author of the revelation. Such prophets as Joachim and others used to affirm, it is true, that not the spirit of the prophets, but only of interpretation, had been given to them, in consequence of a higher illumination—to foretell what they found announced in the prophetical books of the Bible concerning the events of their own and of immediately succeeding ages. But that these announcements were infallibly true, and that every event must certainly come to pass, no one, to my knowledge, affirmed. For it was a generally accepted doctrine, that a seer might mix with the visions imparted by divine illumination, other elements, not genuine, attributable to human agency, merely. Thomas Aquinas accordingly believed, that when the prophetic *illumination* was perfect, it brought with it a divinely assured certainty, and from this conviction might be obtained a guarantee of its heavenly origin, a most unreliable criterion, since strength and liveliness of fancy are frequently the source of this confidence. Yet the rule, that on the whole a prophet has no guarantee against self-deception, must be granted by every one who is even in a slight degree acquainted with the subject of visions and revelations. It was also conceded, on the ground of the Biblical examples of Jonas and Isaiah, that certain prophetic warnings (*prophetiæ comminatoriæ*) were not fulfilled, in case of the conversion of those to whom the warnings were addressed. And it was also admitted, that frequently the full comprehension of the prophecy was not disclosed to him who received it, for the prophet must ever be but an imperfect instrument in the hand of God: so that in many cases the prophecy itself, as given by God, was true; but the organ, the man, gave it a false interpretation.[1]

It was not until the great ecclesiastical and political agitation after the middle of the eleventh century, that individuals, borne up by the waves of this

[1] Aquinas brings this out in his *Summa*, 2, 2 quæst. 173, art. 4. Lambertini, afterwards Pope Benedict XIV., explains it, in his work *De Servorum Dei Beatificatione* (Padua, 1743), c. iii, p. 443, by referring to the unfortunate prediction of St. Bernard. This pope also says: " Fieri potest, ut aliquis sanctus ex anticipatis opinionibus aut ideis in phantasia fixis aliqua sibi a Deo revelata putet, quæ a Deo revelata non sunt."

movement, were carried on, in the full assurance of their hearts to the prophetic announcement of definite events. When one believes himself to live in an atmosphere of miracles, he may easily persuade himself that he possesses the gift of prophecy, and such an one is open to the temptation of foretelling an earnestly-wished-for event, or one in his opinion necessary or suited to the divine plan for governing the world. Such attempts at prophecy have usually failed, it is true, and this may have sobered and deterred those that came afterwards. Peter Damiani prophesied the death of the anti-pope Cadalous, within a year's time. Cadalous lived beyond the year; and Peter knew no better way of answering the scoffs of his numerous opponents than this: "Cadalous was deposed by a synod, and that might be called death."[1] The friend and fellow combatant of Damiani, Pope Gregory VII., publicly prophesied at the Easter festival, 1080, that Henry, the German emperor, unless he should make his submission before June 1st, would be either deposed or dead; if not, no one afterwards need believe him, the pope. The result convicted him also of falsehood.[2] But the later chroniclers, who would vindicate for the pope the right of Caiaphas, to

1. Petri Damiani *Opera*, iii, 410, ed. Bassan.
2. Bonizo, in Oefele, *Script. Rerum Boic.*, i, 819.

prophesy the truth as high-priest, even in opposition to his own opinion, discovered a way of escape. The chronicle of San-Bavo [1] asserts: " The pope simply announced that God had revealed to him, that the false king should die that year. He supposed it was Henry, but the false king was Rudolph, who really died at that time."

There was great excitement throughout Europe, when St. Bernard, so distinguished as a man, and celebrated as a saint, was found to be a false prophet. At the command of Pope Eugene III., he had proclaimed a new crusade in France and Germany, and promised victory and success in the name of God. The contrary occurred. The armies were ruined by hunger, pestilence and the sword of Saracens; the whole Occident was thrown into mourning, and Bernard saw himself brought face to face with the charge of deceiving the people and leading them astray. He could only say that the command of the pope had passed with him for the word of God, and could only appeal to the pope, that he would answer for him. [2] And he scarcely found much comfort in the announcement of the abbot, John of Casa-Maria, who

---

[1] In the *Corpus Chronic. Flandriæ*, ed. de Smet (Brussels, 1837,) 1, 564.

[2] Bernardi *Considerationes*, lib. ii, at the beginning.

assured him that the guardian saints of his cloister, the martyrs, John and Paul, had appeared and disclosed to him, that God had permitted the fall of the christian armies, in order that the vacant places of the fallen angels in Paradise might be filled from the souls of those christian warriors who had lost their lives in this crusade.[1]

Vincens Ferrer, in the beginning of the fifteenth century, was almost as much reverenced in south-western Europe, as a holy man, and fearless preacher of the truth, as Bernard in his times. Vincens felt called to proclaim, before all things, the great fact of the public and speedy appearance of Antichrist, that he might prepare mankind for the dreadful conflict. He was fully aware, when he wrote to Pope Benedict XIII., that the Antichrist was already nine years old; it had been contemporaneously revealed to many; demons had been forced by exorcism to declare it.[2] This eloquent Dominican probably died in the firm conviction that within a few years the truth of his prediction would be palpable to all; and it cost the brethren of his Order, Antoninus

---

[1] *Epistolæ* S. Bernardi, ed. Mabillon, epistle 386. Wilken in his Geschichte der Kreuzzüge, iii, 273, has entirely misunderstood this, in the sense of the final restoration.

[2] The larger part of the prophecy of Vincens is given in Malvenda, De Antichristo, i, 120.

and others, no little pains to rescue the good name of the prophet from the reproach of presumption and superstition.

To Saint Catharine of Siena was accorded by her contemporaries the right to prophesy, as two centuries before to the German Hildegarde. But the world since then must be convinced that she had not a prophetic view of the future development of history. She foretold a great and general crusade for the conquest of Palestine, and endeavored to induce Pope Gregory XI. to prepare for it. The crusade did not follow. She announced that a great and thorough-going Reformation would soon pervade the whole Church.[1] "The bride (the Church)," she said, "now all deformed and clothed in rags, will then gleam with beauty and jewels, and be crowned with the diadem of all the virtues. All believing nations will rejoice to have such excellent and holy shepherds; and the unbelieving world, attracted by the glory of the Church, will be converted to her." How little have these longings of the devout maiden of Siena been transformed into history! In place of this great renovation, this conversion of unchristian nations, and this brilliant sanctity, we have had only a long series of destructive religious wars, and lasting sundering of the greatest and most vital nationalities!

---

[1] *Acta Sanctorum, Bolland.* April III, 924.

CHARACTERISTICS of the PROPHETS.   331

St. Brigitta, but a few years before, had prophesied better and more correctly. She, as the organ of **the Holy Virgin**, announced **a mighty** collapse (*ruina*) **of** the Church, as impending. She portrayed the **breaches in** the walls, the columns levelled to the earth, **the** great gaps in the pavement, and so forth.[1] But Catharine herself also appears to have believed that **the renovation** of the Church would not **in any case come** through the papal chair; for she affirmed, **that if a** pope should attempt to reform the barbarized clergy, a great division would rend and pervade the entire Church.[2]

Two opposing currents ran through the souls of those who in the time of the **14th and 15th** centuries were moved to prophecy. On the **one side the** view, deeply rooted in the general religious consciousness that the state of **the** Church was altogether **unendurable**, and that only the hope of **a** great and **impending** reformation could prop up **the** tottering faith **in** the truth of Christianity. On the other side was the feeling that suitable instruments for this renovation were nowhere to be found; and that **in the source** whence they were to **be** expected, namely Rome, there was

---

[1] *Revelationes*, 78, p. 293, ed. Antwerp.

[2] Facient tunc scandalum universale toti ecclesiæ **Dei quod tanquam hæretica pestis scindet et tribulabit eam**, p. 925.

neither inclination nor capacity for the work. Thus it happened that individual men, as, for exemple, William St. Amour, Ryckel and Jacobus de Paradiso, wearied out and disheartened, believed that there was no hope left for the Church; that she would remain in her degradation until the appearance, so soon to be expected, of the Antichrist. Others, on the contrary,—and they seemed to constitute the majority—foretold with confidence a thorough-going purification and renovation of the Church, which her founder could not possibly permit to go on in such a perverted form.

But also, in harmony with the prevailing popular view, it was expected that a bloody judgment, a bitter persecution of the clergy, and above all, of the highest leaders as the most guilty, would precede the renovation of the Church.

It was often the longing for better things which led men of great spiritual endowments to predict the future. The present seemed to them intolerable. They perceived with pain the contradiction between their situation and the demands of the time, which their religious faith, and their love of country forced them to recognize. As with nations so with individuals. With this longing, a presentiment was generally associated, that the times lay in the pains of child-birth; that humanity stood upon the borders of great changes and transformations. Savonarola at first was himself terrified by the impulse to prophecy which gradually overpowered him and controlled his thinking and action. "I do not desire," said he, "to be taken for a prophet, for that is a weighty and dangerous name, makes a man restless, and arouses against him many persecutions, even though for the love of Christ he may be willing to endure them."[1] "You force me," cried he afterwards to the Florentines, "to be a prophet."[2] "The sins of Italy open my mouth. An inward fire consumes my bones and forces me to speak."

How different from Savonarola, and yet kindred with him, was another prophet of the Dominican order, the learned and profound Campanella, a man of genius. In him also, the prophetic office must go hand in hand with political efforts. To him, a Calabrian, the misfortunes of his narrow native land, Calabria, as well as the condition of the whole of Lower Italy, then oppressed by Spanish rule, weighed heavily upon his heart. He saw his people humiliated by an oppression which a modern writer, well acquainted with Italian affairs, has characterized as perhaps the most wretched that has existed in christian times.[3] He

---

[1] *Compendium Revelationum*, p. 274.
[2] In his *Prediche fatte l'anno del* 1496, f. 359.
[3] See *Ganganelli, seine Briefe und seine Zeit*, by Von Reumont, author of the *Römische Briefe*, Berlin, 1847, p. 32.

said that Southern Italy must become a republic under the theocratic dominion of the Papacy; and in order to gain partisans and confederates, he foretold (basing his prophecies upon the predictions of Joachim, Brigitta, Savonarola, and on his exposition of the Apocalypse), a transformation of Italy, to occur in the year 1600. Like Savonarola, he said at the same time: " I do not make myself out a prophet, and a wonder-worker, and yet I see, perhaps, some great things." [1] Speedily betrayed, his undertaking failed. He spent twenty-seven years in fifty different prisons; he was seven times stretched on the rack, until at last he found an asylum in France. Did then the result, the external quiet of Italy during the year 1600, undeceive him in regard to the truth of his prophecies? In the beautiful and stirring poems in which he breathed forth the changing moods of his long prison life, his anxiety and his hope, his trust in God, and his despair, he raises his complaint towards God: " Shall then the host of the prophets, whom thou sendest, lie? [2] Wherefore dost thou let the stars and the prophets, Thy gifts, alike become delusive teachers?" [3] In the

[1] In the Prooemium to his *Atheismus Triumphatus*, in Struvii Collectanea Manuscriptorum (Jena, 1713), li, 68.

[2] *Poesie Filosofiche di* Campanella, pubbl. da G. C. Orelli (Lugano 1834), Madrigale, viii, p. 161.

[3] Madrigale, i, p. 144.

book which he wrote in prison, "The Spanish Monarchy," Campanella still shows himself full of faith in prophecy; and lays special emphasis on the assertion that St. Brigitta foretold the discovery of America.

A man in whom we may distinctly trace the effects of pain and disappointment produced by earnest reflection ending at last in prophetic vision, was Dionysius Ryckel (or Leewis), styled the ecstatic teacher, a priest of the deepest and most earnest piety, and at the same time the most learned theologian of his age. Like all the men of insight in Germany, like his friend and patron Nicolas of Cusa, he shared fully in the view of the Church as to the necessity of councils and of their authority over the popes. His hopes, like those of all others, rested upon a new council, which he saw at the same time the popes tried to prevent with all their shrewdness and power.

This continual and torturing contemplation of the condition of the Church and the world (in the year 1461) led him to visions and revelations; and he came to see, in converse with the divine Master (what was the product of his own reflections), that the measure of impending chastisements and judgments would be accurately dealt out, according to the measure of the present ecclesiastical corruption.[1] It was revealed

---

[1] *Opuscula Insigniora Dionysii Corthusiani, Doctoris Estatici* (Cologne, 1559), p. 747. Here are found the three " revelationes."

to him that the Church was utterly backslidden and perverted; from the crown of the head to the sole of the foot there was no soundness to be found in by far the larger part. As to her leaders, even should they swear to reform, they would but forswear themselves. It was the time (1461) of the vain attempt of Pope Pius II. to bring about a christian crusade against the Turks, after the loss of Constantinople. Dionysius prophesied that all these efforts must come to naught, as actually happened. It was even expected, with a certain deep sense of guilt, that a Turkish army would soon sweep over the Latin and German nations of the West.

Ryckel's contemporary and friend, the deepest thinker of his time, Cardinal Nicolas of Cusa, like him also became a prophet without precisely claiming for his declarations a high degree of illumination. Cusa also had a clear perception of the deep corruption of the Church, and of its prime cause, the despotic and avaricious Papacy, as it then was. Thus he also came to the convictions, which, after he had outlived the failures of the reformatory councils, he delivered in the form of prophecy: " The Church would sink still deeper, until she should at last seem to be extinguished, and the succession of Peter and the other apostles to have expired.¹ But after that she will be victoriously exalted in the sight of all doubters."²

There were other visionary prophets, to whom the future was only revealed in symbolic pictures, of the signification of which, however, they were assured with inward certainty. Of such were the Dominican Robert of Usez, at the end of the thirteenth century, and the German priest and founder of a monastic order, Bartholomew Holzhauser, in the middle of the seventeenth century. This order affirmed of Robert that he was endowed from his youth with the spirit of prophecy, and had been continually accompanied by the same; that his gift had been formally tested at an assembly of his Order at Carcassone, in the year 1293, and that, on account of the satisfactory character of his answers, he had been commissioned to journey through France, Italy and Germany as preacher and prophet. While Robert beheld, especially in symbols, the corruption of the Church and of the papal chair, Holzhauser's visions reflected the longings of a man of narrow views, desiring to correct the history of

---

1 "Nulla major difformitas ab aliquo poterit exoriri, quam ab illo, qui, suæ magnæ potestatis intuitu licere sibi cuncta credens, in subditorum jura prorumpet," are his words in *Concordia Cathol.*, 2, 27, p. 729, ed. Basel.

2 *Opera*, Basle edition, p. 932.

the world, because the course and the consequences of the Thirty Years' War had assumed quite a different aspect from that which his opinions required. His commentary on the Apocalypse, which formerly had many believing readers, is written in the same spirit.

VI. *The Cosmopolitical Prophecies.*

TURNING now to that class of prophecies which I have styled the "*cosmopolitical*," we may distinguish four periods. The first extends from the Carlovingian times to the end of the twelfth century. The second period, the Joachimist, extends over the thirteenth and half of the fourteenth centuries. The third division covers that gloomy time from about 1347 to 1450; this was the time of the Black Death, the Papal Schism, and of the brightening expectation, soon to be extinguished in darkness, of the renovation of the Church by means of councils. Then followed the fourth prophetic epoch, comprising a period of about 77 years, from 1450 to 1517. In this, the prophecies are wholly filled with the thought of the judgments impending over Rome, popes and clergy, and with longings for the reformation of the Church; so that at last, this prophetic expectation became the common consciousness, the saving anchor of faith, of all earnest religious spirits.

In the first period, in the ninth and tenth centuries, and until the middle of the eleventh, the coming of Antichrist and the approaching end of the world are the well-nigh exclusive objects of men's presentiments. As life in great cities, and popular literature, were not yet developed, and as there were thus no important centres of spiritual growth—we are here restricted to the aid of ideas prevailing in cloisters. In this seclusion, men did not look either backwards or forward, but chiefly from presages, or from physical and moral phenomena not understood, they formed their conclusions as to the speedy termination of the world's history, with no presentiment or comprehension of its goal or of its progressive culture. There was but one fundamental thought in this and the following time, that the existence and duration of the present order of the world were indissolubly bound up with the continuance of the Roman empire, as this was renewed in, or made over to, the Carlovingian dynasty, and after its overthrow to Germany and its kings. It was accordingly styled the Holy Roman Empire of the German Nation, for it was held to be the all-supporting keystone of the christian world, which could not be abandoned until the process of the world's dissolution began. While this kingdom lasted, and the people did not desert it, the last day was still distant,—so they believed and thus they spoke. And hence that general fear or expectation that Antichrist would soon come, and that the end of all things was near (*appropinquante mundi termino*, as the formula run). About the beginning of the eleventh century, the minds of men were distressed, not only because the history of the Church had passed through a thousand years, but still more because the kingdom which Otto I. had exalted to such a position of power and glory, appeared, on the death of his powerless uncle, Otto III., ready to fall in pieces.

The most prominent prophetical authorities of this time were Methodius from the Byzantine Orient, and St. Hildegarde. Under the name of that distinguished Bishop of Patara, in Lycia, who suffered martyrdom in the persecution under Diocletian, the so-called "Revelations" first came to light, probably in the eleventh century in Constantinople. The author's name can scarcely have been Methodius, as was assumed. He simply put his productions into the lips of that teacher of the Church, who had written a celebrated commentary on the Apocalypse. The writing was adapted to the Byzantine Greeks, and was designed to administer comfort, courage and hope, in the time of a manifestly increasing weakness of the Eastern empire, and when the dominion of the Mohammedans was extending its sway over the whole of Asia. Methodius announced the victory and conquests of the Ishmaelites (Arabs) breaking forth from the desert. God had given them victory, and allowed them to subjugate so many christian lands and nations as a punishment for the sins of the laity and clergy. But still the Empire of Rome, as the author and all his countrymen designated the Byzantine (East Roman or Greek) Empire, shall not be eternally overthrown by any power; its weapons are invincible, and it shall subdue all kingdoms at last. Accordingly, an emperor and his son are to fall upon the Ishmaelites, when they fancy themselves most secure, and suddenly wrest from them all their previously conquered lands, and impose upon them a yoke of servitude a hundredfold worse than that with which they have oppressed the Christians. Finally, the last of the Roman (i. e. Byzantine) emperors is to journey towards the emancipated Jerusalem, and there lay his crown at the feet of Christ. Then comes the end of all things, Gog and Magog, and Antichrist, and the last judgment.

This representation of the abdication of the last monarch in Jerusalem is also found in the Occident, in a writing of the Abbot Adso, composed about the year 948, at the request of Queen Gerberga. Since the empire was not until some years later (in 961) transferred to the Germans, one of the Frank kings was here represented as the **last and** most powerful **of the** emperors, who was to bring to a close the course of history in such a devout and humble style. For, said the abbot of Moutier-en-Der, " the Roman kingdom is almost destroyed, to be sure, but it will survive [1] in the kings of the Franks. (A Carlovingian is meant; for the house of Capet had not at **that time yet** arisen.)

But Methodius now essentially **controlled the views** of the Occident concerning the course **of the world's** history; for in the first half of the twelfth century, a Latin translation of his prophecies must have been in circulation. The Turks **had then** displaced the Ishmaelites **(Arabs); the Roman kingdom** and the Roman emperor were **naturally made to refer to** Germany and Italy, **and the emperors of German birth.** Thus was Methodius **the original source of those expectations** cherished **even until modern times, that the** Turks would yet some **time sweep over the whole of** Germany, and their horses drink the waters of the Rhine. Even Otto of Freisingen, in his preface to his Chronicles, addressed to Chancellor Reinhold, introduces Methodius as authority for the continuance of

---

[1] This work is in the Appendix to the Benedictine edition of Augustine, iv, 243.

the Roman empire which was to be fully destroyed only at the end of time.

Another view, deeply imprinted upon the fancy of the Middle Ages, was drawn from the same source. From Rev. xx, 10, it was inferred that heathen nations, from far distant regions, Gog and Magog (Scythians) would, at the end of time, gather together against the New Jerusalem, and be by her destroyed. Now, according to Methodius, Alexander the Great had formerly shut up the race of Gog and Magog in the Caspian mountains by a miracle; but the mountains were some time to open again, and then this stream of wild conquerors and avengers would be poured forth over the world. There was in this a presentiment of the great Mongolian irruption in the thirteenth century, and yet the myth is found in the Syrian poem of a Jacobite of the end of the sixth century. There it is God himself who is described as opening the door of the rocks for the ruin of the nations.[1] Now the chronicles of Alberich in the year 1237[2] announce, that the Minorite Peter de Boreth had from Acre declared, that the Antichrist was already growing up, and would be ten years old in March. It was added in connection therewith, that this was impos-

---

[1] The *Revelation of Jesus* by John Hooper (London, 1861), ii, 438.
[2] In the *Recueil des Historiens de la France*, xxi, 596.

sible, since the tower of Babel must first be rebuilt, the closed Caspian mountains must open, the river Ethan flow, and the idol of Mohammed fall to pieces; that is, Islamism was to die out or decay.

The Latin text of Methodius must also have varied very much, with reference to the last things. That feature, that the last emperor of the Frank race was to go to Jerusalem, lay his crown upon the mount of Olives and there die, is certainly not found in the original Greek. This originated in the tenth century, from a writing by the monk Adso, which was generally taken in the middle ages for a work of the Archbishop Rabanus of Mayence. But this addition was variously given. According to Engelbert of Admont,[1] Methodius said: "The last emperor would be incapable of withstanding the Ishmaelites (Mohammedans), and would lay down his sceptre, crown, and shield on a withered tree, beyond the sea, and there give up the ghost." The history of the world, according to this view, was to terminate (before the Antichrist) with a great victory of Islam over the Christian faith. A view, so dispiriting, so conducive to doubt, led Engelbert to the remark: "The doctors, it is true, out of reverence for the holy martyr (the supposed

---

[1] *De Ortu et Fine Rom. Imperii*, in the *Biblioth. PP. Lugdun.* XXV, 378.

author) did not venture to reject it, and yet attributed little weight to it." It was certainly not found in the manuscripts, for in the printed editions the course of the last days is given quite differently.¹ The Ishmaelites or Turks are completely conquered and subjugated; but the Christians immediately fall, during a long and all too happy condition of peace and prosperity, into fleshly security and luxury, until Gog and Magog set on foot a fearful slaughter, whereupon the Roman king proceeds towards Golgotha, takes his crown from his head, lays it upon the cross, and restores the kingdom of the Christians to God the Father. Thus the shame was at least averted of a final victory over the Christians by their ancient hereditary foe, the Turks, and Methodius remained, especially for the Germans, a book of comfort and of hope. Sebastian Brandt says in the preface, in the year 1497: " I give it over to the press, because, as I hope, the promised triumph of the christian republic over the unbelievers and Turks, is now quite near." And in the year 1518 the warning cry still went forth to Emperor Maximilian,²

> " Give ear, o king, for God hath called
> That thou the suffering christian world

---

1 In the *Orthodoxographa* (Basel, 1555,) p 397, and in the edition of Sebastian Brandt, Basle, 1504.

2 In Liliencron, III, 215.

> May'st bring again unto its right.
> How oft to arm thee to the fight,
> Hath He His holy servant sent,
> Methodius, to this intent." [1]

After this it was added, that it had been prophesied of an Emperor Maximilian, that he should fill the Holy Land with christian faith still,—another of the many hopes which remained unrealized.

In another writing composed by the Dominicans in the year 1474, in order to console the Christians for the fall of Constantinople,[2] Methodius, the "Doctor authenticus", as he is here styled, is again the chief authority,[3] of course not in the form in which Engelbert read him, but in the more encouraging text. Here it was related, that many fathers had subjected Methodius to a careful investigation, the result of which was now imparted. Germany and France would be devastated by internal wars, but should not fall under the

---

[1] Kaiser, schick dich, Gott will dir helf,
Dass du die armen Christenwelf
Widerumb bringest zu einem recht;
Das hab dir Gott den seinen Knecht
Zu schauen manigvalt gesant,
Methodius war er genant.

[2] *Qui pro fide mancipatus carceribus* **angelo** *sibi revelante librum conscripsit*, is added. (Who enslaved for the faith, wrote a book in prison, an angel revealing unto him.) In that case certainly every word must have been infallible, and still be going into fulfilment.

[3] Tractatus quidam de Turcis, prout ad praesens Ecclesia sancta ab eis affligitur (Nuremburg, 1481).

Turkish yoke. Whether Rome would be conquered by the Turks, had been asked by an enlightened monk, worthy to receive divine revelations, to whom Christ had answered, that it was not at present advisable that he should know this, nor who should be the victor in the next Turkish war.

The first of the prophets of more recent times was Saint Hildegarde of Bingen on the Rhine. This German prophetess stands alone, in a peculiar position, actually attained by no other in the entire christian history. No prophet has ever acquired so high consideration, no saint so general confidence, or such unbounded reverence,[1]—not Bernard himself, who paid reverence to her as the more highly gifted, although she was neither spared from attacks, suspicions, nor even scorn and ridicule. Her character and her revelations were investigated at a great assembly of the Church, presided over by Pope Eugene III., and guaranteed and accepted as genuine. Three popes, two emperors, many bishops and abbots came to ask council of her, hoping that divine revelations might be through her imparted to them; and it is worthy of note, that in the letters addressed to her by Popes Eugene,

---

[1] Famosissima illa prophetissa Novi Testamenti, cum quâ familiariter locutus est Deus; so wrote the author of the *Vita S. Gerlaci*, in the *Acta Sanctorum*, 5. Januar. c. 8.

Anastasius and Hadrian IV., there still remains a breath of genuine humility, and recognition of their own fallibility and neglect of duty.[1] Bernard still ventured to write his book, and to warn the papacy, although in vain, against the fearful strides it was making in the path of despotism and centralization. Hildegarde was in this respect a true German prophetess, in that, as none of her sex before or since have done, she portrayed the spontaneous ethical uprising of the Germanic nationalities, rather than of the Latin race, against the degeneracy and the abominations of an insatiable and avaricious hierarchy, corrupting the life of humanity,—a state of things which then was not developed to such a degree as was portrayed, but which was wide spread after the thirteenth century. The time was to come, she said, when princes and people would renounce the authority of the papacy, because religion is found in her no more; then would separate countries prefer their own church rulers to the Pope; the latter, with greatly diminished reverence, would be confined to Rome, and a few surrounding places.[2] Hildegarde also foretold the breaking

---

[1] For example, Eugene III. wrote to her, that he rejoiced that in these times God had illumined her by his Spirit, and given to her s) great insight; sed quid nos ad hæc dicere valemus, qui clavim scientiæ habentes, ita quod claudere et aperire possimus et hoc prudenter facere per stultitiam negligimus.

[2] Quia enim nec principes nec reliqui homines tam spiritalis quam

up of the German Empire; each people and each race would have its own princes, under the pretext "that the magnitude of the kingdom had become rather a burden than an honor;" and just this division, and diminution of the strength of the empire, would entail the fall of the papal dignity.

Hildegarde incontestably had much to do with the fact, that in the middle ages the expectation of a great judgment upon the clergy, and a bloody persecution of the priests, was so deeply fixed in the mind of the German nation. She even foretold a great and universal secularization of the property of the Church, and a return of the clergy, ruined by riches and avarice, to moderate and more equally divided incomes. In a poem of the fifteenth century upon the council of Constance, it was said of her descriptions of simony and clerical luxury:

> "How sadly their course hath marred,
> From Bingen, saith Saint Hildegarde,
> Within her book of wit and taste,
> Who reads, hath well the truth embraced!" [1]

Yet Italy was the land where the prophetic spirit,

---

sæcularis ordinis in Apostolico nomine ullam religionem tunc invenient, dignitatem nominis illius tunc imminent, etc. *Liber Divinorum Operum*, in Baluze, *Miscellanea*, ed. Mansi, ii, 447.

[1] Wie hat den schädlich kläglich Lauf
Gesait von Bingen Hiltgart
In Ihrem Buch, die witz, die zart,
Wer ir Buch liest, dafs man's wol brüst!
(Liliencron, *Historische Volkslieder*, i, 248.)

especially since the beginning of the thirteenth century and without cessation until the end of the fourteenth, grew most luxuriantly. In no country was there then a life so rich and manifold, and such a wrestling of all powers and passions. There Imperialism and Papacy for more than two centuries fought with one another like two giants; there France and Germany contended for the mastery, now openly and now **in secret.** Through entire upper and middle Italy prevailed the irreconcilable feud between the two parties, the Guelphs and the Ghibellines, from which no one high or low could stand aloof. While the mighty devoted themselves to astrology, and not seldom, like Frederick Ezzelino, kept their court astrologers, and never entered upon any important undertaking without first having consulted the favorable constellations, the people rioted in prophetic proverbs. Guelphs as well as Ghibellines had their own prophecies. Merlin and the Sybil had to lend their names, which had become typical, to the continually fresh productions which were called forth by the powerful popular demand for prophecy. Michael Scoto, the astrologer of the Emperor Frederick, Asdenta of Parma, and especially Joachim, stood in high esteem. Sibylline prophecies were all the more confidently trusted since **it was** believed that the Sibylline books were still preserved in the Lateran church at Rome.[1] Scoto and Asdenta were by Dante placed among the damned as false prophets; and the latter, a shoemaker of Parma, he represents as in hell, repenting that he had not kept to his trade. His contemporary, Salimbene, however, reported that he heard much from him which afterwards occurred; and also that Asdenta, solely by the diligent perusal of the writings of the classic prophets of the time, Methodius and Joachim, together with the sayings of Merlin, Scoto and the Sybils, had cultivated the art of prophecy.[2]

In Germany, Hildegarde stood a long time unrivalled. From her death until towards the end of the thirteenth century and even into the fourteenth, no utterances of the prophetic impulse and spirit worthy of mention are preserved among the Germans. All of the German literature, it is true, from the middle of the thirteenth century until its close, was very barren as well in the Latin as in the German tongue, and yet more barren and fragmentary are the historic documents and chronicles which we possess of this period. But one and the same event of worldwide significance was, for both Germany and Italy,

---

[1] Huillard Bréholles, Préface, p. xxxvi, in his edition of the *Chronicon Placentinum*, Paris, 1856.

[2] Salimbene, *Chron.*, p. 284, in the *Monumenta Hist. Parmens.* (Parma, 1857).

equally decisive and momentous; although Italy was at first plunged, in a far higher degree than **Germany**, into incurable disasters in consequence of the **same**. That event was the victory **of the Papacy over the Empire**,—the fall and overthrow **of the House** of the Hohenstaufen, with which was connected the regularly planned weakening **and sundering of the Romano-Germanic** empire **by the popes, resulting to the advantage** of the Curia, of the French kings, and of the Italian Guelphic party. It was clearly seen that the popes, especially the French **popes, and Urban IV.,** Clement IV., Martin IV., did everything to prevent the formation in Germany **of** any unity, of any powerful royal house, of any firm and well ordered government **of** the empire. It was speedily recognized that in consequence of this procedure **of the popes,** an emperor in the true sense could not be obtained by election, and that a Guelph kingdom in **Lower Italy** supported by French authority was impossible. And yet it belonged to the religious consciousness of the **world at** that day, which regarded the empire as an indispensable constituent, an organ of the one Catholic **Church**, that its dissolution **would** lead **to** a general falling away from the papal chair; for a three-fold *discessio* according to 2 Thes. ii, **was** universally accepted viz: *ab imperio, a sede apostolico, a fide;* so that it seemed to many that the popes were laboring, as if driven by a fatality and an irresistible impulse of the stars, to undermine their own authority. Hence the certainty, that the fall of the kingdom would introduce the outbreak of the rule of Antichrist, with all its indescribable series of abominations and apostasies. The judgment of contemporaries presents to us the key to the origin of the prophecies of the time and of their influence.

In England, where there then was more historic insight, and a better historical literature than in the rest of Europe, the contemporary judgment is pertinent and pragmatic: "The Roman Curia, that it may rule alone, has effected the hopeless destruction of the Roman Empire."[1] In Italy the Sibyl was in favor of the Guelph and the French papal party, and it accordingly announced, that on the death of Frederick II., the Germanic Roman Empire itself would go to its grave. The Florentine Guelph, Brunetto Latini, in his work written in French about 1266, gives it as his opinion, that "if Merlin and the Sibyl tell the truth, Frederick and the imperial dignity will end together; yet I do not know whether this is to be

[1] Imperium Romanum, procurante Curiâ Romana, ut sola dominaretur, suspenditur desperatum. *Chron.* Joh. de Oxenedes ad a. 1251 (London, 1860).

understood of his race, or of the Germans, or of both together."[1] We learn however from his contemporary and countryman, Salimbene, that the Sibyl expressed herself very distinctly. "In him," she said, "the kingdom shall come to an end, for although he shall have successors, they shall nevertheless be deprived of the title of Emperor, and of the Roman dignity (*fastigium*).[2] Salimbene himself did not doubt that, for the future, it was **the divine purpose that there** should be no longer an emperor.

Two contemporaries exhibit to us the position of the Germans; the one, the experienced and observing author of a brief anonymous writing[3] of the year 1288, the other, Jordanus of Osnabrück, in his book on the Roman Empire.[4] "Within fifty years," said the first, "the Roman kingdom, which in the year 1220 was still so powerful, has sunk so low as to have lost all consideration. The Papacy, on the contrary, has mounted so high, that kings and peoples, and the whole world lying at the feet of the Pope, have greeted him as monarch of the world. This can now rise no higher, without degenerating into a complete secular domin-

---

[1] *Les Livres du Trésor*, ed. Chabaille (Paris, 1863), p. 93.
[2] *Chron.*, p. 167, 378.
[3] The *Notitia Sæculi*, published by Karajan, in his work, *Zur Geschichte des Concils von Lyon* (Vienna, 1849).
[4] Jordanus, ed. Waitz, Göttingen, 1868.

ion. To such an extent has the clergy, in the service of the Roman Church, and with the co-operation of the French, destroyed the Roman Empire *(Clerici et Gallici nunc parte magnâ Romanum destruxerunt imperium).* Should they fully succeed in accomplishing this work of destruction, such a flood of misfortune and ruin will break forth, preceding the Antichrist, as the world has not yet experienced. In recompense, however, for the shame which the clergy has already brought upon the empire, a judgment will soon be inflicted upon them, because they are so deeply infected with the poison of Simony."

Jordanus expressed himself more cautiously: "Since the Roman Empire has shared in the great honor of constituting the bulwark of the Christian world against the Antichrist, who could not appear until that empire was overthrown, all these forerunners, who assist in this overthrow, are but preparing the way for the Antichrist; and the popes, chief enemies of the Empire, are doing this most of all. The Romans and their popes," then adds Jordanus, "had better beware, lest by a just judgment of God upon their offenses, their authority be taken away from them." The same warning was also delivered by him to the German princes, so gladly enriching themselves at the expense of the empire. The Cardinal

Jacob Colonna, who wrote a preface to this work of Jordanus in the year 1281, addressed Pope Martin V., the tireless opponent of the German and patron of the French power, expressing his fear that if the Roman Church, which had banished its customary prayer for the emperor from its liturgy of the mass, has now gone so far as to be able to say, We have no king or emperor but the Pope, there would break forth a great and bloody persecution of the clergy. (Waitz, 41.)

In still later times, the Belgian chronicler, Dynter, addressed a pathetic warning to the German electors, that they should earnestly consider what dangers and calamities the destruction of the Roman Empire would bring upon the world.[1] This was written in the year 1445, just as Germany had shown to the world, in the Hussite wars, the spectacle of its pitiable impotence, and that its empire was now become an empty shadow.

In the thirteenth century, however, in the midst of all the ruin of Germany and Italy, the hope of an approaching transformation of affairs was still preserved by means of prophecies. Roger Bacon, who, with Dante, was the most richly endowed, the most many-sided and cultivated spirit of his age,

---

[1] *Dynteri Chronicon*, ed. de Ram. (Brussels, 1854), i, 166.

wrote in the year 1267: "It has been prophesied for forty years, and confirmed by many visions, that a righteous, true and holy priest is to arise, as reformer and purifier of the Church, so deeply involved in error. He is to purify the laws of the Church, and establish the practice of christian righteousness, and by reason of his excellence, the union with the Greek Church is to be restored, and the Mongols to be converted, when the annihilation of the Saracens will follow."[1] All this, fancied Bacon, might within the space of a year be accomplished, yea, even in a shorter time, if it pleased God and the pope; and he challenged Pope Clement IV. with all earnestness, to lay his hand to the work,—the very pope, as Bacon must have well known, who, instead of being the leader in the building up of a genuine christian righteousness, was rather only busied with the development of papal absolutism into a purely arbitrary rule, and the confirmation of the tribunal of the Inquisition. But Bacon thought that everything was so corrupt, that either Antichrist would come, or a pope to purify the Church must arise; and he manifestly thinks of the possibility of a great moral and spiritual transformation, to be, as it were, accomplished at one stroke. It is striking to

[1] Rogeri Bacon *Opera Quædem Hactenus Inedita*, ed. Brewer (London, 1859), p. 87, cf. p. 418.

observe, that the men of greatest insight in those days, like Roger Bacon and Dante, believed in a sudden and complete change of disposition in whole nations and periods, and possessed so little understanding of the laws of historic development. This is to be explained from the astrological delusions which prevailed, and which ruled the minds of these men also. The view was held that **the** tone and the ethical tendency of an age were controlled by a change in the reciprocal position of the stars; that sudden transitions, accordingly, from one extreme to the other, from virtue and piety to corruption and sinfulness, and the reverse, were possible. Such changes were **to be** completed in a fatalistic **way, with** unavoidable **necessity,** while yet, to the indi**vidual** was guaranteed his personal freedom of will, to hold fast his **chosen course** in the midst of the stream of ruin. This influence **of** the stars **was** then **called** into the **service of** prophecy. Such men, it was said, as **were** receptive of astral impressions by virtue of their natural temperament, were, for that reason, adapted to prophecy. They were, so to speak, predestined by nature to this calling, and might all the more surely comprehend the twofold revelation of God, the one within them, the other mediated by the constellations.[1]

---

[1] See what Benedict XIV. cites on this from the manuscript of an Italian theologian, appealing to Albertus Magnus and Aristotle: ubi supra, p. 436.

Bacon could, it is true, appeal to the fact, that stupendous religious movements, suddenly bursting forth, were not unheard-of events in his own times. Once certainly had it happened, that a gigantic revival, apparently without previous preparation and entirely spontaneous,—a spirit of repentance and conversion to a new life,—had been manifested. In the midst of the partizan discords and animosities by which Italy was rent, there were times of weariness, in which they tried to shake off the spirit of faction and political hatred which oppressed them as with the weight of Alps, and poisoned all other relations; then a spirit of reconciliation prevailed. Thus in the year 1260, when under the influence of prophecy the first great pilgrimage of the Flagellants arose, thousands of penitents, men and women of every age, scourging themselves and beseeching the mercy of God and peace among men, moved on from city to city. It was as if great towns had emptied their entire population, even twelve or twenty thousand souls, into another town. Those banished were allowed to return, Ghibellines and Guelphs embraced one another and were reconciled; many criminals were pardoned. It was a powerful religious impulse of the nations to help themselves; but the rulers remained unmoved, the pope maintained an attitude of indifference, or even of hostility towards the movement, and so the flame of enthusiasm, which, well directed and fostered, might have led to the salvation of Italy, was allowed to become extinguished.

In the statements of Bacon, we meet for the first time the thought, which was afterwards adopted in Italy, of a "Papa Angelico." It was the expectation laid down by so many subsequent prophets, of a pope who was to restore peace and harmony and bring back the Church again to the purity and freshness of youth. It was the Italian counterpart to the much desired and hoped-for German Emperor Frederick. After the great intermediate empire, the hopes, desires and needs of the German race were concentrated upon the thought of a strong and all-powerful emperor, who was to re-establish the fallen kingdom, humble the grand and despotic papacy, and strip from the clergy its boundless and misappropriated riches. How long was it believed in Germany that Frederick II. was still alive! How many false Fredericks, pretenders trusting to popular favor, deceived the people! When one of these false Fredericks was burned at Wetzlar in the year 1289, the story among the people was: "His bones were not found in the fire; Emperor Frederick was still alive, by the power of God, and is to banish the priests"[1] As these hopes were all at length extinguished, a new prophecy took their place, which promised the appearance of a new Emperor Frederick. It travelled for more than a century in the greatest variety of shapes, and ran like a thread through many other prophecies. In the collections of such predictions, it was usually found in the first rank. It was said to have originated from the most illustrious of the prophets, from Joachim himself. Certain it is, that its influence was deep and abiding. The very name of Frederick became significant, and whoever among princes and monarchs bore it, excited the expectation that he was destined to become the instrument of a great and fortunate change. Earlier, it was a Frederick from the Orient who was expected. The natural son of Frederick II., who died in 1258, appears to have been called Frederick of Antioch for this reason. Later it was simply Frederick, or the third of this name, the Eagle, who was to spread his wings from sea to sea, even to the ends of the earth. By him, or at least in his time, pope and clergy were to be imprisoned, scattered, stripped of their wealth or even killed. Even in the confessions, which the Catharists of southern France made, in the

---

[1] Hagen's *Oesterreich. Chronik,* in Pezii *Scriptores* **Rer. Austr., 1.,** 1105.

year 1321, before the Inquisition,[1] allusion is made to the expectation which they cherished, that Frederick III would arise, extend their Catharist communion, their Gnostic and dualistic church, and while protecting them, violently oppress the clergy and the Church.

In upper Italy, a prophet of the third Frederick excited a bloody religious war. Dolcino, who had attained the headship of an order of mendicants modelled after the Minorites, sent forth from the corner in which he had concealed himself, his prophetic letters, one after the other, in the first years of the fourteenth century. Stirred up by the writings of Joachim, and by kindred ideas relative to the age in which he lived, and its connection with the world's history, he announced that it was revealed to him, that Frederick of Aragon would be called to the dignity of emperor, and that there would immediately ensue a general slaughter of the entire clergy, and the destruction of all religious bodies. Then a holy pope was to be raised up, in whose days the apostolic brethren would enjoy full freedom, and the whole earth be converted to the new and everlasting gospel of the most perfect poverty. Dolcino fixed the occurrence of this event so near that he very speedily outlived the practical refutation of his prophecy. He was so slightly perplexed,

---

[1] In the *Codex Vaticanus*, 97.

however, **that in his** next prophetic manifesto, he simply removed for one year the date of its fulfilment. Persecuted, Dolcino with his 1400 followers took the sword, seized and fortified a mountain in the territory of Vercelli, and a war sprang up, marked by all the atrocities of the times, in which he at last was conquered and **with** his deluded followers came to a horrible end. His adherents, widely scattered, still believing firmly in the judgment to be **visited** upon the clergy **and** his holiness the **pope by the predestined** emperor, fell **into the power of the Inquisition; and,** fifteen years after the **death of the prophet,** several scores of the followers of Dolcino **were burned upon** the market place at Padua.[1]

---

[1] *Historia Dulcini,* cum **Additamento, in** Muratori *Script. Rer. Ital.,* ix, 425.

VII. *The Joachimites.*

WE have, in the teachings of Dolcino, the germs and fruits of a prophetic system, which, like nothing before or after it, was developed into a spiritual power, deeply penetrating the literature of the Church, and for centuries filling the souls of men with hope and fear, controlling their representations of the purposes of God, and of the things to be expected and accomplished. Joachim, the author of this system, and founder of the congregation of monks at Fiore in Calabria, was a profound theologian, cultivated by the most careful biblical studies, although afterwards (that his writings might appear to be the results of a miraculous enlightenment), it was affirmed that he was entirely destitute of education.[1] Joachim himself affirmed, that he was not a prophet, in the strict sense; but that the spirit of understanding had been given to him, or, in other words, the gift rightly to interpret the prophetic contents of the Old and New Testaments, and to construct the course of history, the changeful fate of the Church, from the prophecies,

[1] Accepta, ut aiunt, divinitus sapientia, cum fere esset prius illiteratus: Radulphi Coggeshali *Chron. Angl.*, in Martene, Coll. Ampl., v. 838.

analogies and types of the Bible. He himself describes (*Com. in Apocal.* p. 39) how, meditating one Easter-night, suddenly, by a divine revelation, the entire fulness of the contents of the Apocalypse, and the harmony of the Old Testament with the New, were made perfectly clear to him. It appeared to him, as if a stream of bright light was poured all at once into his soul. He could say, accordingly, to the Abbot Adam of Persigny, at Rome, that all the mysteries of the sacred Scriptures were as clear to him as they had formerly been to the biblical prophets themselves.

Three popes, Lucius III., Urban III. (1185), and Clement III. (1188), advised Joachim not to hide the revelations which God had imparted to him, and to publish the writings which he had subjected to the judgment of the papal chair (the *Concordia*, the *Psalterium*, and the *Commentary on the Apocalypse*).[1] King Richard of England, and English and French bishops of high standing, asked counsel of him.[2] The report of the appearance of so great a prophet as Joachim produced during his life (he died in the year 1202) great excitement even in the remote North,

---

[1] Jaffé *Regesta*, 1085. *Vita Urbani III.*, in Muratori *Ser.* iv, 476. Joachim also names these three writings in his Confessions. See Gregorii Lauri, *Joachim Magnus Propheta* (Naples) p. 166.

[2] Benedicti Abbatis Petroburgens., *Gesta Regis Henrici* (London, 1867), ii, 151-155.

and even where his writings were not yet known. His contemporaries frequently inscribed his name in their chronicles, with the addition: "We must wait to see whether his prophecies are confirmed by the result. Every thing is still uncertain." And yet very little was really known before the year 1220 of the contents of his prophetic writings. It had only been noticed with astonishment that he had said to the English king and his bishops, that the Antichrist whom the apostle Paul had described as the man of sin and son of perdition, would soon appear upon the papal chair;—that he was already born.[1] Since the opinions of Joachim were not yet known in their full extent, this attracted universal attention. It was not known that Joachim had discovered more than one Antichrist in the history of the Church and in the prophetic intimations of the Bible. It was not known that, in consequence of the deep corruption of the Church and the poisonous influence of the Roman Curia, he naturally came to the idea that all these evils met at Rome, concentrated in a single person and a single pope.

Honorius III. likewise declared after the death of the abbot, that since Joachim had submitted in writing

---

[1] Benedict, Petroburg. p. 153. Roger de Hoveden, ap. Savile, Rer. Angl. Script., p. 388.

all his writings to the judgment of the Apostolic chair, and had confessed the faith of the Roman Church, it should be announced throughout all Calabria that the pope regarded him as a good catholic.[1] This decree of the pope was especially directed against the Cistercians, who had taken much pains to secure the condemnation of the man who had separated himself from their order with his congregation, or at least to effect the rejection of his writings; as they had also labored to bring about the condemnation made by Innocent III. of a statement respecting the Trinity, in which Joachim had censured Peter of Lombard.[2] Joachim left behind the reputation of being no less a holy man than one prophetically illuminated. Numerous miracles were related of him; in the churches of Calabria a religious ceremony was dedicated to him as to other saints; and the Bollandists introduced him into their great work upon the saints. Many really cherished the view, that in him, for the first time since the days of the Apostles, the christian world had received a genuine prophet, and that in his writings was first presented the true key to the comprehension of the history of the world and of the church.

---

[1] Lambertini (Benedict XIX.), *De Servorum Dei Beatificatione*, ii., 248.

[2] Gervaise, *Histoire de l'Abbé Joachim* (Paris, 1745), ii., 465.

After the middle of the thirteenth century, other writings appeared, hitherto unknown, under the name of Joachim,—his commentaries on Isaiah and Jeremiah. Had these been genuine, the exact fulfilment of so many historic prophecies, falling into the period from 1202 to 1240, would have presented the most wonderful phenomenon in the history of prophecy. They were composed, however, by Italian Minorites, although entirely in the spirit and method of Joachim. By means of these new writings, especially the commentary of Jeremiah, which was generally accepted with entire confidence as a genuine production of the Calabrian abbot, the doctrines of Joachim were first spread abroad through a wider circle, and formed a school. It was said that an aged abbot of the order of Fiore had entrusted the writings of Joachim to the convent of Minorites in Pisa, for fear that his own convent would be destroyed by the Emperor Frederick. (Salimbene, p. 101.) Hence it was that the Minorites became the most diligent disseminators of his writings. A contemporary affirms that the prophecies of Joachim came to light about the year 1250, when the Cardinal de Porto sent them to Germany.[1] The Minorite, Adam

[1] Conrad of Halberstadt in his (unprinted) Latin recasting of the work of Eicke von Repgow. See Muratori *Antiquitates Ital.*, iii., p. 948.

Marsh, at the same time sent to the Bishop Grosseteste of Lincoln fragments from Joachim, which had just been brought to England from the continent by a Minorite, "in order that he might know whether or not the judgment of God was soon to break over prelates and clergy, princes and people."[1] In Italy Joachimites were found as well among Guelphs as Ghibellines. Salimbene mentions many of them. Notaries, physicians, judges and literary persons regularly assembled at the residence of Hugo de Barcola, one of the most honored of the Minorites, to listen to his lectures on Joachim. A professor of theology, Rudolph of Saxony, abandoned scholasticism in order to devote himself entirely to this theology of prophecy. Now, however, the entire structure of Joachimism was powerfully shaken by events which did not at all correspond with the prophetical reckoning. On the one hand, the death of the Emperor Frederick II., to whose government so significant a position had been assigned in this system, occurred in the year 1250, and brought about the entire triumph of the Papacy over the empire— in total opposition to the prophecy of Joachim, who had assigned a much longer life to the Emperor—

---

[1] Adæ de Marisco *Epistolæ*, p. 147, in the *Monumenta Franciscana*, ed. Brewer.

seventy or seventy-two years, and at the same time had announced to the Church, *i.e.*, according to the Italian and Guelph usage, to the Papacy, a Babylonian captivity of seventy years; in other words, an oppression by the imperial authority for a corresponding number of years. Ten years later occurred another great disappointment. According to the system of Joachim, the second period of the world's history, that of the Son, was to endure **twelve hundred and sixty years.** The second epoch, **accordingly,** that of the Holy Ghost, would begin in **the** year 1260, and in conjunction therewith a great transformation and purification of the Church. By means of their preaching, the Joachimites, belonging to the popular and influential order of the Minorites, had excited in Italy great expectations among the people, and a religious awakening, which manifested itself in the flagellant pilgrimages of that year. **It went,** however, no farther. The world in general followed its ordinary course. The Curia and the hierarchy maintained an attitude **of** indifference **or** hostility towards **the** movement which had seized upon the people. The Minorites could not long remain blind to the conviction that not the slightest inclination to **reform had been** aroused in **the** leading circles **of** the **Church. On the contrary, that evil** condition **of** things, which appeared to them so intolerable, and to be the impelling cause of severe and impending judgments, was evidently ever on the increase. "At this time," said Salimbene, "after the experience of the period between 1250 and 1260, I have entirely abandoned the teachings of Joachim, and I will henceforth believe only what I see."[1] He did not, however, remain steadfast in his determination; for when in his later years (about 1284) he wrote his chronicles, he had again become a believing follower of Joachim. Hugo had said to him that only the carnally-minded rejected the prophecies of Joachim, because he announced disagreeable things, many and severe sufferings and trials. Joachim himself had in fact declared his computations to be uncertain, and declined to fix a definite period for the fulfilment of his prophecies. His followers, however, were ready with expedients. Some said the third epoch, that of the Holy Ghost, had certainly begun with the year 1260, that the Flagellant pilgrimages were the token of its beginning, and that the characteristic of this period, the power and activity of monastic orders, was actually present. Others, like Ubertino of Casale, said that Joachim had rightly announced the

---

[1] Dimisi totaliter istam doctrinam, et dispono non credere, nisi quæ videro. Salimbene, p. 131.

year of the second epoch (1260), but it must, however, be reckoned from the resurrection, not from the birth of Christ: so that the period of the Holy Spirit [1] would begin in the year 1293. In fact, the honor and the prophetic authority of Joachim were cultivated in the heart of every genuine Minorite; for the prophet had not only declared the high ecclesiastical importance and dignity of the order, but had also announced that the Dominicans would be visited with the judgments threatening the rest of the clergy, while the Minorites were to happily continue until the end of the world. (Salimbene, p. 338.) Even John of Parma, the universally respected General of the Order, was obliged, after his retirement from the Joachimites, to submit himself to a severe examination; and his successor and judge, Saint Bonaventura, threatened to damn him as heretic, so offensive were his opinions about the estate and future prospects of the Church. He was only saved by the interposition of the pope.[2] This was all the

---

[1] The formula repeatedly used by Salimbene: *in tertio statu operabitur Spiritus Sanctus in religiosis.* Salimbene, p. 123, 240.

[2] Affo, *Vita del b. Giovanni di Parma* (Parma, 1777), p. 125. Affo will not allow without proof that Bonaventura was present at this trial; because at that time he may have been away from Italy. Besides, John of Parma was canonized by Pius VI., and a festival dedicated to him was introduced into the Order.

more strange, since Bonaventura, as is evident from his commentary on the Apocalypse, held the same views with his predecessors concerning the corruption of the Church, and the chief cause of it, that is, the Roman Curia polluted by simony.

A general survey of the system of Joachim shows us, certainly, the significant germs which it contains, if we take into view the prevailing form of doctrine, and the hierarchical system of the times. The history of the human race, according to Joachim and his school, runs in three great epochs: I. That of the Father (the Ante-Christian period, or, after the type of the three chief apostles, the Petrine period). II. That of the Son, or the Pauline period (from Christ to the year 1260). III. That of the Holy Ghost, or the Johannean period. The two latter periods, however, should not be so sharply separated from one another; for the one passes over into the other by a silent, gradual and imperceptible transition; so that the period from 1200 to 1260 is as much the end of the second, as the beginning of the third period.

The Church has become, chiefly through the ruinous influence of the popes, altogether sensual, a house of prostitution, a den of robbers. Nevertheless, God has left in her a seed of blessing and of grace. The clergy has become despised for its vices; the prelates are adulterers and hirelings; the cardinals and papal legates, the avaricious plunderers of the church, are sucking away its life. Thus is the christian people misled and spoiled by its shepherds. Whoever **goes to Rome** on any mission falls at once among thieves—the cardinals, notaries, &c. Rome, the city destitute of all christian discipline, is the fountain of all the abominations of **Christendom, and upon** her must first fall **the judgment of God.** The chief instruments of the divine **retribution were, besides** unbelievers, the Saracens, the Germans, **the new** Chaldeans, and the Roman Empire, with the emperor. France, the new Egypt, the broken reed upon which **the** papacy leaned, and which pierced its hand through, must be conquered, and its power broken by the Germans, although it is to subjugate the neighboring countries around. For the Italians, who have **so** deeply sinned, the German power is to be a **scourge.** In the bitter conflict between the **Empire and the** Papacy, both these mighty powers will fall in ruin. The pope will seek to destroy the bounds of the **empire, by** arousing the barbarian nations against it, and by arbitrary interference **in the** distribution of the highest dignities.

The emperor, however, is to strip the pope of all temporal dominion, and of all his possessions. Then is to be the time of the conversion of the nations and of the glorification of the true Church. Now it will come to be understood, that the perverse striving of the Church after an unbecoming authority, can only lead to a continually increasing servitude. After the empire has done its work as an instrument of punishment, the avenging judgments will be completed by the Saracens (the beast out of the sea), and by ten kings from the East. The Saracens are then to be annihilated by the Tartars, coming from the North. The instrument which God is to employ for purifying the corrupted Church, and for the bringing in of the great Sabbath, or the epoch of the Holy Ghost, will be an Order[1] of contemplative Eremites, who, by many years of study completed in silent retirement, ripened and illuminated by prayerful reflection, are to be prepared to announce the true gospel of humanity. To this order also will that preacher belong, who, according to the statement of Joachim, either alone or with associates, is to be sent from God as a teacher of love for heavenly things, and

[1] In most passages of the genuine writings of Joachim, only one Order is spoken of, a black-robed society of Eremites. In a few passages, however, he speaks also of two Orders, of which the one was to furnish martyrs for the truth, and the other to devote itself to the contest with heretics. In the commentaries on Jeremiah and Isaiah, two new orders of mendicants, the Minorites and the Dominicans, are distinctly predicted. (Comm. in Apocal. p. 142.)

of contempt for earthly things. *(Comm. in Apocal.,* p. 137) These men, now, will also overthrow the chairs of the carnal teachers, of the Italian "legists," and "decretists," of those flatterers (especially from Bologna, the valley of Tophet) who stimulate the avarice and ambition of ecclesiastical princes by their nefarious doctrines. At last, when the great Sabbath of rest for the christian nations begins, under the guidance of true shepherds, and the contemplative Church celebrates its triumph, then will also come the conversion of the Jews and unbelievers, and even of the Tartars themselves. With reference to the Antichrist, who is meantime to appear, there are contradictory statements in the writings of Joachim, which are however capable of reconciliation since he adopted the opinion that there are to be many Antichrists, partly in succession, partly contemporaneously, and that the nearer the end of the world's history so much the more would they be multiplied.

Such then are the leading features of the prophetic picture of the history of the world, which, sketched by Joachim and completed in sympathy with him (the commentary on Isaiäh was not composed until about the year 1266), controlled directly or indirectly, for centuries, the presentiments and thoughts of mankind respecting the future, especially in Italy.

The views respecting the German people and empire, which are here brought to light, are entirely those of the party of the Guelphs, who saw in the Germans only the warlike and plundering oppressors of conquered nations. They refused to recognize the higher calling of the Empire as it was even then perceived by Dante. "The kingdom of the Germans," it is said in the commentary on Jeremiah, "has been for us hard and oppressive; the Lord must needs annihilate it with the sword of his wrath; that all kings may tremble before the uproar of its overthrow." We recognize in such and similar expressions the language of the Neapolitan Minorites. Of the leading thoughts and events, which the authors of these writings imagined that they beheld in their prophetic mirrors, but very little was ever realized.

Of the two powers which were to destroy each other—the Papacy and the Empire,—the first, the Roman Curia, had just then obtained the most complete victory over the German Empire, which lay at last helpless at its feet. The Papal See, however, sustained no loss either of possessions or of authority from the Germans and their emperors, at least not in the succeeding centuries, and never through an emperor. When, however, in the year 1303, the day of Anagni came, and shortly afterwards the pontificate of Clement V., the Joachimites might well claim the fulfilment of the prophecy of their master, that France was the reed which should pierce right through the hand of the pope who leaned upon it. There exists, however, a noticeable difference of tone and of judgment, which was not observed by contemporaries, between the genuine writings of Joachim and the commentary on Jeremiah and Isaiah attributed to him, especially with reference to the Papacy. Between the former and the latter writings a half century had intervened, during which the Papacy advanced with gigantic strides toward its goal, the dominion of the world. The corruption proceeding from the Curia and pervading all orders and institutions of the Church, had increased in a corresponding degree. Joachim had, so to say, written in the interest, and under the very eyes of the popes. The Minorites, however, who composed the commentaries on Jeremiah and Isaiah, and who used the name of Joachim to conceal their own, and were moreover "Spirituals," and professors of the new doctrine of poverty, inclined rather to unsparing and severe condemnation of the popes and their avaricious and luxurious courts. Joachim, on the contrary, although recognizing in many passages the Roman Curia as the source of corruption, yet always spoke of the Papal Chair in terms of the highest reverence.

It was not in Italy, not by the popes, as might have been expected, but in France, and by French theologians and bishops, that the prophecies of Joachim were first attacked, and characterized as dangerous errors, not to be tolerated in the Church. In Provence the doctrine of Joachim had already produced a literature of its own, when, in the year 1260, a synod at Arles imagined itself called upon solemnly to condemn the doctrine of the three epochs of the Church, and the new outpouring of the Holy Spirit. (Harduin, *Coll. Concil.*, vii., 512.) This, said the bishops, would have been done earlier, had not until very recently the works of Joachim, especially the *Concordia*, lain hidden and unobserved in several cloisters. Certainly, in any other case, they said, the Papal Chair would have condemned and branded, not only the writings of Gherardino, but Joachim himself, the real source.

Somewhat earlier, the Parisian theologian, William Saint-Amour, wrote in opposition to the writings of Joachim, without, however, knowing the later works, the commentaries on Jeremiah and Isaiah. William discovered that all the signs of the coming Antichrist were already present; the Roman kingdom with

Frederick II. had **come to an end**, and the gift of miracles **had been taken** away from the Church. Consequently, not at all Joachim's period of the Holy Ghost, but the very opposite, was to be **expected.**[1] He refused to know anything about a comforting future for humanity and the Church, and it is very characteristic of the times, that **the** Rector of the first university **of** the world **rejected the prophecies** of Joachim, **for the very reason that they** promised the Church and the Christian world a **long** season of peace and prosperity, **and a** prosperous old age, continuing through many centuries. That dark sketch **which he** drew, of **the** sad condition of the **Church** in its deep degradation, was not so different **from the pictures of Joachim, apart** from the mission **of the new** mendicant orders, **which he** regarded as injurious **in their** influence; but **both drew from** the same facts opposite conclusions. **The followers** of Joachim, said : Unless **we** magnify **the brilliant future** of a purified and **well ordered** Church, we must **be wrong** concerning the Church itself, and despair **of its divine foundation and** mission. William assumed, **on the contrary, that** the days of a Church,

---

[1] This work is not **by the** Bishop Oresme de Lisieux, under whose name it is given in Martene *Ampliss. Coll.* ix., 1273, sq.; but by William of St. Amour, as the author by the *Histoire Littéraire de la France*, xxi., 470, has stated.

well pleasing to God and still true to its original destiny and constitution, had long passed by, and that there is no promise of a better future. The Church has now to look for nothing else but the advent of its great adversary.

In the same year in which both the new records of the more fully developed doctrine of Joachim,—the two commentaries on the prophets—appeared, the Minorite, Gherardino of Borgo-San-Donnino, united them in one work, with three genuine writings of the Abbot of Fiore, under the title of the "Everlasting Gospel," and added to them an Introduction, which though conceived in the spirit of Joachim, sounded to the majority of the party like a lamentable perversion of the genuine doctrine. Forbearing as the Papal Chair had hitherto showed itself towards the teachings of Joachim, yet an anathema was now unavoidable. It was accordingly delivered in the year 1255, by a commission of cardinals, at Anagni, on the complaint of the Bishop of Akkon, who came for that purpose from France. Gherardino had announced in his *Introductorius*, the advent, six years later, in 1260, of the third epoch of the world's history, the Era of the Holy Ghost. With this, the New Testament, the epoch and œconomy of the Son, was to be fully closed, abrogated and made void, as that of the first period, or of the Old Testament, had been abrogated by the New. For, he added, no one has been brought to perfection by the Gospel of Christ. Under the guidance of the Order of Minorites, now developed in full proportions, all figures and riddles will vanish in the sunlight of the new Church of the Holy Spirit. As in the beginning of the new covenant there shone three persons, Zacharias, John the Baptist, and the man Jesus; so in **the third, the epoch of the Spirit, the three columns of the structure were to** be Joachim, Dominic, and Francis.[1]

The fate of Gherardino **was** fearful. He **would not recant, and** was **condemned to a** life-long **imprisonment, in which, after eighteen years, he** died. **No one any longer defended the** *Introductorius*, **which after six years was refuted by facts.**

But **the doctrine and** prophecies **of** Joachim were continuously upheld in the Order **of the** Minorites, and two distinguished men, Peter John D'Olive and Ubertino of Casale, gave it a new impulse. Attached **to them** was the influential party of the *Spirituals*, as that class of men was named, in the phrase of Joachim, who desired to retain entire poverty, in the sense of the founder of the order. The authority of

---

[1] Duplessis d'Argentré, in his *Collectio Judiciorum*, i., 163, gives the passages from the *Introductorius*.

Joachim as a prophet remained undiminished, only it was discovered that his dates rested upon pure conjectures, and were therefore not to be strictly taken; although the number 1260, according to the theory of the apocalyptic days taken as years, was always retained as indicating the great turning point.

The entire duration of the world and the Church was now divided into seven periods, in each of which a great and severe contest was to occur. The fifth period, extending into the thirteenth century, was the time of the complete corruption of the Church, in which the Roman Chair, risen to the highest degree of power, also contributed most to the general corruption. With the sixth period, the third great era, that of the Holy Ghost, had begun. In reality it began with the appearance of Saint Francis, a hundred years before; but it was then still flooded with the dregs of the fifth period. The carnal Church, however, with its false popes, was ripening for judgment, and the time was not far distant in which the *Spirituals* should conquer, and the spiritual Church should manifest itself, and rule, freed from the poison of temporal possessions. Then the Church was to have entire leisure and complete power, and endure long enough to bring about the conversion of the Jews as well as of the whole heathen world. D'Olive's[1] commentary on the Apocalypse was the favourite book of the *Spirituals* and of their numerous adherents, especially in Italy, and southern France; they were continually upheld by these prophecies, expecting from year to year the victory and the public manifestation of the Church of the Holy Ghost.

As they had declined to recognize **any** pope since John XXII., the popes visited them with **that fearful** persecution in which a hundred and fourteen *Spirituals* were burned **at** the stake, and many more died in severe imprisonment. The bones of D'Olive were dug **up** and burned, and his writings **were prohibited, until** Sextus IV., himself a Minorite, **ordered a new** investigation, and declared them orthodox, since, as was said, the **passages** which had been regarded as objectionable **could be** interpreted in a good sense.[2]

It cannot be denied that these victims of the papal

---

[1] He was styled the *Doctor Columbinus*, since his party chose the dove as its symbol. The commentary is still unprinted, but the articles presented to a papal commission under John XXII., were taken from it, **and** are sufficient to make us acquainted with his views. Ubertino's **chief** work was composed in the year 1305, *Arbor Vitæ Crucifixæ* (Venice, 1484); **here** he declares Boniface VIII. and Clement V. to be false popes.

[2] Flam. Annibali de Latera, *Supplem.* ad *Bullar. Francis.* (Rome, 1778), p. 52.

dogmatic tribunal led a pure and austere life, corresponding with the rule of their founder. So much the deeper, then, was the aversion aroused against Rome and the Curia, who, according to the judgment of the people, had executed the men that were the very flower of the Catholic Church. It had already been said, in the commentary on Jeremiah attributed to Joachim: "As she (the Curia) had murdered, so should she also be murdered," and the prophecies of the succeeding period had a continually increasing anti-papal coloring. And so sprung up the fearful thought, that the Papal Chair might have been for a time the seat of the Antichrist, or yet should be.

For the impression was very deep which Boniface VIII. by his entire bearing made upon his contemporaries; by his audacious announcement of the dogma of the papal supremacy over the world, by his tyranny based on fear and terror, and by his undisguised immorality. The astonishment and dismay of religiously-disposed persons at the appearance of this "new Lucifer" in the Papal Chair was portrayed in glowing words by the distinguished poet of the Order of Minorites, Jacopone of Todi.[1] The view of the

---

[1] This is found in the oldest editions of his poem, but has been left out in the later ones. Yet Tosti has reprinted it in his *Storia di Bonifacio* VIII., Monte Cassino, 1848, i., 286.

Joachimites, that the chair of St. Peter should be for a considerable period the spoil of an adversary of Christ, who was to bear all the marks foretold of the Antichrist, came to appear more probable in the eyes of many persons.

It was still more easily imagined that such "a Man of Sin, and Son of Perdition" was actually sitting in the temple of God and adorned with the papal tiara, when, in the year 1310, Pope Clement V. instituted a public process against his predecessor, Boniface, now seven years dead, which was continued over a year; and when a whole series of men of the highest standing, prelates, abbots, counts and other noblemen, came forth as eye-witnesses to convict this pope of unbelief, of heresy, of the utter disregard of all morality, men of whom Clement himself testified, when he rejected the suit, that they were in the highest degree trustworthy, and had only been moved to their declarations by zeal for the Catholic Church.

The greatest Italian of his time, Dante, who, although in a way peculiar to himself, was nevertheless a Joachimite, gave utterance to the words (Paradise, 27, 22-24) :

> "He who usurps upon the earth my place,
> My place, my place, which vacant has become,
> Before the presence of the Son of God." [1]

[1] Longfellow's translation.

The poet, however, did not, like the *Spirituals* or Fraticelli, infer from this withdrawal of God from the Papal Chair, that all done on earth by such a usurper was void and invalid. On the contrary, Boniface VIII. was to him the regular representative of Christ upon earth, but in heaven a usurper, as is proved by Dante's renowned expression concerning the seizure at Anagni.[1]

The expectations of the Joachimite *Spirituals*, at the beginning of the fourteenth century, embraced, accordingly, the following points: (1) A general, severe and bloody judgment upon the Church, which had become altogether carnal, in which only few good persons could be found, like a few grains of gold in a great heap of sand. (2) A pope given to simony (the so called mystical Antichrist), who, a living pattern and picture of the abominations of the Church, claimed for himself divine attributes, and received divine honors. (3) A pouring forth of the Holy Ghost upon the *Spirituals*, to rally them for the conflict with the great and last Antichrist. Such were the events which numberless adherents of the same

---

[1] [The seizure and imprisonment of Boniface VIII. by the troops of Philip the Fair at Anagni (Alagna). See Dante's *Purgatory* xx, 87.

"I see the flower-de-luce Alagna enter,
And Christ in his own Vicar captive made." H. B. S.]

party of Minorites looked forward to at that time and long afterwards in Italy and Southern France.

Another prophecy circulated contemporaneously with that of Joachim, and afterwards, gave much occasion for reflection, and was firmly trusted, in the passages which could be understood. As the legend says, it was received from the hands of an angel in 1192 by Cyril, a Greek from Constantinople (a Carmelite, and General of the Order), and it was written upon two silver tables. This prophecy of Cyril, in language designedly ambiguous, and for the most part hardly intelligible, with many foreign words and bombastic flourishes,[1] is one of the numerous fictions of the order of Carmelites; for which reason it is frequently, though in contradictory senses, elucidated by members of this Order.[2] It starts from the year 1254, and first announces the conflicts between the houses of Anjou and Aragon, about Naples and Sicily. Then the fall of the Church and of the Roman Chair, the severe burden of the sins of the degenerated clergy and the

[1] *Ex. gr.* To express the idea that the Holy Ghost has departed from the church, it is said: "*Evolavit palumba nidificans in corona.*" The mendicant monks are called **Pocotrophitæ** (*i.e.*: *Ptochotrophitæ*), *etc.*

[2] *Divinum Oraculum*, S. Cyrillo Carmelitæ solanni legatione Angeli missum, cui adj. Commentarius Philippi a Trinitati (Lyons, 1663). The other commentaries are in the *Bibliotheca Carmelitana* of Cosmas de Villiers (Aurelian. 1752, i., 358).

clerical orders, together with the judgments impending upon them, are portrayed. The Imperial Eagle is exhorted to "awake, spread out thy wings, hew down with thy beak." The stress of the whole seems to lie in the last chapter, where an admonitory sermon is preached to the three corrupt orders, the Minorites, the Dominicans, and Carmelites; and the impositions of the mendicant monks, and their illicit ways of acquiring property, are portrayed.

The author himself has supplied a key, though it is a very inadequate one, for the solution of his riddles; for he has foisted upon the Abbot Joachim an interpretation of the prophecy, with the fiction that Cyril sent to him in Calabria this prophecy from the East, and asked him to interpret it. The text is so obscure, that with a little fancy it can be made to apply to every conceivable event, and therefore it long continued in high esteem. Rienzo believed that in it his mission was clearly outlined; and Telesphorus seized upon it for other ends, and made it a part of the basis of his prophetic scheme.

The famous physician, Arnold of Villanova, held this prophecy of Cyril in so high esteem, that he maintained in his writings that it was more precious than all the books of the Bible;[1] he probably meant,

---

[1] See the *Censura* of his writings by a tribunal of the Inquisition

that it must be placed higher than these, since it was written upon a tablet by the hands of angels, while the books of the Bible came only from men. Arnold was, besides, a zealous Joachimite, one of the *Spirituals*, and altogether too bold a prophet. It seemed to him that the whole Western Church was already completely ruined, beyond redemption, by the excess of its sins; and so he thought that everything must rush quickly to perdition; and therefore (about 1297), he put the coming of the last great Antichrist in the year 1316, and the end of the world in 1335. His positions were afterwards condemned by a tribunal of the Inquisition in Spain.

Spiritual corporations, like the Minorites and the Dominicans, that attain great power in the world, when they come to the height of their importance naturally imagine that their history must have been foretold by divine appointment. The Minorites had taken good care that, in the Joachimite writings, there should be found a very distinct prediction declaring that two Orders were to spring up, one out of Umbria (Assisi), and the other in Spain, brilliant stars for the preaching of the Gospel.[1] Joachim had

at Tarragona, 1316, in Villanueva, *Viage Literario a les Iglesias de España*, xix, 321.

[1] Compare Gregorius de Lauro, *Joachimi Mirabil. Veritas defensa* p. 170.

even depicted the garbs which were to be worn by these two fraternities, in a painting of the cloister of Fiore, and admonished his monks, that when men came to them thus clad, they were to be welcomed with friendliness and reverence.[1] By this means the Joachimites received new support in spite of the unfavorable judgment of the great Dominican theologian, Thomas of Aquinas, about Joachim himself; for Thomas would only let him pass as a well-meaning man who had foretold some truths by happy conjecture, although in other things he was deluded. (Thomas in lib. iv. Sentent. dist. 439, 1, art. 3.)

[1] Gerardus de Fracheto, *Vita Fratrum*, p. 7, ed. Duacen.

VIII. *The Prophetic Spirit from the Fourteenth Century to the Beginning of the Reformation.*

THE silver tables of Cyril exercised no small influence upon the circle of ideas of the Roman tribune, Cola di Rienzo, who had been educated by the *Spiritualists,* and Fraticelli, living as hermits in the Apennines. "The tables of stone were given to Moses on Sinai," wrote Cola to the Emperor Charles IV., "and so these silver tables were delivered to Cyril on Carmel,"[1] and he must believe these prophecies, since Dominicans, Franciscans and the present pope were so plainly designated therein. So, too, Merlin and Joachim, as well as Cyril, had told beforehand of the present persecution of the poor Eremites by the pope and his inquisitors.

In Rienzo were united, in fact, the brooding spirit of the fanatical Joachimites with political insight and a gift of domination which bordered on genius. Like all the Joachimites he firmly believed in the near approach of the third epoch, the Church of the Holy Ghost. We find in him already the idea of a future

[1] Papencordt, *Cola di Rienzo und seine Zeit,* (1841), s., 228.

holy pope, accustomed to the poverty of the Gospel, the "Papa Angelicus," as he was soon afterwards called,—another Celestine, not like him abdicating, but supported by a pious emperor, accomplishing the renovation of the Church and the purification of the clergy. At the same time, however, Rienzo understood how to regulate Rome as a republic, and rule it almost like a dictator; and he strove to unite dissevered Italy into a confederation under the leading of Rome. Yet, in this son of an inn-keeper on the Tiber, the fanatic and the visionary were stronger than the statesman. Even after his first fall, when imprisoned by the Emperor Charles, he firmly maintained the belief that Cyril had predicted his sufferings (Papencordt, p. 241), and that he was still to be the chosen instrument of God, through whom, at the approaching great regeneration of the Church, should be accomplished the political task of raising up the fallen Roman Empire, and the restoration of united Italy to Rome its capital. His views were fundamentally the same with those of the *Spiritualists* or Fraticelli, who at that time, and long afterwards, as soon as they could be got hold of, were sentenced to death at the stake. He too was accused of heresy, yet no sentence of death was passed upon him at Avignon, at least none was carried into execution.

Later, ruling in Rome for the second time, and now sent there by the pope himself, he ended his life as "a tyrant" by the hands of the Roman populace. It can hardly be doubted that the classically educated Petrarch, who joyfully greeted Rienzo as the saviour of Italy, also shared the tribune's prophetic faith. Only, as he had lived so long in Avignon, and there seen the corruption of the Papal Curia and the degradation of the Church by public simony, he was more likely to look for a great and prolonged judgment, than to indulge the assured hope of a simultaneous political and ecclesiastical regeneration with which Rienzo was filled. In a sonnet[1] that became famous, he declares that Rome and the Roman Chair

[1] L'avara Babilonia, etc. *Rime di Petrarca*, ed. Carrer (Padua, 1837), ii, 434. [Sonnet C V I., Macgregor's translation, in *The Sonnets, Triumphs, and other Poems* of Petrarch, London, 1849:

"Covetous Babylon of wrath divine
By its worst crimes has drain'd the full cup now,
And for its future gods to whom to bow
Not Power nor Wisdom ta'en, but Love and Wine.
Though hoping reason, I consume and pine,
Yet shall her crown deck some new Soldan's brow,
Who shall again build up, and we avow
One faith in God, in Rome one head and shrine.
Her idols shall be shatter'd, in the dust
Her proud towers, enemies of Heaven, be hurl'd,
Her wardens into flames and exile thrust.
Fair souls and friends of virtue shall the world
Possess in peace; and we shall see it made
All gold, and fully its old works display'd." H. B. S.]

will at some future time (not so soon as he could wish, he says) be swallowed up by a Mohammedan empire, whose monarch will reside in Bagdad;[1] then will its proud towers be consumed, and its idols be dashed in pieces upon the ground; but then too will begin a golden age: he means the age of the Holy Ghost prophesied by Joachim.

The peculiar prophetic spirit of that period, a mixture of the Joachimite and Minorite *Spiritualism*, was incorporated in the person of the unfortunate Franciscan, Jean de la Rochetaillade; but his visions brought him into a prison where Pope Innocent VI. thought he would be harmless. Like most of the seers of the later centuries he did not claim to be an actual prophet, but only an enlightened investigator, to whom the Holy Ghost had disclosed the meaning, first of the Apocalypse, and then of the prophecies of Merlin and Joachim. Froissart, who upon the whole judges him very favorably, describes him as a pious and spiritually-minded priest, and Petrarch probably derived from the visions of this man his anticipation

---

[1] Petrarch uses the word "Baldacco." Italian commentators do not seem to have known that this means Bagdad, which at that time was reputed to be the chief city of the whole new Christian world, the Rome of heathendom. Thus Baldwin of Ninove says in his *Corpus Chronicor. Flandriæ.* ed. Smets, ii., 713: " Haec civitas Bandas (Bagdad) est caput totius Paganismi, sicut Roma Christianismi."

of the spread of the Mohammedan dominion over Western Europe, or at least over Italy. Jean de la Rochetaillade felt that he was strongest where Joachim had shown himself weak, that is, in exact dates about the immediate future; and he compressed into the narrow period of a few years, from 1356 to 1370, a wonderful series of extraordinary complications, decisive catastrophes and sudden revolutions. In a few months there were to be changes that demanded centuries, according to ordinary historical experience. To him, as a genuine Minorite *Spiritualist*, the observance or transgression of the strict rule of poverty enjoined by his Order is the very heart of the whole history of the world.[1] According to his fancy, the transgressors of this strict rule of poverty are the true cause of all the calamities and maledictions with which the race is now visited. The salvation of the world and of the Church can only come from two " poor rope-wearers" (*Cordelarii*, Franciscans), one of whom is to be pope, the other a cardinal; though such severe and destructive conflicts are to precede that the whole Church would be annihilated by them, were this at all possible. And

[1] He says literally in his *Prophetic Commentary*: Transgressores ordinis fratrum minorum sunt in causa, quod omnes praefatae tribulationes infundentur in orbem." Johann de Rupescissa, *Liber inscriptus: Vade mecum in tribulatione*, in Brown, *Fasciculus*, ii., 403.

then, before the year 1370, the universal "restoration" will begin, the whole world will be converted, gathered into one Church and cordially submit to the dominion of the pope. The monk put the time of his prophecies so near at hand that people were soon undeceived, and the court at Avignon thought itself justified in keeping in prison until his death a prophet proved to be false. Froissart reports from hearsay, that many of his prophecies were fulfilled.

Two prophetic women, who flourished only a short time apart in the latter half of the fourteenth century, were greatly reverenced in life and death. One of these, Catharine of Siena, was and remained an authority chiefly for the Italians, while the other, Brigitta (of Sweden), was honored in the whole of Western Christendom as a divinely illuminated seer, and was diligently read. St. Brigitta became in some measure, for her own and the subsequent times, what Joachim had been before; and in fact from the close of the fourteenth century, Brigitta and Joachim were usually named together as the two leading prophetic authorities. The visions and revelations which she left behind were examined and sanctioned by popes and councils, and defended by famous theologians, like Torrecremata. But it remains a striking circumstance that these writings, which are full of solemn monitions about the prevailing corruptions of the Church, should have been so highly honored by the leaders and spokesmen of the Church itself, that is by the very persons who were doing nothing to remedy the evils that were denounced. These writings contain the severest complaints against the popes; the Roman Curia is painted in black colors, its general corruption, its simony and its traffic in sacred things are condemned; repulsive pictures are presented of the degeneracy of the clergy, and of the great spiritual orders: and Brigitta puts all these charges into the mouth of God himself. And yet the Roman See caused Joachim to be reverenced as a saint; and it canonized not only Brigitta, but also Bonaventura, who in pithy and cutting words designated the Curia as a wanton clad in scarlet, and Vincens Ferrer, who, fifty years after Brigitta, painted the ecclesiastical decay and corruptions in yet darker colors.

These prophets pointed out usually as in the distance, but sometimes as near at hand, a comprehensive and wonderful purification and renovation of the Church, to be brought about by the manifest interposition of heavenly powers (though this is not the case with Vincens and Bonaventura). But when this revolution and universal conversion did not occur, or seemed to be kept too long in suspense, then it naturally came to pass that those men who despaired of the vital energy of the Church as no longer sufficient for its own reformation, at last took the matter into their own hands, determined to carry out the work of reform, if necessary, in the convulsions of a violent and unsparing revolution. It is only lately that attention has again, in Italy, been directed to the visions of St. Brigitta, which for a long time were almost forgotten. She testifies that she was shown the Leonine City, or, as she expresses it, that part of the city from the Vatican and St. Peter's to the Castle of St. Angelo and thence to St. Spirito, spread out like a plain surrounded by a massive wall, in which the different dwellings stood alongside of the wall (as in a Belgian Beguine court). At the same time she heard a voice from heaven saying: "The pope who loves the Church as well as I and my friends have loved it, will take possession of this abode so that he can call his counsellors to himself in freedom and peace." (*Revel.*, 6, 74). This has not been overlooked in these latter days, and St. Brigitta, whom the Church placed so high and canonized for this very gift of prophecy, would say to the present pope, that he will have more peace and freedom for ecclesiastical consultations with his adherents, if restricted to the Leonine City, than as the ruler of a State.[1]

[1] See the work of Gennarelli, recently published in Florence, *Capitoli per la Libertà Religiosa e Pontificia.*

In the fourteenth century, when what was unnatural and horrible was as easily believed as it was frequently enacted, and when the history of the European States was moving on in morbid throes, the prophecies, too, were very apt to go astray as soon as they were applied to definite dates and concrete events. One example of this : the year 1348 and the two following years are among the most extraordinary and fatal of that period. The diary of Michael de Leone [1] communicates a prophecy of a "great astrologer" for the year 1348 : "There will be a single master, the Roman Empire will be aggrandized. The tyrant, the king of France, will fall with his barons, the pope with his cardinals will be destroyed." To this he adds famine and mortality, some common-places about meteorological disturbances, and a few unintelligible phrases. Here, perhaps, an allusion may be found to the fearful pest of the Black Death, which then filled all Europe with terror ; but all the rest failed. So little was the Roman Empire at that time aggrandized, that, on the contrary, the first years of the reign of Charles IV. can only be described as a period of growing decline. King Philip of France did not fall, and the

---

[1] In Böhmer, *Fontes Rer. German*, i., 434. Of the Pope with the cardinals it is said, *Dissipabitur*.

pope with his cardinals sat at ease in Avignon. Here, too, we have only wishes turned into prophecies.

The unfortunate issue of the Crusades, and the general dislike to abandoning the long-cherished hope of regaining Palestine and the Holy City, gave birth in Southern Europe to a special order of prophecies. In a work composed in 1205, entitled " The Seed of the Scriptures," [1] it was predicted that in a hundred years the Holy Land would be regained, and the Church delivered from that simony which was the cause of its loss. Somewhat later, in Southern Italy, a whole series of similar prophecies was fabricated, more and more positive and palpable. The Carmelites, who thought that they had claims to certain places in Palestine, were especially active in this affair. They gave out that Christ had made a revelation to one of their mythical saints, St. Angelus, to the effect that a holy and powerful king of the French house would undertake a *passagium* together with the pope, and deliver the City from the hands of the infidels. [2] When the Spanish house of Arragon began its reign in Naples, other prophecies

---

[1] *De Semine Scripturarum.* See the *Notitia Sæculi*, in Karajan's book, *Zur Geschichte des Concils von Lyon*, s., 104.

[2] *Vita St. Angeli Carmelitæ*, in the *Acta Sanctor.* Bolland, Maii, ii., 821.

were invented, **promising** to these princes or their successors **a great Empire,** brilliant conquests in the north and south, **and in** addition the taking of Jerusalem.[1]

For this purpose Joachim had to be again used, and along with him Johannes Aquitanus and Johannes Rala were adduced as authors of such prophecies. It was well for those pious women, Catharine and Brigitta, and in general for all those who were then troubled about the condition of the Church, that they lived only in the visions of the future, while the past and the sequence of **causes** and effects which had produced the present condition of the Church, were unknown to them. The corruption, as it lay before their eyes, they held to be accidental, the product of recent times; so that it might vanish away in a sudden revolution, under a fuller outpouring of divine grace. They would have been lost in a labyrinth of doubts and struggles of conscience, and wholly disheartened, had they clearly seen that the present condition of the Church was the consequence of a regularly planned perversion of ecclesiastical ordinances and institutions. Those well-meaning prophets of the "Papa Angelicus," then so common in Italy,

---

[1] See the Bollandists, as above, p. 822, who have taken it from the work of Johannes Bonatius, *De Prophetis sui Temporis*, Naples, 1660.

had the fancy that a single, pious man, spending a life of voluntary poverty and austerity, a second Celestine V., a stranger to all political complications, would be sufficient, if raised to the Papal Chair, to effect a thorough reformation of the Church in the shortest time. In point of fact, for several centuries, not one of the popes had effected any earnest and permanent improvement in the affairs of the Church. And in the long series of popes, from A.D. 1300 to A.D. 1500, there was not one whom the popular belief, even for a day, imagined to be the foretold " Angelic Pope."[1]

But he was expected with ardent longing in all Italy, as the true Emperor Frederick was expected in Germany. In the year 1514, Julius de Medici (afterwards Pope Clement VII.), then Vicar General of the Bishop of Florence, imprisoned a monk named Theodore, who had represented to the people that an angel had declared to him that he, Theodore, was the "'Papa Angelico' expected by the Italian people."[2] When Savonarola appeared publicly as a reformer in Flo-

---

[1] This name came from a misunderstood passage in the old Latin poem ascribed to Tertullian. There the Hermas, who wrote the Pastor or "Shepherd," is spoken of, and this "Shepherd" or angel is designated as the *angelicus pastor*.

[2] Cambi, *Storie Fiorentine*, iii., 60. Moreni, *Memorie della Basilica di S. Lorenzo*, ii., 311.

rence, he was accused by his opponents of really intending to have himself made " Papa Angelicus ; " and his adherents actually believed that God had chosen him for this. And all the more, as one Prospero Pitti, a priest of Florence, believed to have prophetic illumination, had a long time before, together with other events, foretold the coming of this bold preaching monk, and the simultaneous elevation of the "Angel Pope." Savonarola himself afterwards, on the rack, declared that his object had not been to become pope, but to bring about a general Council for the purification of the Church.[1] As early as 1491, in the very midst of Rome, a poorly clad street preacher had appeared, with a wooden cross in his hand, proclaiming that the revelation of the "Pastor Angelicus" was near at hand, together with heavy judgments upon Florence, Milan and Venice. The citizens of Rome, however, did not show the slightest longing for such a pope, who must of course begin with stopping their most fruitful sources of revenue; and the prophet was laughed at as crazy.[2]

This expectation of an "Angel Pope" manifestly sprang up on Italian soil. By the simplest means and in the shortest time, although, as it was for the

---

[1] Guicciardini, *Storia d'Italia*, 3, 7.
[2] Steph. Infessura, *Diarium*, in Muratori, *Scrip. Ital.* iii., 2, p. 1250.

most part believed, after a great shedding of blood, and after the secularization of the Church property, which had become the mere rental of the priests, he would accomplish the gigantic work of reformation, restoring the Church to the truth of the gospel. It was soon found that a single "Angelicus" was not sufficient for this, so the prophecies soon became broader, and towards the end of the fourteenth century the single elect one was enlarged into a series of four Angel-Popes. The first who predicted this was the venerable Rabanus, Archbishop of Mayence, who, by the accidental error of being mistaken for the author of Adso's work on Antichrist, obtained the name of a prophet, and was credited with the origin of a prediction which briefly designated the four popes who were to bless the Church. Joachim, in a work ascribed to him, the Book of Fiore, and also a so-called Dandalus, who was supposed to have been the author of a "Revelation of the Popes," bore witness to the four expected popes.[1] The third was to uproot the temporalities of the Church (here is betrayed the Minorite-Joachimite origin of the prophecy); and the fourth was to wander through the whole world as a preacher and propagator of the

[1] Bishop Berthold of Chiemsee, in his *Onus Ecclesiæ*, 60, 8, 9, gives the passages.

Christian faith. Then would begin the catastrophe of the end.

This antagonism of the two schools or tendencies, the Joachimites and the anti-Joachimites, the hopeful and the pessimists, was prolonged for centuries. The monk Giovanni delle Celle, of Florence, in a work written against the Fraticelli, summed up this contrast in a concise and conclusive manner.[1] "The former say the world must be renewed, I say it must go to the ground." Both agreed that the Church was in a most woful condition, desperately diseased, and so defaced as to be scarcely recognised. But, the one said, it can and must be restored; fearful and bloody judgments will first come, but there will follow a long and blessed time of ecclesiastical prosperity. The other said, this decrepitude of the Church will not end in restored health, but all signs indicate death; and the catastrophes, which, according to biblical and traditional prophecy, are partly to precede the coming of the great adversary and partly to attend it, are already begun or are near at hand. History proved both to be wrong. At the time of the Great Schism (1378-1455), Henry of Langenstein reported the prophetic

---

[1] Costoro dicono che'l mondo si dee rinovellare, edio dico che dee rovinare. In the *Compendio di Dottrina*, in the *Scelta di Curiosita Lett.* (Bologna, 1861), disp. 86, p. 351.

spirit as in full blossom.[1] There were soothsayers in abundance who made predictions from the course of the stars, or from conjectures after rules of their own, and found a hearing; their vaticinations were copied and illuminated, as though they were the literal revelations of the Holy Ghost. In short, they were floating in a sea of prophecies as to the end of the schism, all of which came to confusion. Henry relates the fate of one of these prophets: There came from France to the cloister of Eberbach a learned monk, esteemed a saint; he had received revelations as to the short duration of the schism, and was sure that it would continue only a few years. As the years flowed on and the schism still continued, he said that he had not weighed the words of the Holy Ghost with sufficient care; he now knew the end would come somewhat later. But this limit also passed by, and the double schism became a triple one. Then such a feeling of shame got hold of him, that he threw away his monastic garb, fled from the cloister, and wandered around the neighboring forests in wretched lay clothing.

One of the late fruits of the ideas and prophetic spirit of the Joachimite school is the writing of a

[1] Henrici de Hassia, *Liber contra Vaticinia Telesphori*, Thesaur. Anecdot., i., 2, 516.

so-called hermit Telesphorus, who was born, as he says, at Cosenza, in the time of the great ecclesiastical rupture, towards the end of the fourteenth century; and he gave out that he dwelt in the neighborhood of Thebes, that is, where Thebes, now in ruins, once stood. He relates that by the advice of an angel, who appeared to him in 1386, he buried himself in the study of the prophecies of Cyril and Joachim, of Merlin and Dandalus, of the Sibyls and of the papal chronicles. The fruit of his study is the glorification of France and its king and the French pope. He said that the schism would come to an end by the killing of the Anti-Pope (the Italian), which would be in the year 1393 at Perugia; then would follow a great renovation of the Church and a return of the clergy to apostolic poverty, for all their wealth and estates would be taken from them. At the same time great wars would be waged between the nations of Europe, in which the two allies would be victorious, viz: the true (French) pope and the French king. For the true pope is the one for whom this king has declared himself, since the kings of France in all the papal divisions have always contended for the legitimate pope; and he must conquer whom the pope helps, that is the French king.

Only it is remarkable that this Joachimite, with

his Guelph sympathies, who hides himself under the name of Telesphorus, revived and appropriated the legend, now more than a hundred years old, about the Emperor Frederick III., **who was to** be the **restorer** of the Empire and the Church,—but gave it an opposite sense. About the year 1409—so runs **his prophecy,—this** German Frederick, of the seed of **the** second Frederick, **will** be raised to the imperial throne, will subdue the Roman Church and set up a German Anti-Pope, will destroy the clergy in a blood bath, and then march from Italy into France. King Charles is to be his prisoner; but, miraculously set free from the prison, he will fight with and kill this German Emperor. Whereupon the "Pastor Angelicus," meanwhile raised to the Chair of Peter, will forever deprive the German princes of their rights in the election of the Emperor, and will elect and crown King Charles as Emperor. The Emperor and the Pope are then to march to Palestine and conquer it. Whereupon all the children of men will be converted, and the world will be at peace.[1] And so the mask is taken off from this prophecy, pro-

---

[1] This work, ascribed to Telesphorus, was printed at Venice in 1515; but this edition is so rare, that Papenbrock and Mosheim know the work only in manuscript. This Venetian edition is before me. Muratori, in the *Antiquitates Ital.*, iii, 949, has copied the beginning.

claimed with such pretensions upon the authority of an angel, and widely read and believed; and it seems to be only a programme of the French aspirations and political aims. It had long been a cherished scheme of the French princes and statesmen, to connect the Empire with the royal house of France. The Germans now tried to weaken the effect of this vaticination in a twofold way, **by a counter-prophecy, and by a** theological refutation.

The German Anti-Telesphorus prophet is **said to** have been one Gamaleon, a relation of Pope Boniface **VIII.**, and to have imparted to the latter his outlook **into** the future in the year 1390.[1] Like Telesphorus, he represents that a French king was crowned Roman Emperor by the Pope. This king is to wrest the empire from the restless Germans; Rome and Italy are to be his confederates. The clergy, **the prophet** goes on to say, has already levelled to **the ground all** the kingdoms of this world and all principalities. It will at last wrest the empire from the German nation, and strive for the annihilation of the secular princes. Then the Roman Emperor will march **forth** from the field of lilies, subdue Rome, destroy all the lords and tyrants, the Roman Empire, take the French king

---

[1] His prophecy is in the collection of Wolfgang Lazius: *Fragmentum Vaticinii cujusdam Methodii*, etc. (Vienna, 1547), f. hij.

prisoner, and in future the kingdom of France will no longer be honored, but only the German empire. A German patriarchate will then be established at Mayence, the German land and people be raised to high honor, and live with their new shepherd (by whom is probably meant the patriarch of Mayence, raised to the papal dignity); then comes an expedition to the Holy Land, the last of the Crusades. Lazius in quoting this prophecy leaves out the long description of the ecclesiastical corruptions; yet here are found allusions to thoughts and aims, which afterwards became prominent in the great Peasants' Wars.

The theological refutation of Telesphorus was undertaken by Henry of Langenstein, the most famous German theologian of that time. His book shows more than all else, that the Joachimite views had decided opponents in Germany as well as in France. Henry declares it is a heresy on the part of Joachim and his disciple Telesphorus, to speak about the "leprosy of the Church that has committed whoredom,"—a representation current among the Italian Joachimites, especially since the Guelph party had become accustomed to confound Pope and Church, and to call itself the party of the Church. But in Germany this still sounded strange and gave great offense; it was conceded that the Roman Curia might well deserve this apocalyptic description, but they could not endure to have the whole Church so called. Henry did not find it any the less objectionable, that the prophet of Cosenza should say to laymen, that by confiscating ecclesiastical property and robbing the clergy they were executing the divine will.[1] Henry saw clearly that the prophet reverenced and flattered the French court, without being aware of the real connection of things. For there was then on foot a plan for bringing Genoa under French domination, which was carried out at Christmas, in the year 1386. Just before this, Telesphorus sent his book with a dedication to the doge, Antonio of Genoa, doubtless in order to teach him that the republic, which still accepted the Emperor's sovereignty, would do better to submit to the French King Charles VI., since he was soon to be emperor himself.

At last, as the human race approached the great epoch of the Reformation and the rupture of Christendom, the prophetic voices became more threatening,

[1] If he had had a more intimate acquaintance with the Spirituales and Fraticelli, still numerous in Southern Germany, he would have recognized in Telesphorus a member of this community. For among the things which, according to his prediction, were soon to be fulfilled, belonged the dissolution of all the spiritual orders, to be followed by the founding of a new one, which Joachim had already foretold; and all future popes were to come from the latter.

and the thrusts against the papacy more sharp. The Irish used to relate about their St. Columba, that God was pleased to give him the spirit of prophecy in the shape of a wonderfully beautiful queen (*Acta Sanctorum*, Bolland. Januar. ii., 330); and so we may say that the prophetic spirit of those times had a stonied gorgon-like brow, or at the best appeared like a sorrowful widow clad in garments of mourning. There was no longer need of any special prophetic gift, for every one believed that he could announce with certainty the breaking forth of a great catastrophe. Centuries before this the revered Bishop Grosseteste of Lincoln had declared upon his dying bed, that the evils of the Church could be healed only by fire and sword; and now Macchiavelli, a man of a very different spirit, but the most acute observer of his times, declared that one of two things must come upon the Roman Church, destruction, or a terrible chastisement.[1] At the same time Pico of Mirandula believed, as he declared in his Oration to Leo X., that in Italy, of whose ecclesiastical condition he drew a fearful description, the severe and bloody punishment of an avenging Providence had already begun, and still worse evils were to follow.

---

[1] Esser propinquo senza dubbio o la **rovina** o il flagello: *Discorsi sopra Livio*, i., 12 *Opere*, Firenze 1843, 273. Roscoe, in his *Life and Pontificate of Leo X.*, gives the oration of Pico.

Just before this, Italy had seen in one of its great men **the most renowned** prophet since Joachim, Girolamo Savonarola, the preaching monk, who atoned with his life for his firm faith in his mission as a seer, and for the boldness of his warnings. As to the prophetic gift of Savonarola, the judgment of his contemporaries was as divided as is that of later times. But it is more and more conceded, **that this extraordinary man actually possessed a peculiar** gift of divination, as the best of his biographers, Villari, has declared. The historian Comines, **who** always speaks of him with high veneration, asserts that he had told him things which nobody believed, and which had all been confirmed. Even Macchiavelli did not venture to deny his prophecies, " because we must speak with reverence of so great a man." (*Discorsi*, i., 12, p. **272**.) Guicciardini withholds his judgment until time shall have decided about his predictions.

Two statesmen have boasted that in the communities in which they lived nothing important ever occurred which they had **not** foreseen. Cicero claims this for himself ; and the other one, the French Du Vair, goes still further and asserts that not only in the State, but also in his private life, nothing ever came to pass which he had not beforehand seen to be coming.[1] It seems to me that Savonarola had a similarly organized nature.

Savonarola's prophecies were partly the result of his natural insight and rare penetration, in part they were the conclusions he drew from the course of Jewish history as applied to the Christian Church; and, in fine, they were also the interpretations of visions which he had had,—as he himself tells of one such vision of two immense crosses, which were shown him on Good Friday night, 1492, with other wonderful pictures; and he gives an interpretation of them.[2] The future holy pope, in whose speedy coming he believed, was brought in vision before him; he saw his face and form, without knowing who he was among the living, whether an Italian or a foreigner.[3] That this disposition to believe in visions, his own and those of others, was in him developed

---

[1] Cicero's statement is in his *Epistolæ Famil*, 6, 6. Du Vair was President of the Parliament of Provence, and the first parliamentary orator of his century; he lived in the times of Henry IV, and of the Burgher wars. His declarations referred to above are quoted in Ménage, *Observations sur la langue Française*, ii., 110. There is, however, this difference between the Roman and the Frenchman; Du Vair ascribes his anticipations to a sagacity which nature had given him, while Cicero believes himself indebted for his *divinatio* to prolonged study and political experience gradually attained by many years of service.

[2] *Compendium Revelationum*, Ulm, 1469, Fol. 9.

[3] *Oracolo della Renovazione*, Fol. 115.

even to superstition is proved by his reliance upon the angelic voices, which Marelli, a comrade of his Order, maintained that he had heard. (See Villari, i., 296.) Thus it came to pass, that his political prophecies were fulfilled, but his religious ones were not fulfilled. His reputation as a prophet was confirmed and widely diffused by his prediction of what nobody was looking for, viz: the French invasion of Italy under Charles VIII., and the expulsion of the Medici from Florence. But he also foretold with all definiteness a speedy and entire devastation of Rome by fire and sword, because Rome was the great deceiver of all Christendom and the source of its crimes.[1] This destruction never occurred. He further maintained that after many grievous visitations and woes, with which God was about to chastise his Church, it would again be built up as it was in the times of the apostles. Savonarola starts with the idea that when the Church had sunk so deep, and was so thoroughly gangrened as was then the case in Latin Christendom, especially in Italy, there must ere long be a renovation; or else we must suppose that God will forever cast off his bride, as he formerly did the Synagogue, and

[1] *Oracolo della Renovazione della Chiesa* (Venice, 1543), fol. 101. In this work the Florentine Dominican, Luca Bettini, brings together all of Savonarola's prophecies about the Church.

consign it to a hopeless and helpless perdition ; this, however, is inconceivable on the principles of faith. But such a reform as he had in mind and longed for never occurred. He was no more successful in his assurance that a universal conversion of unbelievers would follow the ecclesiastical renovation. On the other hand, he clearly foresaw that his prophetic mission, and the whole position into which he did not force himself so much as he was forced by others, would inevitably result in his own destruction. He longed, he said, to return from the deep sea on which he was afloat to the haven from which he came, but it was no longer possible ; the cause he represented would be victorious, but he would suffer death from it ; for the master, who bore the hammer, would cast him away when he had made use of him. At the end of March, 1498, he was still preaching thus: "Rome will not quench these flames, and if these be quenched God will kindle others, and they are already kindled all around, only you do not know it." On the 23d of May, 1498, he was executed, the Pope said, because he was a heretic ; his Order and his numerous adherents said, because he was a witness of the truth. A sacred office has been dedicated to him as a holy martyr, and persons, whom Rome itself has canonized, like Catharina Ricci and Philip Neri, have reverenced and called upon him by this name.

In Germany, down to the period of the Reformation, a certain popular treasury of prophecies was gathered up, which was at once the expression and the nutriment of the national wishes and anticipations. Methodius, Joachim, Brigitta, Hildegarde, and the so-called Sibylline Revelations, they had in common with the whole western world. There has never appeared in Germany a man like Savonarola, who claimed prophetic endowments and was received as possessing them. But the names of mythical personages were attached to the prophecies which had sprung up in the heart of the people. Thus they had an Eremite prophet, John Lichtenberger. It is said in a poem on the war of Cologne in 1745:

> "This thing three years before to pass it came
> One in Mayence did publicly foretell:
> John Lichtenberger is the prophet's name,
> In the whole kingdom is he known full well." [1]

This only means that the Lichtenberger prophecies were known through all Germany, but not that the prophet in person was universally known. The prophecies which bore his name were a widely-circulated

[1] Liliencron, *Histor. Volkslieder*, ii., 58:
  Das hat vor dreien Jahren offenbar
  Geweissaget einer von Mainz für war,
  Johann Lichtenberger ist er genannt,
  In dem ganzen Reich wol bekannt.

and favorite **book, as is** proved by the great number of editions down to 1528. They are a mixed collection, dating from the end of the fifteenth century, relating to Germany and particularly to the Netherlands, and are not the work of any single man.

A Lollard praying-brother, named Reinhardt, published a book on "The Great Tribulations," introducing the Sibyls and Brigitta, and predicting great bloodshed among the clergy in the time **of the** Emperor Maximilian. Luther, who re-published the Lichtenberger book **in 1527**, remarked in the **preface** that since the war of the Peasants in 1525 **the minds of the clergy** had been at rest, as they **believed that the Lichtenberger** prophecies had been **fulfilled, and that the danger was over.**

There had been **for some time** a general feeling **of** anxiety among the German clergy in regard **to the** impending catastrophe; it was felt that among all classes of the nation there was great hatred and contempt **of the class whose morals** were so debased and whose system was so thoroughly corrupt. **Two South-German** priests, Wolfgang Aytinger in Augsburg, **and Joseph Grünpeckh** in Ratisbon, gave utterance to this anxious foreboding, **the former** in the year 1496, in **a commentary on** Methodius;[1] the latter in the year 1508, in a "Mirror of Vision,"[2] whose title-page exhibited a church falling in the midst of flames. While Aytinger attributed the chief guilt to the profligate condition of the Roman Curia, which he says had become an all-destroying hellish abyss, Grünpeckh declared that for years there had been an expectation of an approaching tempest, which was to burst over Church and clergy, throughout all Germany. Wherever men, women and children assembled, there it was said, "The clergy is shortly to be attacked." Such prophecies were spread among the people, partly by pious and well-meaning persons, who, in spite of some divine illumination, were yet narrow-minded, and partly by the malicious, who longed for the spoils of the ecclesiastical property. Grünpeckh thought that a more fatal corruption than that prevalent in the Church could hardly be imagined; still he warned the laity not to rejoice too much over the threatened visitation upon the priests, since they too must at last drink the dregs and poison of the cup given to the clergy. Another priest, John Hagen,[3] dean of St.

---

[1] *Tractatus super Methodium*, (Augsburg, 1496).

[2] *Speculum naturalis, celestis et propheticæ visionis.* Nuremberg, 1508.

[3] Johannis ab Indagine *Zuschrift*, etc., in the *Neue Beiträge von theologischen Sachen.* 1752, p. 456-477.

Leonard's in Frankfort, spoke still more plainly. He predicted, as the result of his astrological studies, a great revolution in the Church, and the exposure and humiliation of the arrogant clergy. " There is good reason why we clergy should be the object of universal hatred ; we deserve it."

Fear, grief and bitterness gave origin to many a prophecy in Germany, after the middle of the fifteenth century. The disaffection of the clergy itself was as great as that of the laity, since the Papal Chair had disappointed all the hopes of Church renovation, founded on the Council of Basle. One such prophetic voice from the clergy was ascribed to the most renowned German theologian of his time, Henry of Langenstein (commonly called Henry of Hesse), although it was of later origin. It charged with simony every pope and every bishop since Nicolas III. (1277), and promised a reformation of the Romish Church by means of the Germans, the French and their Emperor. [1]

The feeling constantly grew stronger, that though help for the Church must in general come from the laity, it must above all come from a pious emperor. It was even reported that Christ said to St. Brigitta : " The king (for whom she had just been praying)

[1] Denis, *Codices MS. theologici Biblioth.* Vindob., p. 1572.

shall assemble wise and religiously-enlightened men, and consult with them how the fallen walls of the Church can be rebuilt, the clergy be delivered from its pride, and become again humble and modest. "For, verily, my Church has wandered far from me." (*Revelationes*, 6, 26, p. 436.)

So it came to pass that German prophecies dwelt much upon a pope who was to arise in Germany. According to one prophecy, he was first to be appointed by the princes and patriarch of Mayence, and afterwards crowned as pope upon German soil. As Patriarch of the German Church, he would place the crown upon an emperor chosen from the Rhine provinces, then take arms against the emperor with the lilies (the French usurper of the imperial dignity, as Telesphorus had called him), kill him and take possession of Rome. This was proclaimed from the pulpit, in 1409, by John Wünschelburg, a priest of Amberg,[1] that is at the time of the schism, when the thought had sprung up in many a mind whether this schism, brought about by the conflicting claims of France and Italy for the possession of the Papacy, could not be best adjusted by the election of **a German pope**.

A work of Bishop Berthold, "The Burden of the

---

[1] Jo. Wolfii, *Lectiones Memorab.* i., 728.

Church," [1] may be considered as the close and limit of mediæval prophecy. The author's views are those of the Joachimites; he holds to the theory of the seven periods of the Church. His authorities and sources, besides Methodius, are Cyril and the Abbot of Calabria, the canonized prophets Vincens Ferrer, Catharine of Siena, Brigitta, and Hildegarde. As in an impressive way he gives a dark view of the greatness and universality of the degradation of the Church, and holds up a mirror to the Roman Curia as the chief transgressor, so, also, his views and expectations of the immediate future are the darkest that can be imagined. He had no conception of the historical import of Luther's doctrines, and mentions the Lutherans only as a new and mischievous sect. He had no doubt as to the uprooting of the Papal Chair (*exterminium*), which, however, was to be succeeded by a re-establishment and glorification. He shows plainly how strong at that time, in Germany, was the conviction that the Italian nation, incorporated on its worst side by the Papal Curia, had committed a great political as well as social and religious crime against Germany; and that now both nations, the Italian first, since the year 1510, and the German soon after, must do penance for it in bloody wars and revolutions.

---

[1] "Burden," after Is. xiii., meaning a prophetic utterance.

Kindred to this, and yet pervaded by an entirely different spirit, is the "Rollhart" of the Swiss poet, Pamphilus Gengenbach.[1] All the prophetic personages so familiar to the Germans, Methodius, Cyril, Joachim, Brigitta, Reinhart, are there presented; the pope, the emperor, the kings of France, the Turk, put questions, and the answers they receive form an entire prophetic course of past and future events down to the appearance of Antichrist. The object seems to have been to make the Emperor Maximilian feel obliged to fulfil the prophecy that a German emperor or king is to conquer Rome and reform the Church.

"Who can this emperor be?" asked Maximilian, when Brigitta told him that a king was to reform the Church entirely and repair the losses of the kingdom. Thereupon his own name was given: and Methodius also comforted him with the assurance that the Roman Empire would never fall.

"My thoughts are not your thoughts; as the heaven is higher than the earth, so are my thoughts higher than your thoughts." (Is. iv., 8, 9). With these prophetic words, which must already have occurred to many a reader, we close this account of the prophecies current for fifteen hundred years after Christ.

---

[1] Pamphilus Gengenbach, von Gödeke (Hannover, 1856), p. 77 etc.

APPENDIX A.

THE story of the Papess, as given in the Tegernsee manuscript in the Royal Library at Munich (*Cod. lat. Tegerns.*, 781), is as follows:—

"Item papa Jutta, qui non fuit alamannus, sicut
"mendose fabulatur chronica martiniana. Glan-
"cia puella, fuit filia ditissimi civis Thessalici,
"cujus omnis meditatio æquivoca nota sapientiæ
"versabatur; hujus erat intellectus perspicax et
"ingenium docile, quam penitus assidua legendi
"solertia vegetabant; hæc tempore brevi sibi
"famam per omnes circuitus vindicabat; sed
"prædicatas laudes rei veritas excedebat. Erat
"Pircius in scholis illi juvenculus coævus. Huic
"noto discendi capacitatis ingenio, paternis opi-
"bus et omni quasi frugalitate, consiliis **hos**
"ambos, quos ætas æquaverat, exæquat amor,
"de jugalitate tractatur, parentes abnuunt. Cres-
"cit inter hos ardor et concupiscentia, cum
"diebus sensim pullulat ætas, in oscula veniunt
"et amplexus impatientes. Denique latibulum
"petunt et ardentes junguntur. Ludo veneris
"consummato de recessu tractant. Hæc inter
"mulieres, hic inter homines virtutum dotibus

The true story of Pope Jutta. Glancia was the daughter of a Thessalian, a clever and studious child. At school she fell in love with Pircius, and eloped with him, dressed in man's clothes. The two went to Athens, where they remained as students

for a long time. She displayed great ability, and became proficient in all the arts and sciences. He also gained a name for learning. Thence they moved to Rome, where they attracted a large number of scholars. On the death of the pope, Glancia was unanimously elected to succeed. Pircius was made	"ac disciplinarum studiis optant fieri singulares, "et Athenas ire deliberant inter ipsos. Uterque "se quot potest opulentiis munit ; habitus gestusque capit illa viriles et similes animo simul "habitus mirandos ac spectabiles illos facit. "Nulla mora properant Athenas, ubi longo "tempore student, et illa doctior, quidquid est "divinæ facultatis, aut humanæ disciplinæ vel "artium studiosa capescit, et ille similiter est "omni sapientia gloriosus. Hos non Athenæ "solum, sed universa Græcia veneratur. Hi "Romam veniunt, in omni facultate studium "pronunciant, ad hos omnes conveniunt tam "scholares quam quarumcunque scientiarum "doctores et quo profundiores accedunt, quas "hauriant venas, uberiores inveniunt. Hos "omnes et omnium facultatum doctores adorant, "hos omnes cives venerantur et horum mores "modestiamque, virtutes et sapientiam prædicat "omnis Roma, qui amplius in omnem terram "penetrat sonus eorum. Denique functo pontifice mulier nominatione omni labio vocatur "et voce non impugnata, Romanis hortantibus, "ad apostolatus apicem promovetur. Cardinalatur Pircius amasius, vitam sagaciter agunt et "in eorum gubernatione tota lætatur ecclesia.

APPENDIX A.

"Sed quum status **adulteri raro** radices figunt, *cardinal,*
"vel si **germinent,** non roborant, et si roborent, *After a while*
"non perdurant, accidit **ergo,** quod antea nun- *Glancia became*
"quam, fucata mulier papissa prægnatur et *pregnant,*
"**insueta** tempora partus ignorans ibat ad eccle- *and gave birth to a*
"siam sancti **Johannis** Lateranensis cum uni- *child on*
"verso clero missam solemnem celebratura. Sed *her way to mass,*
"inter Colosseum et ecclesiam s. Clementis *dying on*
"coacta doloribus cecidit et puerum peperit et *the spot, which the*
"pariter expiravit. Hæc viam papa semper *popes now always*
"evitat et ante **coronationem papa** semper ma- *avoid.*
"nibus virilia palpantibus **exploratur,**"etc.

> "**Vide,** quos ad gradus virtus **et sapientia** extollit
> Pusillos sic altos in sapientia protexit; sed nihil
> Est omnis nostra sagacitas vel **industria** contra Deum.
> Vide carmina, quæ sequuntur.
>
> Disceret ut leges peregrina **juvencula** plenas
> Glancia clara seges mulierum transit **Athenas**
> Cum juvene cupido vir facta, sed ista cupido
> Militat in turbis ac doctores docet urbis.
> Papa fit et puerum pariens et moritur prope clerum.
>
> ### Moralitas.
>
> Nil mage grandescit quam doctus jure fruendo,
> Nil mage vilescit quam vir sine lege fruendo.
>
> **Papa, pater pauperum, peperit** papissa papellum,"etc.

APPENDIX B.

The following additional particulars about the fable of Pope Joan, gathered mainly from Baring-Gould's *Curious Myths of the Middle Ages*, the notes to Soames's edition of Mosheim's *Ecclesiastical History*, and the article *Papesse* in Peter Bayle's *Dictionnaire*, will be of interest to those who care to pursue the subject further.

It is greatly to the discredit of Mosheim that he should write as follows of this monstrous story: "Between *Leo IV*., who died A.D. 855, and *Benedict* "*III*., a woman, who concealed her sex and assumed "the name of John, it is said, opened her way to the "pontifical throne by her learning and genius, and "governed the Church for a time. She is commonly "called the *Papess Joanna*. During the five subse- "quent centuries the witnesses to this extraordinary "event are without number ; nor did any one, prior "to the Reformation by Luther, regard the thing "as either incredible, or disgraceful to the Church. "But in the seventeenth century, learned men, not "only among the Roman Catholics, but others also, "exerted all the powers of their ingenuity both to "invalidate the testimony on which the truth of the

APPENDIX B. 431

"story rests and to confute it by an accurate com-
"putation of dates. There are still, however, very
"learned men who, while they concede that much
"falsehood is mixed with the truth, maintain that
"the controversy is not wholly settled. Something
'must necessarily have taken place at Rome to give
"rise to this most uniform report of so many ages;
"but even yet it is not clear what that something
"was." Book III., part 2, chap.'ii., § 4. Tant il est
certain que les mêmes choses nous paraissent véritables ou fausses à mesure qu'elles favorisent, ou notre parti, ou le parti opposé. One can hardly doubt that it was Protestant prejudice which made Mosheim "*wish* to believe" (as Gibbon says of a dubious story which pleases him) that the myth of Pope Joan might be true. It matters little to Protestants, as Bayle remarks, whether the Papess existed or not; it matters much that they should not give a handle to people to regard them comme des gens opiniâtres, et qui ne veulent jamais démordre des opinions préconçues. Mosheim says, "During the five subsequent centuries "the witnesses to this extraordinary event are with-
"out number;" he omits to add that they occur in the *last* of the five centuries. For more than 350 years after the death of Leo IV. there is absolute silence about the Papess. Nor is it true that "no one prior

"to Luther's time regarded the thing as incredible or disgraceful to the Church." Most people regarded it as a grievous scandal, and some doubted the fact. Platina, who wrote before Luther was born, after telling the story, says, "hæc quæ dixi, vulgo feruntur, "incertis tamen et obscuris auctoribus; quæ ideo "ponere breviter et nude institui, ne obstinate et per- "tinaciter omisisse videar, quod fere omnes affirmant." —*Lives of the Popes*, John VII.

It is almost slaying the dead to argue against the story of Pope Joan; but it is worth while to give a specimen of Bayle's mode of reasoning. Is it conceivable that five centuries hence there will not be a single historian extant of the sixteenth or seventeenth century who mentions the abdication of Charles V., or the assassinations of Henry III. and IV. of France; but that the earliest mention of these great events will be in some "misérable annaliste" of the nineteenth century? If it should be so, the twenty-fourth century will be very credulous if it believes in these events. To show how impossible it would be for the historians of the ninth century to have suppressed a fact so tremendous as a female pope, who was detected as Pope Joan is supposed to have been detected, Bayle supposed a writer of the eleventh century to narrate as follows:—Charles the Great was very desirous that his successor should be his son; it was therefore a great grief to him that his wife was barren. When at length there were hopes of a child, he was beside himself with joy; but when the child proved to be a girl, he was almost as grieved as before. He determined, therefore, to pass the child off as a boy, and gave it the name of Pepin. Six years later his wife bore him a son; but the parents still felt bound to conceal the sex of the first child, who on Charles' death was crowned as his successor. She reigned for three years without detection. The *dénouement* took place as she was addressing the parliament. The woman-king died in childbirth in the midst of the august assembly; and the nobles, in horror, passed a law which would render such an imposture impossible in future. Imagine half a dozen different accounts of the way in which Queen Pepin died, and you have a narrative as like that about Pope Joan " comme " deux gouttes d'eau." What amount of credence should we give to this eleventh century writer?

Some writers appear to have believed that the child which the Papess bore was Antichrist! An eminent Dutch minister considers it as immaterial whether its father was a monk or the devil.

The German and French Protestants of the sixteenth century delighted in the story, embellishing it with details of their own, in order to make capital out of it against the Papacy. Nor did their fancy exuberate in words only. Some of their accounts are illustrated with woodcuts, which would seem to be more curious and graphic than decent. Mr. Baring-Gould gives a copy of one in which the Papess is strung up to a gibbet over the mouth of hell; rather against the version of the story, which says she was allowed to choose whether she would have the public exposure, or burn for ever in hell.

The *raison d'être* of the myth, as given by Dr. Döllinger in the text, is probably sufficient. Mr. Baring-Gould, however, has little doubt " that Pope
" Joan is an impersonation of the great whore of Re-
" velation, seated on the seven hills, and is the po-
" pular expression of the idea prevalent from the
" twelfth to the sixteenth century, that the mystery of
" iniquity was somehow working in the Papal Court.
" The scandal of the anti-popes, the utter worldliness
" and pride of others, the spiritual fornication with the
" kings of the earth, along with the words of Revela-
" tion prophesying the advent of an adulterous woman
" who should rule over the Imperial City, and her con-
" nection with Antichrist, crystallized into this curious
" myth, much as the floating uncertainty as to the
" signification of our Lord's words, 'There be some

"'standing here which shall not taste of death till 'they see the kingdom of God,' condensed into the myth of the Wandering Jew."

He gives the following "jingling record" of the Papess, which is worth re-quoting. It is a fragment of the rhythmical *Vitæ Pontificum* of Gulielmus Jacobus of Egmonden, preserved in *Wolfii Lectionum Memorabilium centenarii*, XVI. :—

"Priusquam reconditur Sergius, vocatur
  Ad summam, qui dicitur Johannes, huic addatur
  Anglicus, Moguntia iste procreatur.
  Qui, ut dat sententia, fœminis aptatur
  Sexu : quod sequentia monstrant, breviatur
  Hæc vox ; nam prolixius chronica procedunt.
  Ista, de qua brevius dicta minus lædunt.
  Huic erat amasius, ut scriptores credunt,
  Patria relinquitur Moguntia, Græcorum
  Studiose petitur schola. Pòst doctorum
  Hæc doctrix efficitur Romæ legens ; horum
  Hæc auditu fungitur loquens. Hinc prostrato
  Summo hæc eligitur ; sexu exaltato
  Quandoque negligitur. Fatur quod hæc nato
  Per servum conficitur. Tempore gignendi
  Ad processum equus scanditur, vice flendi,
  Papa cadit, panditur improbis ridendi
  Norma, puer nascitur in vico Clementis,
  Colossæum jungitur. Corpus parentis
  In eodem traditur sepulturæ gentis,
  Faturque scriptoribus, quod Papa præfato,
  Vico senioribus transiens amato
  Congruo ductoribus sequitur negato
  Loco, quo Ecclesia partu denigratur,
  Quamvis inter spacia Pontificum ponatur
  Propter sexum."

APPENDIX B.

The literature on the subject is abundant. The arguments of those who maintain the truth of the story are collected and stated by Frederick Spanheim in his *Exercit. de Papa Fœmina* (Opp., tom. ii., p. 577), and L'Enfant has given a French translation and better arrangement of them, with additions: *Histoire de la Papesse Jeanne*, La Haye, 1736; two vols. 12mo.

The arguments against the myth are given in Blondel's[1] famous treatise, *Familier éclaircissement de*

---

[1] Baring-Gould, in his *Curious Myths*, etc., has the following statement in respect to this work of Blondel:

"[Blondel, the great Protestant writer, who ruined the case of the Decretals, says that he examined a MS. of Anastasius in the Royal Library at Paris, and found the story of Pope Joan inserted in such a manner as to convince him that it was a late interpolation. He says, 'Having read and re-read it, I found that the eulogium of the pretended Papess is taken from the words of Martinus Polonus, penitentiary to Innocent IV., and Archbishop of Cosenza, an author four hundred years later than Anastasius and much more given to all these kinds of fables.' His reasons for so thinking are, that the style is not that of the Librarian, but similar to that of Martin Polonus; also that the insertion interferes with the text of the chronicle, and bears evidence of clumsy piecing. "In the eulogiums of Leo IV. and Benedict III., as given to us in the manuscript of the Bibliothèque Royale, swelled with the romance of the Papess, the same expressions occur as in the Mayence edition; whence it follows that (according to the intention of Anastasius, violated by the rashness of those who have mingled it with their idle dreams) it is absolutely impossible that any one could have been Pope between Leo IV. and Benedict III., for he says: 'After the Prelate Leo was withdrawn from this world, *at once* (mox) all the clergy, the nobles, and people of Rome hastened to elect Benedict; and at once (illico) they sought him, praying in the titular church of St. Callixtus, and

la question, si une femme a été assise au siége papal de Rome, Amsterdam, 1647-9; in Bayle's *Dictionnaire historique et critique*, article *Papesse*. See also *Allatii Confutatio Fabulæ de Johanna Papissa*, Colon., 1645; George Eccard, *Historia Franciæ Oriental*, tom. ii., lib. xxx., § 119; Michael Lequien, *Oriens Christianus*, iii., p. 777; Chr. Aug. Heumann, a Lutheran writer, *Sylloge Diss. Sacrar.*, tom. i., pt. ii., p. 352; J. G. Schelhorn, *Amœnitates Literar.*, i., p. 146; Jac. Basnage, *Histoire de l'Eglise*, i., p. 408; Schroeckh, *Kirchengeschichte*, xxii., p. 75-110; J. E. C. Schmidt, *Kirchengeschichte*, iv., p. 274-279; A. Bower's *Lives of the Popes*, iv., p. 246-260.

having seated him on the pontifical throne, and signed the decree of his election, they sent him to the very invincible Augusti Lothair and Louis, and the first of these died on 29 September, 855, just seventy-four days after the death of Pope Leo." Pp. 179-181. H. B. S.]

APPENDIX C.

The story of Popiel, king of Poland, which is so similar to that of Bishop Hatto of Mayence, is thus given by Mr. Baring-Gould :—" Martinus Gallus,
" who wrote in 1110, says that King Popiel, having
" been driven from his kingdom, was so tormented
" by mice, that he fled to an island whereon was
" a wooden tower, in which he took refuge; but
" the host of mice and rats swam over and ate him
" up. The story is told more fully by Majolus
" (*Dierum Canic.*, p. 793). When the Poles mur-
" mured at the bad government of the king, and
" sought redress, Popiel summoned the chief mur-
" murers to his palace, where he pretended that he
" was ill, and then poisoned them. After this the
" corpses were flung by his orders into the lake
" Gopolo. Then the king held a banquet of rejoicing
" at having freed himself from these troublesome
" complainers. But during the feast, by a strange
" metamorphosis (mira quadam metamorphosi), an
" enormous number of mice issued from the bodies of
" his poisoned subjects, and rushing on the palace,
" attacked the king and his family. Popiel took
" refuge within a circle of fire, but the mice broke

APPENDIX C.

"through the flaming ring; then he fled with his wife and child to a castle in the sea, but was followed by the animals and devoured."

He also gives other stories, more or less parallel to that of Bishop Hatto; for instance, the one of Freiherr von Güttingen. This baron is said to have possessed three castles between Constance and Arbon, in the canton of Thurgau, namely, Güttingen, Moosburg, and Oberburg. During a grievous famine he collected the poor on his lands together, shut them up in a barn, and burnt them, mocking their shrieks by exclaiming, "Hark how the rats and mice are squeaking!" Not long after a huge swarm of mice came down upon him. He fled to his castle of Güttingen, which stood in the lake of Constance; but the mice swam after him and devoured him. The castle then sank into the lake, where it may still be seen when the water is clear and the surface unruffled (*Zeitschrift für Deutsche Mythologie*, iii., p. 307). Again, there is a mouse-tower at Holzölster, in Austria, with a very similar legend attached, except that here the wicked nobleman locks the poor people up in a dungeon and starves them to death, instead of making a bonfire of them (Vernaleken, *Alpensagen*, p. 328). Another instance is referred to by Dr. Döllinger in the text.

The Wörthsee, between Tonning and Seefeld, in Bavaria, is also called the Mouse lake. A count of Seefeld once starved all his famishing poor to death in a dungeon during a famine, and laughed at their cries, which he called the squeaking of mice. An island tower was as little use to him as to Bishop Hatto or King Popiel, though he took the additional precaution of having his bed swung from the roof by chains. The mice got at him from the ceiling, and picked his bones (*Zeitschrift für Deut. Myth.* i., p. 452). The Mäuseschloss in the Hirschberger lake is another instance of a very similar story. Legends abound in which rats or mice are made instruments of divine vengeance, but they do not always contain the feature of the island tower, which is essential for our present purpose. Sometimes the avenging vermin are toads and frogs instead of rats and mice.

The tendency which a story of interest has to attract round itself as evidence circumstances which have no connection with it whatever, is so strikingly illustrated by the famous incident of the so-called "Thundering Legion," that I venture to call attention to it. For the sake of clearness I give the outline of the story. The Emperor Marcus Aurelius, in his celebrated war against the Quadri, was reduced to the greatest extremities by a failure of water, just on

APPENDIX C.

the very eve of a battle. A large body of Christians in one of the legions fell on their knees, and prayed to heaven for help. A sudden storm followed, which by its thunder and lightning terrified the barbarians, and by its heavy rain relieved the thirst of the Romans. The truth of the narrative does not concern us; but probably no one who examines the evidence, as collected by Dr. Newman in his *Essays on Miracles* (Essay II., chap. v., section 1), will dissent from his very moderate statement of the result. "On "the whole, then, we may conclude that the facts of "this memorable occurrence are as the early Christian "writers state them; that Christian soldiers did ask, "and did receive, in a great distress, rain for their "own supply, and lightning against enemies; "whether through miracle or not we cannot "say for certain, but more probably not through "miracle in the philosophical sense of the word. All "we know, and all we need know is, that 'He made "'darkness His secret place, His pavilion round "'about him, with dark water and thick clouds to "'cover Him; the Lord thundered out of heaven, "'and the Highest gave His thunder; hailstones and "'coals of fire. He sent out His arrows, and "'scattered them; He sent forth lightnings, and "'destroyed them.'" Just as the story of Pope Joan fastened on the fact that pontifical processions never passed through the narrow street between the church of St. Clement and the Coliseum, and just as the story of the Count of Gleichen made capital out of the big bed and the jewel which the Turkish princess was supposed to have worn in her turban, so this history of the "Thundering Legion" has incorporated with itself two utterly irrelevant circumstances, and that so completely, that some persons have supposed that by exposing the irrelevancy they have necessarily demolished the story—" as if evidence were the test of truth." Claudius Apollinaris, Bishop of Hierapolis, was a contemporary of Marcus Aurelius. His statement of this incident in the war against the Quadri is preserved to us by Eusebius (*Hist.* v., 5), and he alleges as evidence that the legion to which these Christian soldiers belonged was thenceforth called the Thundering Legion. Tertullian, writing some five and twenty years later (about A.D. 200), states by way of evidence that the emperor in consequence passed an edict in favour of the Christians (*Apologeticus*, chap. v.; cf. *Ad Scapulam*, cap. iv.). Now there certainly was a Thundering Legion (Legio Fulminatrix), viz., the twelfth; but then it was as old as the time of Augustus. It was one of the nineteen legions levied by him. And as regards Tertullian's

APPENDIX C. 443

argument, there is some **evidence** that Marcus Aurelius did issue a rescript favouring the Christians, but in the period of **his** reign which *preceded* the battle. And **it is** notorious that he persecuted the Christians both before **and after that event.** Here, then, we have a story, **almost certainly true** in itself, claiming **as** evidence circumstances which, however well attested, **have nothing whatever to do with it.**

Instances of **strange and unusual objects** giving rise to myths might be multiplied almost *ad infinitum.* Thus the story of Arion arose **from** the **figure of a** man on a dolphin, which was the customary offering of one saved from shipwreck; **the** dolphin being a mere emblem of the sea. The story of the Horatii and Curiatii seems to be an attempt **to** explain five barrows. The custom **of representing** martyrs with the instruments or marks of their sufferings, produced the legend of **St.** Denys walking with **his head under** his arm. The allegorical picture of Michael **the** Archangel conquering the **Evil** One in the presence of the Church, gave rise **to** the myth of **St.** George rescuing Saba from the dragon, **&c.**

APPENDIX D.

Pope Hadrian's Letter to Henry II., King of England, A.D. 1154.

Adrianus Papa gratum **et** *acceptum habet quod Henricus Rex Angliæ Insulam Hyberniam ingrediatur ut populum illum legibus* **subdat,** *ita tamen ut annua Petro solvatur pensio.*

ADRIANUS Episcopus, servus servorum Dei, carissimo in Christo filio illustri Anglorum Regi, salutem et Apostolicam Benedictionem. Laudabiliter satis et fructuose de glorioso nomine propagando in terris et æternæ felicitatis præmio cumulando in cœlis, tua magnificentia cogitat, dum ad dilatandos Ecclesiæ terminos, ad declarandam indoctis et rudibus Populis Christianæ fidei veritatem, et vitiorum plantaria de Agro Dominico extirpanda, sicut Catholicus Princeps, intendis, et ad id convenientius exequendum consilium Apostolicæ sedis exigis et favorem. In quo facto, quanto altiori Consilio, et majori discretione procedes, tanto in eo feliciorem progressum te, præstante Domino, confidimus habiturum, eo quod ad bonum exitum semper et finem soleant attingere quæ de ardore fidei et religionis amore principium acceperunt.

Sane Hiberniam et omnes Insulas quibus sol justitiæ Christus illuxit, et quæ documenta Fidei Christianæ receperunt, ad jus beati Petri et sacrosanctæ Romanæ Ecclesiæ (quod tua etiam nobilitas recognoscit) non est dubium pertinere, unde tanto in eis libentius plantationem fidei fidelem et germen Deo gratum inserimus, quanto id a nobis interno exadistrictius prospicimus exigendum.

Significasti siquidem nobis, fili in Christo carissime, te Hyberniæ Insulam ad subdendum illum populum legibus, et vitiorum plantaria inde extirpanda, velle intrare, *et de singulis domibus Annuam unius denarii beato Petri velle solvere pensionem* et jura Ecclesiarum illius terræ illibata et integra conservare; nos itaque, pium et laudabile desiderium tuum favore congruo prosequentes, et petitioni tuæ benignum impendentes assensum, gratum et acceptum habemus, ut, pro dilatandis Ecclesiæ terminis, pro vitiorum restringendo decursu, pro corrigendis moribus et virtutibus inserendis, pro Christianæ Religionis augmento, Insulam illam ingrediaris; et quæ ad honorem Dei et salutem illius spectaverint exequaris; et illius terræ populus honorifice te recipiat; et sicut Dominum veneretur (*jure nimirum Ecclesiarum illibato et integro permanente, et salva beato Petro et sacrosanctæ Romanæ Ecclesiæ de singulis domibus* annua unius *denarii pensione*).

Si ergo, quod concepisti animo, effectu duxeris prosequente complendum, stude gentem illam bonis moribus informare, et agas, tam per te, quam per illos quos ad hoc fide, verbo, et vita idoneos esse perspexeris, ut decoretur ibi Ecclesia, plantetur et crescat Fidei Christianæ Religio, et quæ ad honorem Dei et salutem pertinent animarum taliter ordinentur, ut et a Deo sempiternæ mercedis cumulum consequi merearis, et in terris gloriosum nomen valeas in seculis obtinere.—Rymer's *Fœdera, Conventiones*, &c., I., p. 15.

It is interesting to compare with the claims made by the above document the decision of the recent Council of the Vatican:

"Si quis itaque dixerit, Romanum Pontificem habere tantummodo officium inspectionis vel directionis, non autem *plenam et supremam potestatem jurisdictionis in universam Ecclesiam*, non solum in rebus, quæ ad fidem et mores, *sed etiam quæ ad disciplinam et regimen Ecclesiæ per totum orbem diffusæ pertinent*; aut eum habere tantum potiores partes, non vero totam plenitudinem hujus supremæ potestatis; aut hanc ejus potestatem non esse ordinariam et immediatam sive in omnes ac singulas ecclesias, *sive in omnes et singulos pastores et fideles;* anathema sit."—*Constitutio Dogmatica* **prima de** *Ecclesia Christi*, cap. iii.

APPENDIX E.

Decisions "ex Cathedra."

" Quelles étaient alors les conditions de l'acte *ex*
" *cathedrâ* ? Qui peut dire ce qu'elles sont au-
" jourd'hui ? Connaît-on deux théologiens bien
" d'accord sur ce point ? Nous parlerons des actes
" *ex cathedrâ* quand nous saurons ce que veut dire
" le mot *ex cathedrâ*."

Most persons who have endeavoured to discover
what the exact meaning of decisions *ex cathedrâ* is,
will be inclined to sympathise very heartily with the
above words of Père[1] Gratry.

Archbishop Manning tells us[2] that the Vatican
Council has defined the meaning. What the Council
says is this: " We teach and define that it is a dogma
" divinely revealed ; that the Roman Pontiff, when he
" speaks *ex cathedrâ*, that is, *when in discharge of the
" office of Pastor and Doctor of all Christians, by
" virtue of his supreme Apostolic authority he defines a
" doctrine regarding faith or morals to be held by the
" Universal Church*, by the divine assistance promised

---

[1] *Troisième lettre à Mgr. Deschamps*, p. 13.
[2] *The Vatican Council and its Definitions*, London, 1870, p. 57.

"to him in blessed Peter, is possessed of that in-
"fallibility," [1] &c.

But some persons have been able to accept the new dogma, that the Pope has the Church's infallibility when he speaks *ex cathedrâ*, precisely because neither the nature of the Church's infallibility nor the meaning of *ex cathedrâ* have ever been defined. It would seem, then, that the definition of the Vatican Council is itself in need of definition. We must fall back, therefore, on the explanations of the phrase which have been attempted elsewhere.

Those not already committed to a position, with which the meaning of *ex cathedrâ* must at all hazards be made consistent, will probably agree with "Janus," [2] that beyond excluding off-hand remarks on dogmatic and ethical questions made by a pope in the course of conversation, the distinction *ex cathedrâ* has no meaning. "When a pope speaks

---

[1] "Docemus et divinitus revelatum dogma esse definimus: Romanum Pontificem, cum ex cathedrâ loquitur, id est, cum omnium Christianorum Pastoris et Doctoris munere fungens, pro supremâ sua Apostolica auctoritate doctrinam de fide vel moribus ab universa Ecclesia tenendam definit, per assistentiam divinam, ipsi in beato Petro promissam, ea infallibilitate pollere, qua divinus Redemptor Ecclesiam suam in definienda doctrina de fide vel moribus instructam esse voluit," &c —*Constitutio Dogmatica Prima de Ecclesiâ Christi*, cap. iv., sub. fin.

[2] *Der Papst und das Concil.*, p. 127. English translation, p. 101.

"publicly on a point of doctrine, either of his own accord, or in answer to questions addressed to him, he has spoken *ex cathedrâ*, for he was questioned as pope, and successor of other popes, and the mere fact that he has made his declaration publicly and in writing makes it an *ex cathedrâ* judgment. . . . . The moment any accidental or arbitrary condition is fixed on which the *ex cathedrâ* nature of a papal decision is to depend, we enter the sphere of the private crotchets of theologians. . . . . Just as if one chose to say afterwards of a physician who had been consulted, and had given his opinion on a disease, that he had formed his diagnosis and prescribed his remedies as a private person, and not as a physician. . . . . Thus Orsi maintains that Honorius composed the dogmatic letter he issued in reply to the Eastern Patriarchs, and which was afterwards condemned as heretical by the sixth Œcumenical Council, only as 'a private teacher;' but the expression *doctor privatus*, when used of a pope, is like talking of wooden iron."

Some have maintained that before a pope speaks *ex cathedrâ* he must have thoroughly discussed the question to be decided, conferring with bishops and theologians. This *appears* to be the present view of Bishop Hefele, judging from his recent most disappointing letter to the clergy of his [1] diocese. But the learned author of the *Conciliengeschichte* does not tell us whether the consulting a synod is an indispensable condition of a definition *ex cathedrâ*, or only a piece of ecclesiastical etiquette. If the latter, the statement is nugatory; if the former, we have the startling paradox that the infallibility of an infallible Head is dependent on consultation with fallible subordinates.

Bellarmine and his fellow Jesuit, Endæmon Johannes, make it a *sine quâ non* that the Pope should address what he defines *ex cathedrâ* to the whole Church. Thus a decree or definition addressed to the Church in France or in Germany would not necessarily be infallible. But surely what is truth for

---

[1] The words of our Constitution (*Constitutio Dogmatica Prima de Ecclesiâ Christi*, cap. iv.): "Romani autem Pontifices, prout tempo-"rum et rerum conditio suadebat, nunc convocatis œcumenicis "conciliis aut explorata Ecclesiæ per orbem dispersæ sententia, "nunc per synodos particulares, nunc aliis, quæ divina suppeditabat "providentia, adhibitis auxiliis, &c.," contain not only an historical notice of what was done formerly, but also imply the rule, in accordance with which papal decisions *ex cathedrâ* will always be made. — *Rundschreiben an den hochwürdigen Klerus.* Rottenburg, April 10th, 1871.

But will it suffice if the Pope merely consults a synod, and then decrees what he pleases, whether the synod approve or no? Or must at least *some* of the synod agree with him? Or will it be sufficient if he only consults those who are known to agree with him? "This question has become a crucial one since 1713, when Clement "XI. issued his famous Bull *Unigenitus*, which he had drawn up "with the assistance of two cardinals only."—(Janus).

one is truth for all. How can a proposition be an article of faith for France or Germany, if it is not an article of faith for the whole Church?

Others again, would make it of the essence of an *ex cathedrâ* decision that the document should have been affixed for a certain time to the door of St. Peter's, and in the Campofiore.

[Bishop von Hefele, in his essay on Honorius, against De Margerie's pamphlet, *Le Pape Honorius et le Bréviaire Romain* (Paris 1870), takes the ground that Honorius spoke *ex cathedrâ* on the question in hand. He says:

"Who does not know that it is extremely difficult to determine when the Pope speaks *ex cathedrâ?* De Margerie propounds two criteria by which this may be known:

"*a.* When the Pope proclaims in *positive* terms an opinion as an article of faith. Honorius, he argues, did not do this. But is not the following dictum *positive:*

"We confess one will of our Lord Jesus Christ. (Unam voluntatem fatemur domini Jesu Christi. *Mansi*, T. xi., p. 539).

"Further, Honorius says: 'We have not learned from the Holy Scriptures that Jesus Christ... has one or two *energies;* but that He acts in *manifold* modes,' (*multiformiter* cognovimus operatum, *Mansi.* p. 542). And is not Honorius prescribing this as a matter of faith? Toward the close of his epistle, he says: 'This, my brethren, you will with us proclaim... and we *exhort* you (hortantes vos) that you *avoid* the new way of talking about one or two energies, etc.' (*Mansi*, xi., p. 543).

"In the second epistle he is still more clear: 'As to the ecclesiastical *dogma*, and what we are bound to hold and to teach (quantum ad *dogma* ecclesiasticum pertinet quæ *tenere* vel prædicare *debemus*), we are not bound to define that there is in the Mediator either one energy or two.'

"Thus Honorius in fact proclaimed his thesis *positively, and prescribed* it.

"*b.* But, says Margerie (p. 43), he did not enjoin it upon the *whole world*, and this is the second requisite of a dogma *ex cathedrâ*.

"I do not know that a formal address to the whole Church is absolutely necessary to an *ex cathedrâ* definition; for if that be the case, the famous dogmatic epistle of Leo I. to Flavian was not given *ex cathedrâ*. But there is no doubt about the fact that Honorius would have the whole Church, and not merely the Church of Constantinople, believe what he propounded." (See the *Presbyterian Quarterly and Prince-*

ton Review, April, 1872, pp. 299, 300.) Bishop Hefele, however, published the Vatican decree on Papal Infallibility in April, 1871, and gave in his adhesion to it, accompanying it with an interpretation on several points, as *e.g.*, that this "infallibility extends only to revealed truth about matters of faith and morals;" that "the *definitions* alone are infallible, and not the introductory statements and arguments;" and, in fine, that the reason why a papal definition is infallible "is not to be found in the person of the Pope, but in the divine aid." This last is certainly a remarkable interpretation: for if that was the real sense of the decree, none of the minority of the Council could have opposed. See a sharp criticism on these points in von Schulte's *Stellung der Concilien, Päpste und Bischöfe*, Prag. 1871, s. 336-8. H. B. S.]

Another necessary condition, according to some, is that the Pope should anathematize those who dispute the decision.

Lastly, the Bishop of St. Pölten maintains [1] that

---

[1] *Die falsche und die wahre Unfehlbarkeit der Päpste*, von Dr. Joseph FESSLER, Bischof von St. Pölten, Wien, 1871. The pamphlet contains some strange inconsistencies; as professor Berchtold has already pointed out, e. g.. On p. 34 Bishop Fessler maintains that the well known brief of Pius IX , *Multiplices inter* (June 10, 1851), in which certain doctrines are condemned as heretical, is not a decision *ex cathedrâ*; and the bishop ridicules professor Schulte for supposing that a definition of an article of faith could be made in

the pope must expressly state that he is defining, in virtue of his office, as supreme teacher in the Church. Hence he would contend that it is still doubtful whether the present Pope's *Syllabus* is *ex cathedrâ*, and therefore infallible. Would *Rome* allow that it is doubtful?

In considering these various, and in some cases extraordinary conditions, we can scarcely avoid the conclusion that they are for the most part artificial restrictions, invented for the purpose of excluding certain awkward utterances of popes from being *ex cathedrâ*. Such efforts reach a climax when the view is deliberately put forth, that,[1] as no pope ever has spoken *ex cathedrâ* from the beginning of time till now, so it is probable that henceforth till the end of time none ever will so speak. And nothing short of this desperate theory can save the Bull of Paul IV.— "*Cum ex Apostolatus officio,*" March 15th, 1809 (one

condemning a book. On p. 41, however, he tells us that in theology it is a sure sign (sicheres Kennzeichen) of a dogmatic decision, when any doctrine is declared by the Pope to be heretical. The pamphlet in style is perhaps scarcely what one would have expected from a prelate.

[1] *What is the Meaning of the late Definition of the Infallibility of the Pope? An Enquiry.* By W. MASKELL, p. 10. Noticed by the Dean of Westminster in his recent pamphlet on *The Athanasian Creed.* Dean Stanley justly remarks, " Whether such interpretations " are respectful to the documents which they profess to honour may " well be doubted." (p. 95.)

APPENDIX E.

of the most terrible ever issued by a pope)—from being *ex cathedrâ*. Every[1] condition, even down to the affixing it on the doors of St. Peter's, is fulfilled. The Bishop of St. Pölten attempts to exclude it, because it is not a decision in matters of faith— "keine *Glaubens*entscheidung;" but it is most undeniably a decision in *matters of morals*, and these are claimed as within the sphere of papal infallibility no less than matters of faith.

[1] It is perhaps worth while to quote the passages which prove this :—" Cum *ex Apostolatus officio* nobis, meritis licet imparibus, " divinitus credito, cura Dominici gregis nobis immineat *generalis*, " et exinde teneamur pro fideli illius *custodia*, et salubri *directione*, " more Vigilis *Pastoris* assidue vigilare," &c.

" Habita super his cum venerabilibus fratribus nostris S. R. E. " cardinalibus *deliberatione* matura, de eorum consilio, et *unanimi* " *assensu*," &c.

" Hac nostra *in perpetuum valitura* constitutione,.... *de Aposto-* " *licæ potestatis plenitudine* sancimus, statuimus, decernimus et " *definimus*," &c.

" Ut autem præsentes literæ ad omnium quorum interest notitiam " deducantur, volumus eas,.... in *Basilicæ Principis Apostolorum de* " *Urbe et Chancellariæ Apostolicæ valvis atque in acie campi Floræ* " per aliquos ex cursoribus nostris publicari et *affigi*," &c.

" Si quis autem hoc attentare præsumpserit, *indignationem omni-* " *potentis Dei*, ac Beatorum Petri et Pauli apostolorum ejus se noverit *incursurum* "—" hoc" being the infringing or opposing of the Bull. See an able article in the *Allgemeine Zeitung* (Beilage, April 11, 1871), *Die römische Frage, die päpstliche Sittenlehre und die europäische Rechtsordnung.*

APPENDIX F.

The Latest Defenders of Honorius.

In order to be convinced how fatal the case of Honorius is to the claims of papal infallibility, one has only to read a few of his apologists. The means resorted to in the vain attempt to overcome the insurmountable difficulty, are *so extraordinary* and *so various*, that one feels that the truth must be on the side which is so fiercely and irrationally assailed. The controversy is one more proof of the simplicity of truth and the multiplicity of error. We are only concerned now with that mode of argument, lately renewed in high quarters, which would demolish the case of Honorius as an instance of papal fallibility, by maintaining that the letters of Honorius are *not* heterodox. This method has at least the advantage of being bold. Three general councils have declared that these letters *are* heterodox, in fact, damnably heretical; and pope after pope has confirmed the decision of these councils. But, in spite of that, three Roman archbishops publicly assure their clergy that the epistles of Honorius are perfectly orthodox. Protestant "private judgment" can scarcely go farther.

A recent pastoral of the archbishop of Baltimore contains the following "excellent passage," quoted with approbation by Archbishop Manning: "The case "of Honorius forms no exception; for 1st, Honorius "expressly says in his letters to Sergius that he "meant to define nothing, and he was condemned "precisely because he temporized and would not "define; 2nd, because *in his letters he clearly taught* "*the sound Catholic doctrine*, only enjoining silence as "to the use of certain terms, then new in the Church; "and 3rd, because his letters were not addressed to a "general council of the whole Church, and were "rather private than public and official; at least they "were not published, even in the East, until several "years later."

The Archbishop of Westminster goes even further than his American brother. "I will, nevertheless, here "affirm that the following points in the case of Hono- "rius can be abundantly proved from documents:—

"(1.) That Honorius *defined no doctrine* whatsoever.
"(2.) That he forbade the making of any new "definition. (3.) That his fault was precisely in this "omission [1] of Apostolic authority, for which he was

---

[1] Would the council have solemnly cursed Honorius for mere "omission of Apostolic authority?" And would Pope Leo have spoken of such omission as a "profana proditio," an attempt to subvert the faith?

"justly censured [i.e. anathematized]. (4.) That *his
"two epistles are entirely orthodox;* though, in the
"use of language, he wrote, *as was usual*, before the
"condemnation of Monothelitism, and not as it
"became necessary afterwards. It is an anachronism
"and an injustice to censure his language before that
"condemnation, as it might be just to censure it
"after the condemnation had been made;"[1] an
anachronism of which three general councils and
various popes have been guilty. One is not ashamed
of being similarly guilty in company so respectable.

It is difficult to decide which statement is the most
audacious, that the letters of Honorius are entirely
orthodox, or that the language for which he was
anathematized was usual at the time.

Similarly the Archbishop of Malines maintains of
Honorius, that "non-seulement il n'a pas enseigné le
monothélisme, mais *il a formellement enseigné le
contraire.*"

Let us very briefly review the facts.

Of the four Oriental patriarchs three had declared
for the famous *Nine Articles*, which were an attempt
to make peace by means of a doubtful expression.[2]

---

[1] *The Vatican Council and its Definitions:* a Pastoral Letter to the Clergy, London, 1870.

[2] Θεανδρικα ἐνεργεια—words capable of an orthodox, but also of a monophysite interpretation. They occur in the seventh and crucial article. The first six are introductory; the last two are anathemas.

The new patriarch of Jerusalem, Sophroniscus, disregarding the promise which he had made **as a** private theologian, had called a synod and solemnly condemned the *Nine Articles*. Now came the **time** when Honorius, hitherto quite passive, could keep silence no longer. He was formally asked for his decision. ·**It** would seem as **if he never** clearly understood **the** question. He gave *four* [1] different

[1] (1). " Unde et UNAM VOLUNTATEM FATEMUR D. N. JESU CHRISTI, " quia profecto a divinitate assumpta est nostra natura, **non culpa** " [in] illa profecto, quæ ante peccatum creata est, non quæ post præ-" varicationem vitiata." (2). " Nam *lex alia in membris,* **aut** *voluntas* " *diversa* non fuit, **vel** *contraria* salvatori, quia super legem natus est " humanæ conditionis." **(3).** " Utrum autem propter opera divini-" tatis et humanitatis una an geminæ operationes debeant deri " vatæ dici vel intelligi, ad nos ista pertinere non debent, relin-" **quentes ea** grammaticis, **qui solent parvulis** exquisita derivando " nomina venditare. Nos enim non unam operationem vel duas " dominum Jesum Christum ejusque sanctum Spiritum, sacris literis " percepimus, sed multiformiter cognovimus operatum." Honorii PP., Ep. III., *Ad Sergium Constantinopolitanum Episcopum.* Labbe, *Concil* , VI., 929, 932. (4). " Auferentes ergo, sicut diximus, scanda-" lum novellæ adinventionis, *non nos oportet unam vel duas opera-* " *tiones definientes prædicare,* sed pro una, quam quidam dicunt, " operatione, oportet **nos unum** operatorem Christum dominum **in** " utrisque naturis veridice confiteri ; **et pro duabus** operationibus, " *ablato geminæ operationis vocabulo,* ipsas potius duas naturas, id est " divinitatis et carnis assumptæ in una persona unigeniti Dei " Patris, inconfuse, indivise, atque inconvertibiliter nobiscum prædi-" care propria operantem." "Scribentes etiam communibus fratribus " Cyro et Sophronio antistitibus, *ne novæ vocis, id est, unius vel* " *geminæ operationis vocabulo insistere vel immorari videantur :* sed " abrasa hujusmodi **novæ** vocis *appellatione,* unum Christum dominum " nobiscum in utrisque naturis **divina** vel humana prædicent operan-

answers. (1.) We must confess that Christ had only one will. (Which was heretical.) (2.) We must not say that Christ had two conflicting wills, of which the divine will compelled the human will to act in harmony with it. (Which no one had ever dreamed of saying.) (3.) It would be better not to talk either of one will or of two wills, but to leave such a mere question of language to grammarians. (Which was no answer at all.) (4.) We *must* not talk either of one will or of two wills. The question cannot lawfully be discussed. (Which was a return to the absurd and disastrous policy of Zeno's *Henoticon*; attempting to settle a vexed question by forbidding its discussion.)

In the *Ecthesis* the Emperor gave this fourth dictum of Honorius the authority of an imperial decree. The *Ecthesis* was received with great favour in the East; and Honorius would no doubt have accepted it. He died, however, before it reached Rome, October, A.D. 638.

[The literature about the case of Honorius has had an addition of some forty or fifty works and pamphlets

---

" tem." Honorii PP. Ep. IV., ad eundem. Labbe, *Concil.*, VI., 969. A fresh discussion of the case of Honorius has just appeared in Germany —*Die Irrlehre des Honorius und das vaticanische Decret.* By A. Ruckgaber, Stuttgart, 1871. The book has been placed on the Index, and the author has submitted to the condemnation.

APPENDIX F. 461

within the last few years. See the article by Bishop von Hefele, already referred to, translated in the *Presbyterian Quarterly*, April, 1872; also Hefele's *Conciliengeschichte*, vol. iii., pp. 129, 145, 264, 285. Mgr. Maret, *Du Concile Général et de la Paix Religieuse*, 2 Tome, Paris, 1869. The *Case of Pope Honorius*, by P. Le Page Renouf, London, 1869, is a reply to articles of Dr. Ward in the *Dublin Review*, 1868,-9—and to a work by Father Bottala. The work entitled *Monumenta quædam Causam Honorii Spectantia*, Rome, 1870, is from the press of the *Civilta Cattolica*. Hefele says of it, that "the notes appended are almost worthless, and wholly insufficient to justify Honorius." Another more recent work by Professor Joseph Pennachi, of the Roman University, *Liber de Honorii I. Romani Pontificis Causa*, is written in a worthier spirit, but it attempts to prove that "the epistles of Honorius are *absolutely* catholic and give no countenance to the Monothelite heresy." In an Appendix to the German edition of his essay on Honorius, Bishop Hefele effectually disproves Professor Pennachi's position. H. B. S.]

APPENDIX G.

[Malachias was Archbishop of Armagh, and a special friend of St. Bernard, who wrote a work *De Vita et Rebus Gestis S. Malachiæ;* see Fabricius, *Bibl. Med. et Inf. Latin.*, vol. v, under the word "Malachias." Of his prophecies about the popes a full and interesting account is given by H. Weingarten of Berlin, in the *Studien und Kritiken,* 1857, S., 555-573. He was a man of singular virtue and austerity. Bernard spoke of his prophecies, which were not, however, published until 1595, by Wion, a Benedictine, in the works of his Order, under the title *Lignum Vitæ, Ornamentum et Decus Ecclesiæ,* Venet. A controversy and a prolific literature sprung up about them. Protestants, like Bengel, extolled Malachias. Frörer published the work anew in his *Prophetæ Veteres Prendepigraphi,* Stuttg. 1840. In these predictions 111 popes are described by 111 concise sayings, some of which are quite characteristic, while many of them are simple allusions to external facts and relations with play upon words. **Lucius II. is** described as *inimicus* ***expulsus*—** his family name was *Caccianemico (caccia,* chase, *nemico,* foe); and the Romans, too, expelled and stoned him. Innocent III. is *comes signatus;* **he**

APPENDIX G. 463

came of the counts of Conti, who had possessions in Segni. Pius II. (Æneas Sylvius) is *de capra et albergo*, for he was once secretary of the cardinals Cápranica and Albergati. More characteristic are the words about Gregory XI. *de tribulatione pacis*,—for he lived just before troubled times (1621), and about Alexander VIII., *custos montium*, for he bore six mountains on his coat of arms, which led the daughter of Gustavus Adolphus to apply to him the proverb—"parturiunt montes, nascetur ridiculus mus." (Weingarten, p. 564.) The mottoes of some of the coming popes (eleven in all) are, "Lumen in cœlo" (for the successor of Pius IX.); then, "religio depopulata," "fides intrepida," "pastor angelicus," "pastor et nauta," "flos florum," etc. The last one reads thus: "Petrus II. Romanus, qui pascet oves in multis tribulationibus, quibus transactis civitas septicolis diruetur et judex tremendus indicabit populum suum." Weingarten thinks it probable that the Benedictine Wion is the real author, or finisher, of these prophecies, by which he sought to elevate his Order, and that they were ascribed to Malachias, partly on account of the similarity of his name with that of the last prophet of the Old Testament. H. B. S.]

END.

www.ingramcontent.com/pod-product-compliance
Lightning Source LLC
Chambersburg PA
CBHW051237300426
44114CB00011B/774